D0594271

SHANAHAN LIBRARY
MARYMOUNT MANHATTAN COLLEGE
221 EAST 71 STREET
NEW YORK, NY 10021

The
Garland Library
of
War and Peace

SHANAHAN LIBRARY
MARYMOUNT MANHATTAN COLLEGE
221 EAST 71 STREET
NEW YORK, NY 10021

HD
9743
.A2
I58
1972

The
Garland Library
of
War and Peace

Under the General Editorship of

Blanche Wiesen Cook, *John Jay College, C.U.N.Y.*

Sandi E. Cooper, *Richmond College, C.U.N.Y.*

Charles Chatfield, *Wittenberg University*

The International Trade in Armaments Prior to World War II

comprising

The Bloody Traffic

by

A. Fenner Brockway

Mixed Commission on Armaments
League of Nations

The Secret International
Armament Firms at Work

Union of Democratic Control

with a new introduction
for the Garland Edition by

Richard Dean Burns

SHANAHAN LIBRARY
MARYMOUNT MANHATTAN COLLEG
221 EAST 71 STREET
NEW YORK, NY 10021

Garland Publishing, Inc., New York & London
1972

The new introduction for this
Garland Library Edition is Copyright © 1972, by
Garland Publishing Inc.

———

All Rights Reserved

Publ, 42.00 | March 84

Library of Congress Cataloging in Publication Data
Main entry under title:

The International trade in armaments prior to World
    War II.
    (The Garland library of war and peace)
    Reprint of The bloody traffic, by F. Brockway, first
published 1933; of Report of the Temporary Mixed Commission on Armaments, League of Nations (in French and
English), first published 1921; and of The secret international, by Union of Democratic Control, first published 1932.
    1. Munitions. 2. Firearms industry and trade.
3. Firearms industry and trade--Great Britain.
I. Brockway, Fenner, Baron Brockway, 1888-   The
bloody traffic. 1972. II. League of Nations. Temporary Mixed Commission for the Reduction of Armaments.
Report. 1972. III. Union of Democratic Control. The
secret international. 1972.
HD9743.A2I58 1972   338.4'7'35582   74-147550
ISBN 0-8240-0331-4

Printed in the United States of America

Introduction

As in a recurring nightmare, the American people of the 1970s find themselves again confronted with some of the major problems that bedeviled earlier generations during the 1920s and 1930s — the activities of armament industries and arms merchants. Popular phraseology has evolved considerably during the past half-century — from condemnation leveled at the "Bloody Traffic" and the "Merchants of Death" to those now hurled at the "military-industrial complex" and the "warfare state" — but the basic concerns would seem to remain.

Two of these basic concerns may be stated here: is the problem of international "arms transfers" (modern arms control experts feel this to be a more useful term for analysis than "arms traffic" or "arms trade") a substantive one which still warrants public attention? And do these "arms transfers" contribute in any significant measure to international instability and are they, consequently, disruptive of world peace?

I

Since the beginning of the twentieth century, we seem to have been living in an age dominated by weaponry and war. In the years since World War II, *for example, there have been at least fifty-five wars of significant intensity — about one every five months. And there seems to have been a ready supply of military hardware with which to carry on these martial outbreaks, one testimonial to man's industrial creativity. George W. Thayer, in his recent account* The War Business: The International Trade in Armaments *(1971), estimates that in 1970 there were some 750,000,000 useable military rifles and pistols in the world — one for every living adult male — together with tens of millions of machine guns and mortars, millions of artillery pieces and tanks, hundreds of thousands of military aircraft, and tens of thousands of missiles and naval craft.*

It is difficult to draw reliable cause-and-effect relationships between the availability of weapons and the outbursts of martial violence for most wars are the product of a multiplicity of factors. Indeed, while they hint at a direct relationship, very few of the critics of the arms traffic assert that a relationship exists nor do they bring much evidence to support such a direct connection. The "Bloody Traffic" or "transfer of arms," nevertheless, has been frequently singled out as one of the basic causes of international instability and, as such, deserves close examination.

To impress upon us the several dimensions of this problem, not the least of which is its durability, the editors of this volume have brought together three items which reveal the early concern with international traffic in weapons during the decades be-

INTRODUCTION

tween World Wars I and II. Two of these documents are of particular value: the League of Nations' report (1921) and the Union of Democratic Control's The Secret International *(1932).* (Brockway's The Bloody Traffic [1933] *is largely a popularized extension — without much further illumination — of the Union's argument and evidence.) The significance of these first two documents is that they reveal certain fundamental characteristics of the problems involved, reflect the human passion that has become traditional with the critics of the continuing practice of merchandising armaments, and show (when compared with the post-1945 era) the essential shifts which have taken place in the management of the arms trade.*

The League of Nations' Temporary Mixed Commission on Armaments suggested, in 1921, that the manufacture "by private enterprise of munitions and implements of war" was open to at least six objections:

> *1. that armament firms have been active in fomenting war-scares and in persuading their own countries to adopt warlike policies and to increase their armaments;*

> *2. that armament firms have attempted to bribe Government officials, both at home and abroad;*

> *3. that armament firms have disseminated false reports concerning the military and naval programmes of various countries, in order to stimulate armament expenditures;*

7

4. that armament firms have sought to influence public opinion through the control of newspapers in their own and foreign countries;

5. that armament firms have organized international armament rings through which the armament race has been accentuated by playing off one country against another;

6. that armament firms have organized international armament trusts which have increased the price of armaments sold to Governments.

The authors of The Secret International *(as well as most other opponents of the interwar decades to the arms trade) have concluded that "these are definite charges and it is a pity that the evidence on which they were based has not been published." A more careful reading of the League's report indicates that these statements were* not *an indictment but rather were put forward as a summary of the contemporary "strongly prejudiced" public mind; consequently the League probably never attempted in these early years to corroborate these prejudices. One man who attempted to do so was Philip Noel-Baker, and his* Private Manufacture of Armaments *(London: Victor Gollancz, 1936) contains probably the best detailed examination of each of these six contentions.*

The essence of the arguments of those men and women who challenged the armament merchants and their practices was that this traffic constituted an immoral undertaking which was stimulated by the "free enterprise" ethic. They generally granted that the State had the right, even the obligation, of maintaining armed forces for its survival and that, in the maintenance of such forces, the State had the legitimate right to call upon its citizens to make sacrifices through service and taxation in the common defense. "...This system is all built upon a conception of patriotism which makes loyalty to the State and to its interests the highest virtue," Noel-Baker acknowledges, "a virtue and a duty against which no other consideration must be allowed to stand" (p. 55). However, he argues

> It is not easy to fit into such a system the fact that, while some citizens are called upon to die, to leave widows and children unprovided for and unprotected, other citizens are allowed to make great profits from selling the arms which their less fortunate compatriots carry into battle. It is not easy to fit into such a system the fact that in time of peace some citizens are engaged in countering the spies of other nations, while under the private patent system the manufacturers of arms are selling secrets which may be of incomparably greater value to an enemy State than any that his spies could possibly discover. It is not easy to explain why the sacrifice of some citizens should be rendered vain by the financial gain of others. (p. 55)

To these critics, it was impossible "to reconcile the moral values of patriotism and of the accepted system of national defense with the moral values of the system of Private Manufacture of arms and implements of war" (Noel-Baker, p. 55).

The targets under attack by opponents of the arms traffic varied somewhat: those who were motivated by emotional outrage or pacifist ideals usually focused on the activity of individuals and manufacturing firms, the Sir Basil Zaharoffs and the Vickers companies, while those who were stimulated by a fundamental reformist impulse usually challenged the basic "system" of capitalism which permits such practices and were, usually, aligned with some "socialist" movement. But regardless of the assumptions arousing their displeasure with the "bloody traffic," they were unanimous in their belief that the production of war materials must be nationalized or, at the least, placed under close government supervision. Such action, they contended, would greatly enhance the prospects of peace, particularly in the less developed parts of the world where arms industries did not exist and where martial strife was fueled by the importation of armaments.

II

If those who wished to see the production of armaments come under governmental control were not successful prior to the Second World War, they have to be less than enthusiastic with the accomplishments during the years which followed. While it is true that the production of armaments after the war was transferred to governmental supervision and sponsorship, the results were even worse. Indeed, the United States and the Soviet Union — under the pressure of the Cold War — have developed the armaments industry far beyond what it ever had been and have vastly increased the exportation of armaments to all areas of the globe. The result is that, today, the Pentagon is the world's largest arms merchant while the Kremlin is a close second.

While it is difficult to obtain reliable, precise figures relative to the sales, loans, and grants of weapons from governmental sources, several methods currently are being employed to chart the statistical estimates of today's "arms transfers." Some investigators use quantitative dollar costs; some employ more qualitative criteria which emphasize the nature of the weaponry and its impact within a given geographical region; and still others utilize the armament expenditure figures versus gross national products, and major weapons imports versus national exports. But no matter what statistics one applies to this issue the end result is the same — discouraging.

According to a recent, exhaustive study by SIPRI (Stockholm International Peace Research Institute), The Arms Trade with the Third World *(1971), the increase of weapons stocks in third world countries "is one of the new and disturbing features of the post-war world" for, among other things, it links arms races in these regions to the major East-West confrontation. Also, the developing countries are devoting more and more of their meager resources to the procurement of weapons. While their gross national products have increased at an average of five percent a year since 1950, the military expenditures of these third world countries have grown at the yearly rate of seven percent and their importation of weapons at a rate of nine percent. Although these figures do not necessarily represent an "arms race" in North Africa, sub-Saharan Africa, and most of Latin America, they do constitute at least what Lincoln Bloomfield termed an "arms walk." [1]*

It would be far too simplistic, however, to hold the "Cold War" solely responsible for this expanding arms traffic in the third world, for even without this East-West confrontation these emerging and developing countries would be seeking weapons. Indeed, for the major powers now to attempt to shut off the supply of armaments, without an overall, general program of world disarmament, would bring a shout of protests from the third world states. They would claim, with considerable justification, that the big powers were once more unfairly meddling in their affairs. It has been for just this reason — self-sufficiency — that such nations as Israel, South Africa, and Argentina have been striving, at considerable expense, to develop their own armament industries.

12

INTRODUCTION

There are several reasons why the smaller nations and the countries with low defense technology object to the imposition of any rigid international control over the transfer of armaments. (1) Many of these states are virtually defenseless against external military aggression without foreign-made arms. (2) In other countries, foreign arms are sought to protect the government from rebellion and to maintain general order. (3) Several new states, and even some of the more established ones, have unresolved disputes — such as frontiers — with their neighbors. (4) Almost all of these states are moved by the force of nationalism to obtain the hallmarks of independence, modernity, and prowess — sophisticated military hardware.[2]

One should not ignore this last factor — nationalism — as a powerful stimulant in the traffic of major weapons systems. A few years ago, for example, the United States attempted to dissuade several small South American nations from using their precious resources to purchase supersonic military aircraft for which they had no real need or use. The Pentagon was told, in blunt fashion, that if the United States did not supply these modern aircraft, similar to those held by their larger neighbors, they would begin negotiations to purchase French Mirages. President Johnson capitulated and the new aircraft were delivered to bolster national pride.

While, as mentioned earlier, specific figures regarding the transfer of arms are sketchy and incomplete,

13

it has been estimated by the SIPRI study that some eighty-seven percent of the major weapons, supplied to third world nations between 1950 and 1969, came from four countries — the United States, the Soviet Union, Britain, and France. (During the past four years, this figure has increased to over ninety percent.) While the United States began shipping arms to these nations in the early 1950s,[3] the Soviet Union got into the "market" considerably later; yet today the U.S.S.R. is the world's second largest arms supplier with over some twenty client states and ranks second only to the United States.

Yet other statistics reveal that six-sevenths of the world's weapons is produced for the major contestants in the Cold War, and that two-thirds of this amount is produced by and for the countries of the Western Alliance. Thus, excepting the Vietnam conflict, almost four-fifths of the United States' military sales during the 1960s went to its NATO allies, with West Germany as the largest buyer.[4] (And it should be noted that the sales of arms to West Germany has been part of a financial "trade-off" aimed at reducing the United States' cost of maintaining its troops in Europe.)

Nor has the prospects of profit in arms sales escaped the attention of post-1945 private entrepreneurs. Samuel Cummings' Interarms, Inc., controls some ninety percent of the world's private arms sales, which amounts to an estimated forty million dollars per year. Thayer believes that Cummings' organization has enough weapons on hand at any one time to equip forty infantry divisions, most of which is surplus equipment obtained from the United States government or its client states. Privately obtained arms have appeared in many parts of the world; lately they have apparently found their way into the hands of the rebels in Northern Ireland. If the British government is correct, most of these contraband weapons were supplied by private arms dealers in the United States.

The international transfer of armaments is, then, one of those continuing, complex problems for which there seems to be no simple or certain answer.

III

One example of the complexity of this problem may be seen by the attempts made in recent years at the United Nations to impose some controls upon the shipment of conventional armaments. On two different occasions, it has been suggested that a first step toward such controls should be the establishment of an international weapons register. Malta initially proposed this device in a draft resolution to the U.N.'s First Committee on November 30, 1965; it was narrowly defeated (18 for, 19 against, and 39 abstentions) on December 2, 1965. The second attempt came in a joint draft resolution to the same U.N. committee by Denmark, Iceland, Malta, and Norway on November 21, 1968. After running into

INTRODUCTION

bitter objections, principally from the small nations, the sponsors withdrew their resolution on December 5, 1968.

So the efforts of earlier generations continue with, unfortunately, a similar lack of success. The accounts which follow focus on these earlier efforts, and it is hoped that they will enable students to examine the origins of the international arms transfer issue in some depth. Also, it can only be hoped that these same students will similarly address themselves to today's dimensions of this same dilemma.

March, 1972   Richard Dean Burns
                                              California State College
                                                    Los Angeles

NOTES

[1] *U.S. Senate, Committee on Foreign Relations Staff Study, "Arms Sales and Foreign Policy," January 25, 1967, p. 1.*

[2] *See, for example, "Working Papers: Conference on Arms Trade and International Politics," Occasional Papers No. 12, School of International Affairs, Carleton University, May 1971.*

[3] *Senator Frank Church recently declared that, since 1950, the United States had disposed through give-away programs, credit advances, and other means some 36.5 billion dollars worth of arms.* Los Angeles Times, *November 5, 1971.*

[4] *Additional statistics for U.S. Military Export Sales, 1962-1969, appear in the* Congressional Record — Extension of Remarks *(October 15, 1969), p. E8503.*

THE BLOODY TRAFFIC

THE BLOODY TRAFFIC

by

FENNER BROCKWAY

LONDON
VICTOR GOLLANCZ LTD
14 Henrietta Street Covent Garden
1933

First published August 1933
Second impression November 1933
Third impression June 1934

Printed in Great Britain by
The Camelot Press Ltd., London and Southampton

To L. B.

who initiated the Movement of
Resistance to the World War
in Britain

AUTHOR'S ACKNOWLEDGMENT

I N   T H E   compilation of this book I am specially indebted (among other works and reports) to Dr. Lehmann-Russbüldt's *War for Profits* (a study of the armament industry from the German angle), Mr. Seymour Waldman's *Death and Profits* (an exposure of American armaments organisation during the World War), and to *What Would be the Character of a New War?* (a collection of essays by experts).

But most of all I am indebted to a remarkable brochure, *The Secret International*, published at sixpence by the Union of Democratic Control. The Union of Democratic Control has carried out the most thorough research on the subject of armaments since the World War, and the main results of its work are compressed into this pamphlet. In many of the chapters of *The Bloody*

Traffic I have obtained help from *The Secret International*, as the footnotes indicate, and its analysis of the organisation of the industry is so detailed that the chapters devoted to the Armament Firms in Britain and the Armaments International are almost completely based upon it.

CONTENTS

CHAPTER I

THE TRAFFIC *IS* BLOODY

" War on a large scale to-day would mean a conflict in which masses of civilians were blotted out in scarcely conceivable conditions of horror. One single bomb filled with modern asphyxiant gas would kill everybody in an area from Regent's Park to the Thames."—LORD HALSBURY.

SOME THREE months before the World War I wrote a play, which I called *The Devil's Business*. The subject was a Cabinet Meeting at Downing Street during a war between Britain and Germany. The principal character was an armaments salesman who played off one country against the other.

Before the play could be published, war was declared between Britain and Germany, and the proofs had to be corrected so that Britain and Germany became " two civilised and Christian " Powers. Mr. Asquith, Mr. Lloyd George, and Sir Edward Grey were made unrecognisable ; only the armaments salesman remained the same, threatening to sell the latest death-dealing inventions to the other side if the price demanded were not forthcoming.

As soon as the play was published, the police seized every available copy, and, after trials at the Mansion House and the Guildhall, the entire stock was ordered to be destroyed.

I still see the horror of the chairman of the magistrates. The Devil's Business. *The Devil's !* What a way to describe the making of munitions for a holy war for liberty and democracy and justice ! What blasphemy to suggest that the patriotism of the armament-makers was a sham, and that profit-making was their one concern !

That attitude of mind seems incredible to-day ; but let another war return and the attitude of mind will return.

Even now there will be some who object to my title, *The Bloody Traffic*, just as the magistrate objected to *The Devil's Business*.

Bloody Traffic. Bloody is such a nasty word !
I mean it to be nasty. The traffic is nasty.
It's the filthiest and bloodiest of all traffics.

Face it in plain terms.

The purpose of the armaments industry is to produce the most effective instruments of death and destruction that human invention can devise. The more human beings a product of an armament firm can shatter to bits the more valuable the product.

The Bloody Traffic. Let us look at what the products of armament firms do.

General J. F. C. Fuller tells us in that remarkable book, *What Would be the Character of a New War?* that " In the Third Battle of Ypres, which took place during the summer and autumn of 1917, the British fired 4,283,550 shells, costing £22 millions, in the preliminary bombardment before the battle opened."

It is impossible to depict the horror and tragedy which this statement of statistical fact involves—the instantaneous slaughter of thousands of youth ; the sorrow of those who

loved them ; the destruction of the promise
of their lives ; the torture which thousands
underwent before they died ; the mutilation
of thousands for the rest of their lives ; the
blinding of others. I do not want to stress the
horror, but read this extract from Corder
Catchpool's *On Two Fronts* and then judge
whether the title I have given this book is
justified :

" I wish you could see the hospital . . . a
man with a buttock torn off by a bit of a
shell, who has been lying two or three days
on a stretcher in a pool of urine. . . .

" Perhaps the blinded men are the saddest,
if one excepts those who have gone mad."

Is " Bloody " too nasty a word to describe
the traffic which made a profit of twenty per
cent out of the shell which tore that soldier's
body to pieces ?

Over four million shells in the preliminary
bombardment of the Third Battle of Ypres.
Costing £22 millions. Each shell yielding
someone a monetary profit.

I take another passage from General Fuller's chapter :

" On April 24, 1918, seven British tanks, manned by 21 officers and men in all, over-ran three German battalions and slaughtered over 400 of their men. This is not war, but massacre."

Twenty-one men slaughtered over 400 by the use of a new device of the Bloody Traffic. Each tank costs £5,000. The more successful in slaughter, the larger the number of orders—and profits.

In this book we shall examine the poison gas organisation of the Bloody Traffic. The first poison gas used to any extent was chlorine. It was experimented with at Ypres in April 1915, when it killed 6,000 men. How did those 6,000 men die ? Here is a medical description of the symptoms which are characteristic of the effects of chlorine :

" The body of the victim seeks by contin-uous torturing coughing, accompanied by difficulty in breathing, to rid itself of the poisoned tissues in the lungs and respiratory organs. The destruction of the blood-vessels in these organs leads to a terrible agony of suffocation which may continue for hours, days, or even weeks, and ends with the coughing of blood which means death. It is said that nothing stirred up the feeling of hatred towards the enemy so much as the sight of these unhappy victims of the first gas attack struggling against death, their faces blue and bloated with suffocation, and blood-flecked foam issuing from their mouths and noses."[1]

Out of this torture the Bloody Traffic makes profit.

Even when the instruments of the Bloody Traffic have done their cruel work, the mutilated human beings whom they leave alive are treated primarily from the point of view of whether there is hope that they may be utilised again for the purpose of slaughter. " There are two points of view of the problem of wounded soldiers, the military and the humanitarian," says Mr. H. S. Soutter,

---

[1] Dr. G. Woker in *What Would be the Character of a New War* p. 368.

who was Surgeon-in-Chief of the Belgian Field Hospital at Antwerp and Furnes during the World War. Mr. Soutter defines the military point of view as follows :

" To the military commander the only problem is victory, and unless the medical service helps him to achieve this it is useless for his purpose. For him the wounded fall into two classes ; those who can be made fit for further service in the line, and those who cannot. To him the repair of the slightly wounded man is vital ; seriously wounded only encumber the ground."[1]

Smashed to bits by the instruments of the Bloody Traffic, and then " only encumber the ground " ! They will take a long time to make fit again. Men are wanted in the line to slaughter others. The seriously wounded must be put on one side until those who are slightly wounded have been treated.

Is " Bloody " too strong a word for the Traffic of War ?

There is one great master of this traffic

---

[1] *Daily News*, April 4, 1929.

Bb

whose better self evidently revolted against it. Alfred Nobel, the dynamite king, was also the founder of the World Peace Prize, presented yearly to the man or woman who does most in the cause of peace. He justified his activities in the Bloody Traffic on grounds often repeated.

He once met Countess von Suttner, the author of *Down with Arms*, on the Lake of Zürich. She pointed to a luxurious villa belonging to a silk manufacturer.

" Ah, yes," remarked the manufacturer of dynamite, " that villa was woven by silk-worms."

" Dynamite factories are perhaps more profitable than silk mills," replied the Countess, " and tainted with far more guilt."

" My factories," he said, " stand a better chance to end war than your peace congresses. On the day two army corps annihilate each other in a single second, all civilised nations will shudder away from war and disband their troops."

Since then we have had the World War,

in which the products of armament firms slaughtered ten millions. It is now commonly known that the Bloody Traffic has prepared for use weapons of death which could annihilate more than two army corps in a few seconds.

Yet the Bloody Traffic goes on. The alternative is now clear. Mankind must either destroy the Bloody Traffic or be destroyed by it.

CHAPTER II

THE INDICTMENT

" An average of the military expenditure of 61 countries
during the last four or five years reaches the immense
sum of 4,000,000,000 dollars (over £1,000,000,000) a
year."—ARTHUR HENDERSON, *President of the Disarmament
Conference*, 1933.

THERE is no need for any reader to put
the objection which is in his mind. I know
it. It is that it is not fair to put on armament
firms the responsibility for the horrors of
war, when it really rests with the Governments and peoples who sanction war.

After all, the armament firms only fulfil
the demand. So long as war goes on, nations
must arm. If the possibility remains that
one day the young men of this country will
be called upon to engage in war, it is only
right and proper that they should be provided efficiently with arms.

This is the argument. It has been admirably

stated by Mr. Douglas Vickers, one of the
directors of Vickers-Armstrong, the leading
British armament firm.

" There are people who maintain that
armaments should be taken out of private
hands, and who believe old stories about
the influence which armament firms are
said to have exercised in the past in the
interests of war.

" There is not a shadow of truth in such
stories. Armament firms are the most peaceful of people, and in their own interests do
not want war, but only that we shall be prepared for war.

" They feel it would be absolutely criminal
to send out our men unless they are equipped
and armed in the best possible way, and for
that reason I think that the term ' a national
asset,' applied to our firm during the war,
can still be applied to-day.

" It is useless to expect the League of
Nations to settle all quarrels, and a private
firm making armaments is deserving of the
support I claim for it."[1]

That is the case for the armaments

[1] Speech at opening of Vickers House Showroom, Westminster,
May 28, 1931.

SHANAHAN LIBRARY
MARYMOUNT MANHATTAN COLLEGE
221 EAST 71 STREET
NEW YORK, NY 10021

industry. Before concluding this book, I shall have challenged this case almost sentence by sentence. I shall have proved that many of these " most peaceful of people " have encouraged war. I shall have proved . . .

TEN CHARGES

But perhaps it will be better to formulate the charges at once. Here they are, in direct, unmistakable language :

1. Armament firms have formed international rings to intensify armaments rivalry in order to get large orders.

2. They have exploited their own nations by artificially maintaining exorbitant prices through the operations of armament trusts.

3. Whilst claiming to be patriotic, they have supplied *all* countries with armaments, *including enemy countries.*

4. They have deliberately created war scares.

5. They have influenced countries to be warlike.

6. They have bribed Government officials.

7. They have lied about the military and naval programmes of other nations.

8. They have used their influence over the Press in order to inflame public opinion.

9. They have used their influence in banking institutions in order to finance increased armament programmes in other countries.

10. They have sent representatives to international conferences in order to hinder the achievement of disarmament.

I shall justify these charges in detail, but it may be well, right at the commencement, to meet scepticism by quoting authoritative support for much of the case here outlined.

The League of Nations is a very moderate institution. The Governments of Europe which compose it are in some cases

Imperialist and in all cases Capitalist. Yet the following charges were officially laid before the commission which the League appointed to inquire into the problem of the private manufacture of arms in 1921 :

1. Armament firms have been active in fomenting war scares and in persuading their own countries to adopt warlike policies and to increase their armaments.

2. Armament firms have attempted to bribe Government officials both at home and abroad.

3. Armament firms have disseminated false reports concerning the military and naval programmes of various countries in order to stimulate armament expenditure.

4. Armament firms have sought to influence public opinion through the control of newspapers in their own and foreign countries.

5. Armament firms have organised international armament rings, through which the armaments race has been accentuated by playing off one country against another.

6. Armament firms have organised international armament trusts, which have

increased the price of armaments to Governments.[1]

Unfortunately, the evidence upon which
these charges were made has not been
officially published, but the efforts of investigators and research workers in various countries have revealed sufficient facts to enable
one not only to repeat them, but to add
the other charges which are included in my
indictment.

[1] Report of the First Sub-Committee of the Temporary Mixed
Commission of the League of Nations, 1921.

CHAPTER III

HOW THE TRAFFIC WORKS

" CUSINS : What on earth is the true faith of an Armorer ?
" UNDERSHAFT : To give arms to all men who offer an
honest price for them, without respect of persons or
principles : to aristocrat and republican, to Nihilist and
Tsar, to Capitalist and Socialist, to Protestant and
Catholic, to burglar and policeman, to black man, white
man, and yellow man, to all sorts and conditions, all
nationalities, all faiths, all follies, all causes, and all
crimes."—G. BERNARD SHAW.

ARMAMENT-MAKERS are always great
patriots. Old man Krupp, the founder of
the German firm, once assured the Prussian
Minister of War that if he could not continue
in his business quietly, " without disturbing
the harmony between love of country and
honour," he would give up his work and sell
his factory. And at the very time he wrote
these words he was supplying Austria with
the munitions she used against Prussia in the
war of 1866 !

If the armament-makers did not pretend

to be great patriots and disinterested servants of the public, if they acknowledged that they were just ordinary commercial concerns out to sell where they can, irrespective of the nature of the buyer, and to make profits at all costs—if, in a sentence, they were honest about their business—one might have some respect for them. It is the cant of the combination of patriotism with profiteering that arouses contempt.

You will find the directors of armament firms manning the councils and committees of every patriotic organisation. You will find them on the platforms of the most patriotic political parties. You will find them most bitter in their denunciation of the policies of other countries. You will find them condemning as traitors those who venture to criticise the policy of their own country.

These are their professions. Now let us turn to the reality of their practice.

AN INTELLIGENT SALESMAN'S GUIDE
TO THE ARMAMENTS INDUSTRY

Armament firms are purely profit-making business concerns. They have room for patriotism only when it helps to sell their articles. They have no room for patriotism when it restricts the selling of their articles. They have no room for sentiment or humanitarianism. Their one object is to do business and make profits.

Grasp this realistic conception of the armaments industry and everything else follows. Let us see how it works out.

The purchasers of armaments are Governments. The success of the business, therefore, depends upon persuading Governments to buy.

No Government wishes to spend money. Taxation is unpopular. But every Government will spend money on armaments if convinced that the expenditure is necessary for national defence.

Therefore the first thing an armament firm

must do is to convince Governments that its articles are indispensable for this purpose.

An armament firm produces a new type of death-dealing instrument and submits it to a Government. The instrument is costly. The Government knows that no rival Power possesses it, and turns it down.

The armament firm is not discouraged. It knows that it has only to get *one* Government to buy the new type of death-dealer and immediately *all* governments will buy. Any War Minister who neglected to order the latest weapons in use would betray the sacred cause of national defence.

So the armament firm seeks out some Government which is nervous about the arms of some rival nation. " Take this new invention," says the firm, " and you need fear your rival no longer."

Or the firm seeks out some small nation just launching out in armaments expenditure, with a Government or ruler who will take pride in possessing the first of a new type of armament.

It doesn't matter how insignificant the Government is : once get the new invention on the market and no Government will dare to be without it.

But sometimes there is a difficulty. The Governments of small nations cannot afford to buy. So comes the second principle of armament selling : Governments must be lent money if necessary. That involves a close relationship with the banks.

It will be convenient, therefore, if armament directors happen to be bank directors ; perhaps the armament firm will run a bank itself to facilitate the loan. The loan will be made on conditions that orders are placed with the firm.

The next necessity in the technique of armament salesmanship is the use of Press influence. The heavy sale of armaments depends upon the state of tension in international relations. Therefore public psychology must be kept nervous. This not only involves making the Press of your own country suspicious of other countries ; the

Press of other countries must be nervous of the intentions of your country.

Armament salesmanship therefore requires close connections with the Press. Own newspapers if you can. Some of your directors should certainly also be directors of newspapers. Don't be too squeamish about the truth of your stories. Publicity knows no morals. Good business depends upon war scares. Foment them !

Of course, if an armament salesman can directly approach a Government and convince it that there is danger from another country, or that some enemy Power is arming against it, that is best of all. Occasionally even that has been done.

There are grosser things in armament salesmanship, as there are in most salesmanship, about which we do not usually talk. Those who have the responsibility of giving orders may perhaps be encouraged to do so " for a consideration." When the orders run into millions, the " consideration " is sometimes considerable.

But there is also a more subtle form of technique which may be followed to obtain influence in desirable quarters. If an armament firm can promise a Government official a post when he is due to retire, the firm has a double advantage. The official is immediately friendly, and when he joins your staff he has inside knowledge and contacts of great value.

There are still some parts of the world where war lords, and even industrial concerns, resort to arms in their private quarrels. China and Mexico are examples. In such cases it is the duty of the armament salesmen to keep the private interests concerned well equipped, just as they do Governments.

So much for methods. Now for organisation.

In armaments manufacture, as in every other industry, the tendency is towards trustification. In place of rival competing firms, rings are formed to maintain prices. Subsequently amalgamation takes place, so that the whole national industry becomes one powerful combine.

But in armaments the case for extending this process from a national to an international sphere is particularly strong.

All Governments have to be supplied. Why not an international ring to maintain prices everywhere? International tension and fear must be maintained if orders are to be increased. How much easier to do this if your organisation is international—then you can collect and distribute information ; you can act simultaneously in all countries ; you can influence the Press everywhere ; you can upset the nervous system of the whole world ! One Government must be played off against another. How convenient if you have an international organisation which can be approaching two Governments at the same time !

Armament firms have not been slow to realise the value of this technique. I shall prove not only that they have abolished competition within nations, but that they

Cʙ

have established international contacts which enable them to pursue a common policy all over the world.

Of course, you must have no qualms about arming enemy countries if you are an armament salesman. In every war of modern times (except one), the armament firms have supplied the weapons of death to both sides. The exception was the Franco-German War of 1870, when Krupp, owing to a quarrel with Emperor Napoleon, did not supply France. That was probably why France lost !

The more one considers armaments as a business proposition, the more attractive they become. They are the best business proposition in the world. Indeed, one begins to wonder why any business man of enterprise troubles about any other form of manufacture.

The demand for the goods of most business firms is limited in two ways. First, by the restricted purchasing power of individuals. Second, by the satisfaction of what is required. The market for armaments is not restricted in either of these ways.

The purchasers are Governments, and Governments can command, in the last resort, all the wealth of the world. They will not only pledge the resources of the present time ; they will pledge the future if they can be led to think that armaments are necessary.

Think of what happened in the World War. The British Ministry of Munitions expended £672,164,933 during 1917–18. There was a time when the British Government was spending over seven million pounds a day— and we are still paying a million pounds a day in interest on the national debt.

Even in peace-time the Governments place expenditure upon armaments before everything else. National expenditure upon health and housing and maternity and child welfare and education and unemployment is cut down. Governments tell us that we must all tighten our belts. Yet this year, despite all the stringencies of the economic crisis, the British Government has increased the expenditure upon the armed forces by £4½ millions.

Create the fear that national defence is endangered, and the purse for armaments is limitless.

Secondly, there is no satisfaction point.

The demand for armaments depends upon fear. The stomach can only accommodate a certain amount of bread, but there is no restriction to the fear a mind can accommodate. The brain is not confined by physical limits. Fear can grow infinitely.

Moreover, armaments have this advantage over other commodities : the more you supply, the greater the demand. Sell a new form of armament to one Government, and all the other Governments will immediately demand it. Convince one Government that her expenditure should be increased : all the other Powers will immediately pour orders upon you.

Yes—armaments are a magnificent business proposition. But don't mix up patriotism with it. You must arm your enemy, you must deceive and conspire against your own Government, if you are going to get the most out of the armaments proposition.

And don't pretend that it is anything but a beastly business. It sent ten million men to their deaths in the last war. It mutilated twenty million. It flourishes by maintaining the conditions out of which another war, and the murder and mutilation of millions more, will come.

It is good business ; but it is bloody.

CHAPTER IV

THE MODEL SALESMAN

" If this figure should seem to some imaginations to cast a
very dark shadow upon the human spectacle, the fault
lies rather with the pinnacle he stands upon and not
with himself."—H. G. WELLS.

THE STORY of Sir Basil Zaharoff has been
told before and with vivid detail,[1] but no
book dealing with the Bloody Traffic can
omit it, in brief at least. Sir Basil is the model
example of successful salesmanship in the
armament industry. Upon his journeyings on
strange and secret missions from one part of
the world to another depended the welfare
and destiny of millions.

Zaharoff was born amidst the remotenesses
of Greece, but like a true armament man he
knows no national frontiers. He is as much
an Englishman as a Greek, and as much a

[1] *Sir Basil Zaharoff : The Mystery Man of Europe*, by R. Lewin-sohn.

Frenchman as an Englishman. Both France and Britain have recognised his distinction. The French Government has conferred upon him the Grand Cross of the Legion of Honour and the British Government has knighted him and made him Guardian of the British Empire. The University of Oxford has conferred upon him the degree of D.C.L. Such are the honours held by a triumphant salesman in the armament business.

Zaharoff began working-life in his 'teens as an hotel-porter. Then he became assistant to his uncle, a draper. His uncle cheated him, so he paid himself off and decamped to London. In revenge, his uncle had him arrested on a charge of robbery, and he was only saved from imprisonment at the last moment by discovering in the pocket of an old overcoat a crumpled letter giving him power as a partner to pay out money as he thought fit.

Fate plays curious tricks. If young Zaharoff had gone to prison in these formative years, his adventurous spirit might have found expression in a life of petty crime, as so many young prisoners have done. Instead, he has pursued the honourable and distinguished career of a dealer in the instruments of death to the greater part of the earth, and can boast in his old age that he is one of the richest men in the world.

Zaharoff's first armament job (at £5 a week) was with the firm of Nordenfeldt. He began at a fortunate period—in the 'eighties. Turkey and Russia were struggling for power in the Near East. All the Balkans were in a ferment. He seized his opportunity.

Patriotically he began re-equipping and extending the Greek Army. Then, in accordance with armament technique, he sold Greece (the Great Powers having turned it down) the first submarine ever produced. An immortal honour for the Greek Navy ! That accomplished, his interests widened. He convinced Turkey that, if Greece had one submarine, she ought to have two. Turkey bought. He convinced Russia that Turkey's submarines would menace her shipping in the Black Sea. Russia bought. And so the terror of the submarine was launched under the waters of the world.

At this time, Nordenfeldt manufactured the standard gun, which required four men to work it. Hiram Maxim had the ingenuity to invent one which required only one man. The story of how Zaharoff met this competition has been retold delightfully by Mr. H. G. Wells :

"Hiram Maxim exhibited his gun at Vienna. While he fired his gun at a target and demonstrated its powers, Zaharoff was busy explaining to expert observers that the whole thing was an exhibition of skill ; that only Maxim could fire that gun ; it would take years to train men to use it ; that these new machines were delicate and difficult to make and could not be produced in quantities, and so forth.

"Maxim, after tracing the initials of the Emperor upon a target, prepared to receive orders. They were not forthcoming. He learnt that the Nordenfeldt was simple and strong. This gun of his was a 'scientific instrument' unfit for soldierly hands. His demonstrations went for nothing.

"What had happened? He realised he was vis-à-vis with a salesman, a very formidable salesman. In the end he amalgamated with the salesman.

"Thereupon difficulties vanished. The Maxim gun ceased to be a scientific instrument and became a standard weapon. Nordenfeldt and Maxim consolidated, and the fusion was financed with the eager support of the investing public."[1]

From this point, Zaharoff became active in supplying to the world the blessings of the Maxim gun ; but he was not content with that. He hungered for the big prizes of armament salesmanship : the handling of orders for warships, selling at four and six million pounds. His company merged with Vickers Ltd., and the opportunity came.

It was during the Russo-Japanese war that the international genius of Zaharoff was

The Work, Wealth, and Happiness of Mankind, p. 614.

fully displayed. Britain was the ally of Japan. Vickers was a British firm. But Russia wanted armaments ; and Zaharoff, rising above national prejudices, saw that Russia got them.

Before the outbreak of the war he had laid his plans well. The largest armament firm in Russia was unpopular with its rulers, because its workmen were revolutionary. The Tsar feared to give this firm orders lest the workers, having made the armaments, should seize them and use them for their own purposes. Zaharoff suggested to the Tsar's advisers that it would be much safer to make the armaments in Britain. He got the orders for Vickers.

Then he entered into an alliance with the St. Petersburg Iron Works and the Franco-Russian Company, a turbine company, and through them supplied Russia with guns and heavy material for the cruisers she was building. His next success went still further. He contrived to get an order for two first-class battleships for the Black Sea, and the

Glasgow branch of Vickers—William Beardmore—was given a contract, in conjunction
with a French firm, to build a dockyard and
cannon factories in Reval.

No doubt, if Russia had won the war, Sir
Basil's decorations would have included
honours conferred upon him by the Tsar ;
but, despite the help that Russia had from
the British firm Vickers, Britain's ally,
Japan, was victorious.

Meanwhile, Zaharoff had extended his
armament interests. By the end of the war
he held shares, not only in Vickers, Armstrong-Whitworth, and nine other British
concerns, but in the powerful French firm,
Schneider-Creusot.

Indeed, his control over Schneider-Creusot was considerable. He skilfully applied the
technique of the armament traffic to his
new business. He secured a share in the
control of the *Quotidiens Illustrés*, which
issued the influential journal *Excelsior*, and
he endowed a chair of aerodynamics at the
University of Paris to hasten the day (to

quote Mr. Wells again) " when aeroplanes
(by Vickers) would be a necessary part of
armaments all over the world."

There was a sensational armament
scandal, just before the World War, in
which Zaharoff was concerned. It is a
revealing illustration of the technique of
the trade.

In June 1912 the Russian Duma had voted
the colossal sum of £130 millions for the
building of a new fleet. It was anticipated
that Schneider-Creusot would obtain a considerable part of the order ; first, because
Schneider had invested one million pounds
in the reconstruction of the Putiloff Works in
St. Petersburg ; and, second, because part
of the loan raised by Russia to meet the
cost of the new fleet was contributed by
France.

But in January 1914 the *Echo de Paris*
contained the surprising anouncement that
the German firm, Krupp, was planning to
acquire the Putiloff Works. The report was
false, but it had, of course, a purpose behind

it ; it is said to have been inspired by M. Raffolovich, the Russian Ambassador in Paris, in collusion with M. Suchomlinoff, the Russian Minister of War, after an understanding had been reached between them and Zaharoff.

The purpose of the report was to obtain further finance for the Putiloff Works and a further loan for Russia. It succeeded.

Panic among the armament firms of Britain and France was the immediate consequence of the report. In all innocence the Russians assured France that they would be delighted to get the capital they required for the Putiloff Works—another £2 millions —from Schneider-Creusot. Schneider-Creusot obliged, and, about the same time, a new Russian loan of £25 millions was raised in France.

A curious feature of this transaction was that, although Vickers Ltd. was not a party to raising the money, it secured a considerable portion of the subsequent Russian order for armaments. Many people came to the conclusion that this was in return for the services rendered by Zaharoff.

From now onwards Zaharoff went forward unchallenged as the universal armament provider. His British and French firms became linked in an international trust with the leading firms of Germany, America, and Italy. They sent arms all over the world. It was only the Great War which broke this international organisation into its national sections. Then the peoples proceeded to slaughter each other by the million with the instruments which Zaharoff and his colleagues had so impartially provided.

The World War was Zaharoff's climax of power. He became virtual master of the munition supply of the Allies, and at the same time the products of concerns in which he was interested were being used by Germany, Austria, Turkey, and Bulgaria to shatter the troops of the Allies. Zaharoff developed from a mere armament producer and salesman to the status of a great political power. It was due primarily to his efforts that Greece joined the war. He entered the very inmost circle of the counsels of the Allies.

Zaharoff was, of course, well placed to judge the trend of events before the actual declaration of war. He was one of the group of well-informed persons (they included a number of prominent bankers) who increased their holdings in armament shares during the summer of 1914. Once hostilities began, he devoted his gifts and powers to extending the conflict and opposing a negotiated peace.

He went on a special mission to his native land. At the beginning of the war, Greece disgraced herself in the eyes of the Allies by remaining neutral. Zaharoff went to Greece and, with funds which he provided, organised the propaganda which eventually returned M. Venizelos, the friend of the Allies, to power and brought Greece into the war. One of the methods adopted by Zaharoff was to buy up a number of

the influential newspapers on behalf of
France. It was for this service that he was
decorated with the French Legion of
Honour.

Zaharoff became a close friend and political adviser of the leading statesmen on the
Allied side—Lloyd George, Clemenceau,
Briand. He was, of course, a die-hard and
resisted every suggestion of peace by negotiation. When there was a possibility of
negotiations through the intervention of the
United States in 1917, he was consulted.
His view is recorded in the diary of Lord
Bertie, the British Ambassador in Paris,
under the date June 25, 1917. The entry is
concise and pointed : " Zaharoff is all for
continuing the war *jusqu'au bout*."

There is no need at all to interpret
Zaharoff's war-time activities as motived
by his armament interests. They suggest a
quality of enthusiasm greater than material
considerations can inspire. But the fact
remains that the bullets and shells and tanks
and guns which sent millions to their deaths

DB

meant profits to him. At the end of the war he was one of the richest of living men—thanks to his success in the Bloody Traffic.

CHAPTER V

HOW ARMAMENT FIRMS ARM THE ENEMY

(I) BEFORE THE WORLD WAR

" Patriotism is not one of the distinguishing features of the armaments trade."—VISCOUNT SNOWDEN.

WE HAVE made a general survey of the methods of the armament industry and have seen them exemplified in the life of one of the most successful armament sales-men. Now we will consider these methods in some detail and in concrete instances. In this chapter and succeeding chapters we shall see how, in their hunt for business and profits, armament firms have always been ready to arm enemy countries.

THE CASE OF KRUPP

The name of Krupp retains its sinister power despite the dismantlement of the armament equipment at the Essen works at the end of this war. Let us look briefly at the story of this great German combine.

Alfred Krupp, the founder of the firm, was only a lad of fourteen when his father died, leaving him with a disused factory. He resolved to make it a success, and in 1826, with a staff of seven workmen, he began to make cast-steel. He made a tour of English steel works and returned with the secrets of many new processes ; he was, for example, one of the first manufacturers in Germany to install the steam engine. His enterprise was so great that he was awarded the gold medal by the Berlin Exhibition of Commerce and Industry in 1844.

It was following this that he began the manufacture of new forms of armament. He was not encouraged by the Prussian Government, whose Minister of War embodied the customary conservatism of generals. " The traditional Prussian War equipment is so good that it needs no improvement," he informed Krupp.

Rebuffed by his own Government, Krupp went to the enemy Government of France. From the French Minister of War he received a kindly welcome, and, more important, substantial orders.

Krupp's success with the French Government began to stimulate the interest of the Prussian Government. Krupp produced gun-bores. The Prussian Government was interested, but hesitated. When the Prussian Minister of War delayed his signature to the contract, Krupp wrote angrily to his Berlin agent : " As soon as any other steel manufacturer gets an order for guns, I'll begin to supply the whole world with whatever it needs."

He was better than his word. He began himself to supply the new type of gun to France. Under this menace the Prussian Government ordered. Then Belgium ordered.

Then the British Government gave him an order, through Vickers and Armstrong. He became the manufacturer of field-guns for all the important Governments of Europe and of heavy naval guns for Britain.

At this time the hostilities between Prussia and Austria which eventually led to the war of 1866 were developing. Krupp took full advantage of the situation. He made the most of the armament rivalry between the two nations to get orders from both sides. Although he was a Prussian subject, and his firm was situated in Prussia, he did not hesitate to arm the southern States of Germany, which were openly siding with Austria. Although he had, through the offices of Bismarck, just obtained substantial credit from the Prussian State Bank, he contracted with the Austrian Government to supply it with guns.

At this point the Prussian Government intervened. It begged Krupp not to supply Austria with guns without the consent of the Ministry of War. Krupp replied that such a pledge would constitute " breach of contract." The Prussian-Austrian War broke out. " What followed is now fairly well known," writes Dr. Lehmann-Russbüldt.

" At the famous battle of Königgratz, German soldiers, bound by blood-ties, destroyed each other with German guns which were molten brotherly-wise in the same crucible ; and, likewise in brotherly fashion, the profits flowed into the self-same coffers."[1]

Then another opportunity for good business came. Britain and Russia were engaged in the Crimean War. Krupp supplied both sides with guns.

Throughout this period Krupp was seeking to maintain his trade with the French Government, although the national antagonism which resulted in the Franco-German War of 1870 was already developing. His methods of business were exactly the same as those of any business firm. He developed improved articles—that is, more deadly weapons —boasted their claims in an illustrated

[1] *War for Profits,* p. 42.

prospectus, and then approached prospective buyers, of whatever nationality.

One of his letters to Emperor Napoleon III of France has been published. It is an amusing example of armament advertising :

"Essen, *April 29,* 1868.

"To His Majesty Napoleon III, Emperor of France.

"Encouraged by the interest your Majesty has shown in a simple industrialist like myself, and the happy results of his labours and great sacrifices, I venture once more to ask you humbly to accept the enclosed prospectus.

"It contains a collection of drawings of several newly perfected products of my workshops. I venture to hope that your Majesty will specially glance at the four last pages, exhibiting steel cannon which I have supplied to *several powerful European Governments,* and I sincerely trust that Your Majesty will forgive my audacity in doing so.

"ALFRED KRUPP."

The pivot of this letter was, of course, the

italicised words, *which Alfred Krupp heavily underlined*.

The reply of the Emperor, sent by General Le Bœuf, read as follows :

" The Emperor has received your prospectus with great interest, and His Majesty commands that his thanks be conveyed to you for this. I am requested to inform you that His Majesty extends his lively wishes for the success and expansion of an industry which promises to be of considerable service to mankind."

Of service to mankind ! The manufacture of articles to blow human beings to bits ! Was the Emperor intentionally ironical or was this the customary courtesy of the Court ?

In actual results Krupp's letter failed. A quarrel occurred between him and the Emperor, and French orders for Krupp cannon ceased. Indeed, in the war of 1870 between Germany and France, Krupp was defeated. He only supplied guns to one side.

But this was only an isolated defeat. Alfred Krupp died in 1877. By that time 24,576 guns had been manufactured at Essen. Of these, 10,666 remained in Germany and 13,910 were exported to other countries. After the death of the founder of the firm the policy of providing armaments to all Governments, whether allies or enemies, was maintained. By 1911 the Krupp firm had produced 53,000 guns. Of these, 26,000 remained in Germany and 27,000 were exported to fifty-two countries. When the World War broke out three years later, these guns boomed across the trenches from both sides.

The business principles of Krupp are, of course, the business principles of every armament firm : sell where you can ; it is not your concern how the armaments are going to be used.

During the Boer War there was a considerable public outcry in Britain because British soldiers were being killed by bullets from rifles of British manufacture. We have

already seen, in the story of Sir Basil Zaharoff, how British firms armed Russia during
the Russo-Japanese War, although Britain
was the ally of Japan. But of all examples oi
the complete absence of patriotism in the
Bloody Traffic the World War is the most
remarkable.

CHAPTER VI

HOW ARMAMENT FIRMS ARM
THE ENEMY

(2) DURING THE WORLD WAR

" I once saw this happen, after the war, at Belleau Wood.
An American father and a German father met at the
cemetery. The American stood above a neat grave with
a wooden cross. The German had not even so much of
concrete symbol to console him. All that he knew was
that, years before, his son had fallen there. The meeting
was strangely moving. The two men were clumsily
drawn to each other, embarrassed, at a loss, with only
bald, commonplace words to answer what they felt
within."—PIERRE LOVING.

THE WORLD WAR was the period when
the emotion of national patriotism reached
its height. The armament firms played their
part in stimulating and maintaining this
emotion, but their practice was quite un-
moved by it. They shamelessly profiteered
at the expense of their own nations, and as
business concerns they had the satisfaction
of knowing that their products were spread-
ing mutilation and death on both sides.

This is a summary of what happened.

German soldiers were killed by the thousand with grenades to which were attached Krupp patent fuses. German soldiers were entangled and bayoneted on barbed wire made by German firms. German vessels were sunk, and their crews drowned, by fire from British ships using German gun-sights. German troops were blown to bits by French, Italian, and Russian guns and cannon made with German iron and steel. The Russian Navy was built with German capital. American armaments were constructed with German capital. The infantry of the Allies went into battle wearing German-made shields.

That is one side of the story. The other side is this.

British regiments were shattered by shells composed of gunpowder provided by a trust in which British firms were partners. British crews were sent to the bottom of the sea by torpedoes, submarines, and mines made in the dockyard of a British firm. The British and Australian troops in the Dardanelles were massacred by guns and forts built by a British firm. The regiments of the allies of France in the Balkans were destroyed by guns and cannon supplied to Bulgaria by a French firm.

HOW GERMAN FIRMS ARMED THE ALLIES

The use by the Allies of the German patent fuses for hand grenades was revealed in a legal action brought by Krupp against Vickers after the war. Krupp sued Vickers for 1s. per fuse used. The amount claimed was £6,150,000, which means that 123,000,000 fuses of the German type were used against the soldiers of Germany and her allies. A compromise was reached, under which Krupp was given a large interest in the British-owned Miers Steel and Rolling Mills in Spain.[1]

It is difficult to characterise the callousness of these proceedings. Hundreds of thousands

[1] *War for Profits*, p. 131.

of German boys and men must have been done to death by these 120,000,000 fuses, each duly marked Kpz 96/04 to indicate that the patent was the property of Krupp. Yet Krupp dared to claim royalties upon them ! A pound of flesh upon each grenade which scattered in bloody bits the flesh and bones of German boys and men.

Many instances could be given of the loss of German and Austrian lives during the World War by armaments made by German firms. Here are two examples.

The Skoda Works, in Austrian territory before the war, had a steel-smelting mill in St. Petersburg where Russian guns were repaired. During the war the Austrian troops in Galicia were mowed down by guns made fit, for their murderous work, in this mill.

The second example is little known. *The German U-boat menace during the war was met by the use of airships built on the model of a German airship bought by the British Admiralty in 1913.* The story is told by Rear-Admiral F.

Sueter in a report which he presented to the Admiralty :

" I received permission from the Admiralty in 1913 to conclude an agreement with the Parseval Company in Bitterfeld for a new airship, size 300,000 cubic feet hydrogen gas capacity, 279 feet long, diameter 47.8 feet. . . .

" When the German U-boats began to grow menacing, it was seen that small airships like the Parseval were extraordinarily effective in countering the U-boat danger. A contract was immediately drawn up which called for the quick construction of such airships."

Admiral Sueter states that German U-boats were destroyed by these airships, either directly by bombing, or indirectly by patrol boats which received signals from the airship. The airships also proved of great aid in mine-searching. The German Parseval Company sold their model airships to Japan and Russia, as well as to Britain, immediately before the war. No doubt they were equally useful in the destruction of German lives.

But in one respect many of the other instances of the use of German materials against Germany were worse than the instances of the grenade fuse, the steel works, and the airships. The patent rights in the fuse were sold to Vickers, the Russian guns repaired, and the model airships acquired *before the war*. Other arms and material were supplied to the Allies *during the war*.

Germany's armament problem during the war was to obtain supplies of rubber, animal fat, oil, nickel and copper. In order to get these, Germany had to export, in exchange, iron and steel and manufactured war-materials. The exchange was conducted through neutral countries, despite the restrictions which were supposed to operate.

The German invasion of its northern area deprived France of the products of its mines and mills. Both France and Italy were largely dependent upon these mines and

Eʙ

mills for their iron and steel. When Germany developed its submarine activities, supplies from America became doubtful. It was then the German supplies were secured.

During the first eight months of the year 1916 an average of 150,000 tons of iron and steel were exported monthly by Germany to neutral countries. A fine of five marks was imposed upon each ton exported, but the high prices which France and Italy were prepared to pay for these products made the charge of little account. This export of iron and steel proceeded after the German firms responsible for it had informed the Commissary Department of their Ministry of Munitions that they could not supply an additional 15,000 tons of steel to meet Germany's requirements.

The German firms pretended to be ignorant of the ultimate destination of their coal and steel, but of course this was a pose which deceived nobody. In Switzerland, special workshops were adapted to the process of removing the trade marks from the German

steel rollers destined for France. The industrialists of Switzerland did not trouble to
hide this trade. In 1917, when the Allies proposed to take more stringent action to prevent commerce with Germany, the Swiss
machine and textile industries presented a
statement to the Swiss Federal Parliament
pointing out that one of the advantages of
free commerce was that they were able to
send German iron in large quantities to
France and Italy. A legal case reported
widely in the French Press after the war
revealed that two important French firms
imported without difficulty 60,000 tons of
German steel during the war.

The German Government was aware of
the traffic across the frontiers. On one
occasion the German War Office complained
to the Government that a considerable
quantity of German-made nails were being
sent to France and Italy through Switzerland. No action was taken. The Stinnes
Factory at Differdingen was caught in a particularly flagrant case. Nothing happened.

The Thyssen Company was discovered selling infantry shields to Holland for 68 marks
each, when it was charging the German
Government 117 marks. It was not proceeded against. On another occasion this
firm was found to be sending three thousand
horses across the Dutch frontiers, despite
the fact that it seemed probable at that time
that Holland would side with the Allies !

Finished articles designed for war purposes
got across the frontiers. In his *War for Profits*,
Dr. Lehmann-Russbüldt quotes an army
officer, whose statement was subsequently
authenticated in the Reichstag. This officer
said :

" At the battle of Skagerrak the British
fleet used gun-sights that six months earlier
the Zeiss Company, Jena, and the Goerz
Anschütz Company had delivered to a
Dutch concern. Moreover, German soldiers
at Douaumont found themselves entangled
in barbed wire which the Magdeburg Wire
and Cable Works had exported to Switzerland only two months before."[1]

[1] p. 76.

There was a sensational legal case in Germany during the war, in which a prominent member of the Senate of Lübeck was charged with supplying the Russian armies with steel. The Supreme Court finally decided that he was justified in doing so. The story was this.

Herr Possehl had a large iron and steel business in Scandinavia and Russia. He had mines in Norway and Sweden and factories in Russia. His Swedish mines supplied his Russian factories with the necessary raw materials.

When war was declared, Herr Possehl continued to send iron into Russia, and after a time he was arrested and held in custody for a year, during investigation. His defence was skilful. He argued that by continuing to send iron into Russia, despite his knowledge that inevitably some of it would be used for war purposes, he was abetting Russia's cause less than if he shut down his Russian factories, normally used to manufacture horseshoes and scythes, and thus invited Russia to confiscate them and utilise them entirely for military purposes.

On these grounds he was acquitted of giving aid " of his own free will and through his business to a foreign Power at war with Germany." His justification by the Supreme Court was followed by an official welcome, with honours, on his return to the Senate of Lübeck, and the Kaiser sent him a message of congratulation upon his patriotism.

HOW THE FRENCH ARMAMENTS TRUST ARMED THE ENEMIES OF FRANCE

Now let us look at the reverse side of this traffic. Let us examine what was happening in the countries of the Allies. We will start with France.

Both Turkey and Bulgaria, the allies of Germany in Eastern Europe, were armed by France. Their Governments ordered armaments from Schneider-Creusot, the great French armaments trust, and the French banks made them loans to meet the cost of the orders. The last order given by Turkey to Schneider-Creusot was actually within a month of the declaration of war. In July 1914 the Turkish Minister of Marine visited the headquarters of the firm at Creusot and selected the armaments he required. Unfortunately for the profits of Schneider-Creusot, hostilities were commenced before the deliveries could be made. The Turkish Minister of Marine therefore called upon Krupp at Essen on his return journey and spent the money he had raised in Paris to purchase a German supply of armaments instead of French.

The story was told in the Chamber of Deputies by Paul Fauré, the Secretary of the French Socialist Party. Paul Fauré is one of the most courageous figures in the fight against armaments. Until the last election he represented the constituency of Creusot, in which the headquarters of Schneider-Creusot are situated. Thousands of his constituents were employed by Schneider. Their prospects of employment depended upon Schneider obtaining orders. Nevertheless, with complete fearlessness he repeatedly exposed the intrigues of the Schneider firm. His courage cost him his seat. At the general election in 1932 he was defeated, largely as the result of the propaganda of Schneider-Creusot.

Fauré's account of the arming of Turkey and Bulgaria by France is so astonishing that I quote at some length ; this particular speech was delivered in the Chamber of Deputies on February 11, 1932 :

" Turkey has taken fifteen loans, on thirteen of which nothing is being paid to-day. *The last of these loans was in 1914, to permit Turkey to make war against France.*

" I want to make two or three observations on the Turkish and Bulgarian loans.

" One of these Bulgarian loans was in 1906 or in 1907. I have in my dossier a photograph of Prince Ferdinand visiting the Creusot factories, accompanied by M. Eugene Schneider himself, *and buying arms and cannon which you found later on the Eastern Front for four years.* [Bulgaria, of course, sided with Germany against France and the Allies.]

" What happened ? The order was so exaggerated that when King Ferdinand found himself before the Financial Commission of the Sobranje [the Bulgarian Parliament] it refused to ratify the credits.

" The French Government intervened at this point and declared that, if the Sobranje did not ratify the credits, the Bulgarian loan would not be authorised. *The Sobranje spoke, France paid, and the armaments of Creusot were sent there.*

" I have also in my dossier a photograph showing the Turkish Minister of Marine visiting the Creusot factories [in July 1914], preceded by all the inventors, who showed him the latest developments on the side of defence. The Turkish Minister gave his order.

" He had already used up the last loan lent him by France. Only the war came too quickly. Several days later, war broke out, and the unfortunate Minister could not take away the French cannon. *But, as he had French money, he bought on the way back at*

Krupp's, in Essen, and at Skoda the cannon which were used on the Eastern Front."[1]

From this exposure, which was never contradicted, we find that both Turkish and Bulgarian arms were supplied by Schneider-Creusot by means of a French loan. That is to say, the French financiers subscribed to loans to enable the Turkish and Bulgarian Governments to order, from the French combine, armaments destined to slaughter the soldiers of France and her allies !

HOW BRITISH ARMAMENT FIRMS ARMED THE ENEMY

But Schneider-Creusot was not the only armament firm on the side of the Allies providing Turkey on the eve of the war with arms destined to be used against the Allies. Vickers and Armstrong signed a big contract towards the end of 1913. Under this contract the Turkish Government handed

[1] *The Secret International*, p. 21.

over to these two British firms entire responsibility for maintaining the arsenal and
docks at the Golden Horn, together with
a site for a naval base at Ismid. The contract laid down that " no foreigner, except
British, may be employed."

That arsenal, dock, and naval base,
developed by the two principal British armament firms, were used to decimate British
soldiers. It proved to be for the preparation
of the slaughter of the Australian and British
troops in the Dardanelles that the prestige
of the exclusive employment of British workmen and technicians was enjoyed.

Mr. Hugh Dalton, a soldier during the
war and afterwards the Under-Secretary for
Foreign Affairs in the Labour Government
of 1929, voiced in moving language in the
House of Commons on March 11, 1926, his
view of the morality of the Bloody Traffic
as illustrated in this event. He said :

" Vickers had been supplying the Turkish
artillery with shells which were fired into the
Australian, New Zealand, and British troops

as they were scrambling up Anzac Cove and Cape Helles. Did it matter to the directors of these armament firms, so long as they did business and expanded the defence expenditure of Turkey, that their weapons mashed up into bloody pulp all the morning glory that was the flower of Anzac—the youth of Australia and New Zealand and our own country ? "

In 1926, British armament firms were again supplying the Turkish Government with arms. Sir Austen Chamberlain, who was then Foreign Secretary, acknowledged that licences had been issued for this purpose. " Is not the Foreign Secretary aware," asked Mr. Arthur Ponsonby (now Lord Ponsonby), " that a British battleship was sunk in the Dardanelles by a mine that had been sold to Turkey by an English firm ? "

The Minister admitted the accuracy of this, but declared that " a war with Turkey is out of the question." Let us hope Sir Austen proves right, but the course of foreign politics since that time is not reassuring. If the clouds of war hanging over Europe break, Turkey is likely to be in the camp opposite to Britain, and then once more we shall see British-made weapons destroying British soldiers.

Here is another flagrant instance of the arming of the enemy in the World War by British armament firms.

Vickers and Armstrong had a subsidiary firm for the manufacture of the smaller types of naval armaments. It was known as Henry Whitehead & Co. It had docks at Weymouth in Dorset for the manufacture of torpedoes for Britain. But it also had docks at Fiume in Hungary for the manufacture of torpedoes, torpedo-boats, torpedo-boat destroyers, submarines, and mines. During the World War these docks were confiscated and both Germany and Turkey were supplied from this source. Perhaps that is where the mine which sunk the British warship in the Dardanelles was made.

Or take the case of the Nobel Dynamite Trust Company, manufacturers of gunpowder and explosives. It was registered before the war as a British company. It owned, or was interested in, six British companies, with three of which Vickers shared directors. But it was similarly connected with four German firms, and it was one section of the International Cartel of Powder Manufacturers, which, we shall see later, represented firms in Britain, Germany, France, and Russia. During the war this firm supplied gunpowder and explosives both to Germany and Britain. Its German and British partnership was only dissolved in May 1915.

The method by which this dissolution of partnership took place is significant. Despite the proclamations which were issued for the confiscation of enemy property during the war, the Nobel Dynamite Trust Company succeeded in obtaining passports for its British and German agents to meet to arrange for the exchange of shares. Advertisements were published in the Press of both countries in May 1915, announcing an exchange of shares between the British and

German sections of the trust, and the announcement was introduced by the statement that it was made " with the consent of the two Governments." The shareholders were assured that " ordinary shares of the Nobel Dynamite Co., Ltd., held in Germany, will be accepted in exchange for the same class of shares in the Dynamite Aktien Gesellschaft (formerly the Alfred Nobel Co., of Hamburg) " and vice versa. By this means, British shareholders in the German company, which was producing explosives to shatter British soldiers to bits, were protected against a loss of their interest and dividends.

Similarly there was the Chilworth Gunpowder Company, with headquarters at Vickers House, Westminster. It had thirteen shareholders. Four of these bore the name of Vickers, a fifth (Sir Trevor Dawson) was the managing director of Vickers, a sixth (Mr. Meade Falkner) was a director of Armstrong. But the firm was not only British. Among its other directors were Louis

Hagen and Carl Duttenhofer, directors of the German Arms and Munitions Factory. No doubt the Chilworth Gunpowder Company was as catholic in its distribution of gunpowder in preparation for the World War as in the distribution of its directors.

But it was not only before the war that British firms supplied Germany, Austria, Turkey, and the other enemy countries with materials which were used to shatter the limbs and destroy the lives of British soldiers. The traffic went on during the war itself through the neutral nations, just as it did from the German side.

I shall subsequently deal with the British America Nickel Corporation. Nickel is, of course, of enormous importance in armament manufacture. It is a very hard metal essential in the construction of steel armaments, to which it imparts strength. So far no substitute has been found for it.

During the war the British Government concluded a trading contract with the British America Nickel Corporation to take nickel ore from it for a period of ten years from 1917. At the same time the Government made a loan to the corporation to the value of £620,000. The corporation undertook to pay interest of six per cent on this loan and to repay the principal in five instalments from January 1920.

The managing director of the British America Nickel Corporation, Mr. James Hamet Dunn, was made a baronet by the British Government and became Sir James Dunn. This honour was no doubt conferred for services rendered during the war.

The interests of the British America Nickel Corporation (to use the words of Admiral Consett, naval attaché in Scandinavia from 1912 to 1919) were closely identified with " those of the Kristiansand Nikkel Raffineringswerk, " the one factory in Norway that produced nickel in any important quantity."[1] With this firm the British Government also entered into an agreement. The K.N.R. (as the Norwegian firm was

[1] *The Triumph of Unarmed Forces*, p. 200.

FB

commonly called) was supplying Germany with about sixty tons of nickel a month. The British Government wished to limit the export of nickel to Germany, and with this object paid the K.N.R. £1,000,000.

Let us see how these agreements were fulfilled.

In December 1920 the Select Committee on National Expenditure reported as follows about the contract with the British America Nickel Corporation :

" Up to the present time there has been no delivery of nickel under the contract mentioned in the preceding paragraph ; and, as a fact, the world-supply of nickel has been, and is at present, in excess of the demand. No interest on the loan of £620,000 has been paid, nor any instalment on the redemption of the loan.

" As the British America Nickel Corporation have failed to carry out their agreement, we recommend that an immediate effort be made to recover as much of the capital as practicable, and in particular that no further liability be incurred in the matter."

Now let us see what happened in Norway with the K.N.R., the associated company of the British America Nickel Corporation.

The K.N.R., we have already noted, was " the one factory in Norway that produced nickel in any important quantity." Yet these are Norway's exports figures for nickel, " practically all of which " (states Admiral Consett) " went to Germany " :

1913	1914	1915	1916
594 tons	696 tons	760 tons	722 tons

The Norwegian statistics do not record the imports of nickel from Britain during the war. We cannot, therefore, judge how far the increased nickel supplies exported to Germany came through Britain. But the Swedish statistics give these particulars. The imports of nickel from Britain were as follows :

1913	1914	1915	1916
27 tons	60 tons	328 tons	78 tons

Before the war no nickel was exported to Germany from Sweden. It was utilised in

Sweden itself. But in 1915 the export of nickel to Germany reached seventy tons, and in 1916 was 30 tons. Upon these facts Admiral Consett comments :

" In 1915 the United Kingdom sent to Sweden more than twice her pre-war imports ; of Sweden's total imports of 504 tons in 1915, 70 tons were sent to Germany. The greater part of this quantity was virtually sent by us, the remaining 434 tons being used in the country for Germany's benefit in the manufacture of war materials. We sent Sweden twelve times the amount of nickel in 1915 that we did in 1913."[1]

The Swedish importers of British nickel were required to certify that the supplies were not being used for Germany's war purposes ; but no British firm supplying Sweden with nickel can have had any doubts about the reason for the increased demand as soon as the war broke out. The Swedish factories were a supplementary arsenal for Germany. Even when the nickel was not forwarded to

[1] *The Triumph of Unarmed Forces*, p. 201.

Germany, it was largely used in making war materials for Germany in Sweden.

Let us go from nickel to copper, a metal which enters into every phase of naval and military warfare. Until copper was made contraband in October 1914, Germany obtained enormous supplies through neutral countries. Take Sweden's figures. Her copper exports to Germany and Austria were :

1913	*1914*
1,215 tons	3,960 tons

British firms largely participated in this extra traffic of copper to Germany for war purposes. The British export of copper to Sweden increased as follows :

1913	*1914*	*1915*
517 tons	710 tons	1,085 tons

This book is concerned with armaments, but in passing it may be recorded that the traffic across the neutral frontiers involved every kind of article used for war purposes : cotton, glycerine supplies, cement, hide for the soldiers' boots. Admiral Consett's evidence on the last point is worth quoting :

" During 1915 and 1916, Sweden sent to Germany 3,470 and 2,664 tons respectively of boots and shoes : the boots were of military pattern and for the use of the German Army, and the above figures represent for these two years over 4,500,000 pairs.

" During the same period, in addition to the boots, Sweden sent to Germany and Austria nearly 50,000 head of cattle on hoof, 6,000 tons of hides and skins, and more than 2,000 tons of tanning materials and tanning extracts. *This traffic was assisted by 2,800 tons of hides and skins and 3,400 tons of tanning materials and extracts which Sweden received during 1915 and 1916 from the United Kingdom and the British Empire.*"[1]

Thus we see that, whilst the British Government was sending its soldiers to the battle-field to kill Germans, British firms were providing Germany with the means to kill the same soldiers, and were providing the German armies with their footwear and their other needs.

[1] *The Triumph of Unarmed Forces*, p. 227.

Germany was prepared to pay high prices for nickel and copper and glycerine and boots and the other essentials of war ; and British firms put profits before patriotism.

CHAPTER VII

HOW ARMAMENT FIRMS ARM THE ENEMY

(3) SINCE THE WORLD WAR

" We find M. Schneider (the French armament-maker) arming Bulgaria, M. Schneider arming Turkey, Skoda (a Schneider subsidiary) supporting Hitler ; we find France raising Hungarian and Rumanian loans ; we find Franco-Japanese, Franco-Argentine, and Franco-Mexican banks. This is all extremely suspicious."— PAUL FAURÉ.

SINCE the World War the armament firms have not in any way modified their policies. Indeed, owing to the slump in the demand for war materials which followed the peace, the tendency has been to intensify their methods in order to obtain every possible order. They certainly have not hesitated through any fear that a purchaser might be a potential enemy.

The leading firms have supplied nearly every Government of the world, irrespective of political alignments. In the Sino-Japanese War they have armed both sides ; it has not occurred to them to refrain from arming the Japanese forces because their Governments and the League of Nations have condemned Japan. They have armed both sides in the wars between Bolivia and Paraguay and Peru and Columbia, despite the condemnation which the League of Nations has passed upon the resort to arms. They have helped to arm even Russia, despite the antagonism of their Governments to the Soviets. They have armed nations in Europe in violation of the Peace Treaties. They have armed the private armies of Europe, and the mercenary armies of China and the oil combine armies of Mexico. They have sold armaments wherever they could find a purchaser, without any consideration of the purpose for which they would be used.

We will leave the Sino-Japanese War for a separate chapter ; here we will consider the arming of Russia by German firms, the arming of Hungary by French firms, and the arming of private military ventures by armament firms generally.

HOW GERMAN ARMAMENT FIRMS HAVE ARMED RUSSIA

Russia has declared its willingness to disarm completely if other nations will agree to do so, but, failing such agreement, it is maintaining its armaments efficiently. It has its own nationalised armament works, but sometimes armament firms of other nations succeed in getting orders. For example, Skoda Works, in Czecho-Slovakia, the subsidiary of the French Schneider-Creusot, has supplied considerable armaments to Russia. The most remarkable instance of this, however, comes from Germany.

In May 1928, there was a disastrous explosion of poison gas in a factory at Hamburg. Eleven persons were killed, many were injured, and many more became ill through inhaling the gas. It was only the fortunate direction of the wind away from the town which prevented a much more extensive loss of life.

Questions were naturally asked. For whom is this gas being prepared ? How does a firm in Germany come to be making poison gas, since under the Versailles Treaty it is forbidden ?

Suggestions were then thrown out that it was a war-time stock which had not been used or that it was phosgene, to be used for industrial purposes. To everyone's surprise the French Government did not protest. Indeed, the French expert at the Inter-Allied Commission of Control issued a reassuring explanation to the Paris Press that the phosgene was a dye stuff and that its production did not contravene the Versailles Treaty.

Those in Germany with a knowledge of the facts were puzzled. Dr. Lehmann-Russbüldt states that there can be no doubt that the Hamburg explosion was due to war gas.[1]

[1] *War for Profits*, p. 119.

Then why this whitewashing report by the *Ingénieur en Chef des Poudres?* It was difficult to believe that he had been fooled. The commonly accepted explanation in Germany was that the French interests had hushed up the matter because of their association with the German chemical industry. In a later chapter I shall describe how, immediately after the war, the French Ministry of War and the Société de l'Azote had entered into a fifteen years' contract with the most important German chemical concern.

The general conviction in Germany was that the Hamburg factory was producing poison gas for Russia. A special court of inquiry was set up, out of which a legal case arose between the chemical factory of Hamburg and the Economic Bank of Berlin. This led to some remarkable revelations.

The head of the Hamburg chemical factory was Dr. Hugo Stoltzenberg. He had apparently contracted in October 1923 to establish a factory at Trotsk, in Russia, for the manufacture of poison gas.[1] The real purpose of the enterprise was camouflaged by the formation of a company " to further industrial enterprises," which became known later as the Economic Bank of Berlin. But before the contract fell due the political situation had changed, owing to the Locarno policy of Germany in 1925, and Russia withdrew from it. The result was that Dr. Stoltzenberg lost heavily, and his legal case against the Economic Bank was to recover nearly five million reichsmarks.

At the same time German firms were making arrangements to supply Russia with aeroplanes. Another company was established " to further industrial enterprises." It was known as the " Gefu," a branch of the Reichswehr, and, with 70 million marks at its disposal, it controlled several aeroplane factories in Russia.

In 1922 the Junkers firm, acting under another pseudonym, also entered into agreement to supply Russia with aeroplanes. The

[1] *War for Profits*, p. 141.

real nature of the traffic was hidden under a contract to send sixty " chests " a year to Russia. The " chests " were aeroplanes.[1] Deputy Kuenstler, who exposed this matter in the Reichstag, declared that, in addition to poison gas and aeroplanes, German firms were sending artillery and infantry ammunition to Russia, and that these deliveries continued until 1926.

In this instance it seems evident that the German firms were carrying on their traffic in arms with the support of the German Government. The traffic was secret and illegal, and the official explanation was that it was only known to subordinates in the German Government. The fact was, however, that in a long memorandum General von Seeckt, Chief of the German Staff, had expressed unqualified approval. He was no doubt thinking of the potential value to Germany of an armament industry in Russia should his Government become involved in a war with France ; he wrote of the desirability

[1] *War for Profits*, p. 143.

of industries in Russia " which should be of service to us in the matter of military equip-ment." But at the same time General von Seeckt was in public a rabid anti-Bolshevist, and the development of European politics since that time suggests that the armament factories which German firms have estab-lished in Russia are much more likely to be used against Germany than on the side of Germany.

Russia is not, of course, the only country which German firms have assisted in arming since the World War. Although Germany is officially " disarmed," it does a large export traffic in armaments. In *Lloyds Handbook* a German firm openly advertises " military weapons and war materials of every kind," and announces itself to be a " purveyor to foreign Governments."

In 1927 the firm of Krupp acquired impor-tant shares in the Swedish Bofors Ordnance and Drydock Co., which operates the Krupp patents in Scandinavia. Dr. Lehmann-Russ-büldt states that " the French firm of

Schneider also seems to have bought shares in Bofors."[1] The association of the German and French firms appears to have been profitable. The business of Bofors rose from 9.3 million kroner in 1926 to 42 millions in 1928.

In 1928, when a disused automobile factory near Warsaw was transformed into machine-gun works, the machinery was provided by the Ludwig Loewe Co. of Berlin, and the raw material came from Mannesmann, in the Saar. It is not necessary to emphasise the political tension between Poland and Germany. Should war develop from this political tension, German soldiers will be slaughtered by machine-guns made from a plant provided from Berlin and constructed with steel from the Saar.

[1] *War for Profits*, p. 125.

HOW FRENCH ARMAMENT FIRMS
FINANCED SECRET ARMING OF
HUNGARY

From this interesting glimpse of the methods of German armament firms let us turn to their sister concerns in France.

It will be recollected that the French Government protested strongly in February 1933 against the secret purchase of arms by Hungary in violation of the Treaty of Peace. M. Paul Fauré, to whose courageous exposure of the French armament combine I have already referred, has stated that the secret arming of Hungary has only been made possible by the help of French armament capital. He first made this allegation in a speech in the Chamber of Deputies on December 13, 1931. An official inquiry was set up to investigate his charges. Some astonishing facts were revealed.

The Hungarian Government originally obtained a loan from Schneider-Creusot,

GB

the French armament firm. When Schneider-Creusot asked to be repaid, the Hungarians could not produce the money. Thereupon the French Government secretly lent the Hungarian Government the amount necessary !

This loan was transmitted to Hungary, not by the Bank of France, but by the Union Parisienne Banque, in which Schneider-Creusot holds a controlling interest. I don't know whether secrecy or profit-making was the motive in using the Schneider bank. Perhaps both. The Schneider bank would of course draw commission on the transaction ; its use would also enable the money to pass without outsiders being aware of what was being done. The French Parliament would never have been aware of the loan made in its name, if M. Paul Fauré had not obtained the information which enabled him to expose the matter.[1]

[1] *The Secret International*, p. 20.

HOW ARMAMENT FIRMS ARMED CHINESE
WAR LORDS, OIL TRUSTS, AND FASCISTS

Armament firms are no respecters of
Governments. If there are war lords or
industrial concerns or Fascist leaders
interested in obtaining arms, the armament
firms will, in their ordinary course of business, supply them.

For example, arms have poured into
China for twenty years. The war lords have
sent their officers to visit the works of
Schneider-Creusot, Krupp, and Vickers,
and big orders have followed. The costs of
the orders for munitions, cannon, and
machine-guns have been met by the pillage
of the peasants in the provinces, over which
the armies of mercenaries have swept, or the
crowded populations of captured cities.

" Each general has his sleeping partners,
whose names are to be found in the banks
of Hong-Kong, Paris, London, New York,
Yokohama, or even Moscow," writes M.

Francis Delaisi. " Mere displacements of capital determine the fusion or scission of armies. The sleeping partners change their generals, or the generals their sleeping partners. This system has let loose on this unhappy country all the horrors of the Thirty Years' War."[1]

In Central and Southern America armed revolutions are almost yearly happenings. Behind them are the conflicting economic interests of great industrial concerns which the armament firms do not hesitate to supply with the weapons of civil war. " When the Standard Oil and the Royal Dutch Shell groups were fighting for the Mexican oil-fields " (to quote M. Delaisi again), " if the Government took measures favourable to one of the two rivals a ' revolution ' immediately broke out and the two armies marched regularly upon Tampico, where the naphtha wells were situated. Invariably one was supplied with cannon, machine-guns, and even aeroplanes of American

[1] *What Would be the Character of a New War ?* p. 197.

manufacture, the other with arms of English manufacture. It was in this way that Mexico was for twenty years a prey to civil war. It has only found peace since the two groups discovered that there was too much petrol on the market and agreed to prevent the working of the Mexican oilfields, which had become useless."

The private forces of the Nazi movement in Germany are understood to have obtained arms secretly from the Skoda group of firms before Hitler attained power. Directors of the Skoda Works publicly supported the Hitler campaign. His success could be expected to hasten the re-armament of Germany ; but the Skoda Works are, as we shall see, a subsidiary of the *French* combine, Schneider-Creusot. Thus a section of the French armament combine was actively supporting the champion of German nationalism in a campaign which was defying the Versailles Treaty !

Whilst armament firms do not feel an obligation to restrict their trade because of political considerations, they are always ready, of course, to serve the interests of their Governments if increased business is likely to be the result. When two small nations go to war, there are often powerful industrial interests behind the quarrel, and associated with these interests there are often powerful Governments. Under such circumstances a Government may not be able openly to support the side which it favours by force of arms, but there is nothing to prevent its leading firms from giving support by force of armaments. This may be done on an extensive scale when the Government is officially neutral in the conflict, or even when by treaty it has undertaken to be favourable to the other side.

Here is a recent example. By the Treaty of San Remo, in 1920, Britain agreed to the French occupation of Damascus in return for French acceptance of the British Mandate over the Mosul oilfield. But the British authorities did not want to see the French in Damascus. They had previously promised the city to Emir Feisul as his capital, and they would have preferred to see their puppet in Damascus rather than a rival Power.

Emir Feisul, supported by the Druses, proceeded to make war on the French. There is little doubt that the repeating-rifles and munitions which the Emir and his allies used were supplied by British armament firms.

About the same time Greece and Turkey were in conflict. The British Government was unofficially favourable to Greece ; the French Government to Turkey. From Vickers the Greek Government secured on credit supplies of arms and munitions, and with these it drove back the troops of Mustapha Kemal into the heart of Anatolia. But at this point Mustapha Kemal concluded the Angora agreement with the French Government, and he found himself provided with a supply of cannon and rifles " discarded " by the French Army. With these he drove back the Greeks into the sea.

M. Francis Delaisi quotes an ironical comment made upon this incident by an American war correspondent. He wrote : " I first saw the retreat of the Greeks ; they abandoned cannon and machine-guns all bearing the mark of the British firm of Vickers. Then I witnessed the triumphal entry of the Turks into Smyrna ; they brought with them magnificent Creusot cannon. *That day I understood the meaning of the ' Entente Cordiale.' "*

M. Delaisi's own comment is as follows :

" Officially, France was at peace with Greece, and the Foreign Office knew nothing of the Druses. The British Parliament had agreed to no treaty of alliance and to no credit permitting support of the Greek Army. The French Parliament had approved of no military agreement permitting the arming of the Turks. But there was nothing to prevent Vickers from supplying Greece with artillery on credit, nor certain adventurous traders from selling the Turks French cannon, to be paid for by various concessions after victory had been obtained. It is to be

supposed that neither the officials of the Quai
D'Orsay nor those of the Foreign Office
were completely ignorant of these *private*
transactions. But it was to England's interest
to have the Turks away from the Bosphorus,
and France wanted at all costs to maintain
her mandate over Syria. Thus the two
diplomacies closed their eyes (if not their
hands). And the two Governments, French
and British, made war—within narrow limits
it is true, and through go-betweens—without
the knowledge of the responsible Parlia-
ments."

Thus we see how the Bloody Traffic con-
tinues in peace-time as in war-time. The
armament firms sell their weapons of murder
to whomsoever will buy : to their own
Governments ; to friendly Governments ;
to enemy Governments ; to Governments
which are potential enemies ; to Governments engaged in wars condemned by the
League of Nations ; to countries carrying
on wars which their own Governments wish
to support secretly ; to Chinese war lords ;
to the armies of oil combines ; to Nazis—to

any Government, to *any interest whatsoever,* so long as the money is forthcoming. The purchasers matter not. If they pay they get their goods. Even when they can't pay, they get their goods if their credit, on the security of taxation or pillage, is sufficiently good.

Such is the Bloody Traffic—a quite callous selling of the weapons of murder to any customer who can pay the price.

CHAPTER VIII

HOW ARMAMENT FIRMS HAVE ARMED CHINA AND JAPAN

" The Government should start from the principle that no country loyal to the Covenant will sell arms to Japan. How could it ? In Manchuria, at Shanghai, in Jehol, Japan has made war on China, and the consequences of war in death and destruction are not less hideous because they are remote. Japan is not only destroying innocent flesh and blood ; she is restoring the lawlessness of the jungle in place of the rule of law, which, slowly and painfully enough, we have been trying to build up. We call the League a ' family ' of nations. How odd a name it would be for a group which was found supplying deadly arms to a member whom it had just condemned for pursuing a bitter, long attack upon another member. An obligation, individual and inescapable, rests on every country which is sincere."—*The Manchester Guardian*, February 25th, 1933.

CHINA has for some years been the paradise of the armament firms. She has been the scene of almost continual war, and, since she has practically no equipment for the production of arms, the armament salesmen have had a prosperous time. In recent years

China has imported more arms than any country in the world.

China has been supplied from every armament centre. The largest orders have probably been fulfilled by the Skoda Works, in Czecho-Slovakia, using Hamburg as a port. But the supply of armaments has also been constant from Britain, the United States, France, Germany, Belgium, Norway, and Japan. Although Japan has been the political enemy of China for a generation, and has been more or less continually at war with her for the last two years, the Japanese armament firms as recently as 1930 supplied China with no less than 37.5 per cent of her munitions.

Shanghai is the centre of the armament industry for the Far East. Here the loads of armaments from Europe are discharged and sorted out—some for China, some for Japan. The same seamen and dockers handle both. Often they have been made by the same firm and the same workers. But they are destined to be used in two opposing armies, bringing death and destruction both to Chinese and Japanese.

Japan has the advantage over China of a large, efficient, and up-to-date armament industry. She can build the most modern weapons for land, sea, or air. She can build warships and aircraft carriers. She has had the service of British experts, and one of the firms associated in her Mitsui combine is actually a subsidiary of Vickers-Armstrong. The same combine has the advantage of possessing the Far Eastern patent of the American Curtiss-Wright engines for aeroplanes.

Under such circumstances, Japan has a considerable advantage over China, but, despite the condemnation of her invasion and occupation of Manchuria by the League of Nations and the Government of the United States, the European and American armament firms have continued to render her assistance. During 1932, British armament firms exported 5,361,450 small-arm cartridges, 4,909 cwt. of high explosives, and other explosives to the value of £40,239 to Japan. During 1931, American firms sent Japan armaments valued at 48,197 dollars.

Following upon the unanimous condemnation of the Japanese Government by the European nations associated with the League, the British Government for a time announced its intention of putting an embargo on all munitions to the Far East, whether destined for Japan or China. But when other nations showed no sign of following this example, the embargo was withdrawn. The war in the Far East has since resulted in heavy orders for armaments, both in Britain and the Continent of Europe.

The French armament firms appear to have done particularly well. In March it was reported that 200 pieces of heavy naval artillery (French 75's), 10,000,000 rounds of naval ammunition, 12,000,000 rounds of machine-gun ammunition, and 2,000,000 shells for light calibre artillery had left the

Schneider-Creusot works for Japan and China. " The armament firms of France," we were told in the Press, " are working their employees night and day in the biggest munitions drive since the war."

Another French firm upon whom heavy demands have been made by the war in the Far East is the Hotchkiss Company, of whose shareholders a considerable number are English. The Hotchkiss Company benefited not only from the unofficial war in the Far East, but from the wars in South America, also condemned by the League of Nations. Whilst her machine-guns left Marseilles for Japan and China, other machine-guns from her factories left Boulogne and Rouen for the unofficial wars conducted by Paraguay and Bolivia. " The night haunts of Montmartre," a descriptive Press writer informed us, " are filled with workmen from the Hotchkiss machine-gun factories, who come to Paris for the week-end to spend their overtime earnings just as they did during the war."

The one booming industry amidst the economic collapse of Europe prospers by providing munitions to both sides in two wars which the Governments of Europe have condemned as outraging international conventions !

One of the Press reports records that a retired British captain was acting for the Japanese Government at the Schneider-Creusot works. It stated that in November the Japanese representative " coolly gave an order for the entire stock of munitions on hand in the factories and warehouses of the Schneider-Creusot Company to be sent immediately to Japan. Now the 12,000 employees in this great armament town are working on a fresh order so large that workshops usually reserved for the manufacture of tractor wheels, locomotive parts and rails, and other instruments of peace, have been converted into munition shops."

The Japanese Government can afford to ignore the political condemnation of the Governments of Europe when the armament works of Europe are so readily at its disposal. In war it is weapons, not words, that count.

The Skoda Works in Czecho-Slovakia, a subsidiary of Schneider-Creusot, enjoyed the same prosperity as a result of these unofficial wars in the Far East and South America. They were working night and day, with a largely augmented staff, in March. From these vast works a regular supply of death-dealing weapons was pouring forth, not only to the Far East, but to Bolivia, Peru, Ecuador, Brazil, and Uruguay. Skoda's European orders were also up considerably, as the result of the political tension in every part of the Continent. In the Far East, Skoda's weapons rain death on Japanese and Chinese alike. In South America they destroy the forces on both sides. If the smouldering embers in Europe burst into flame, Skoda's munitions will fall into both camps.

Thus the infamous traffic continues. Profit from death—who dies does not matter.

Many firms were engaged in the simultaneous production of armaments for Japan

HB

and China. Arising from this there arose a curious incident at a British armament works which Mr. Morgan Jones, M.P., described in the House of Commons on February 27. "At a certain factory," he said, "armaments were being prepared in one part of the building for Japan and in another for China. By an unfortunate chance, the representatives of the Governments arrived at the factory at the same time and were shown into the same room. There they began to discuss the charges made by the firm for their munitions, with the result that they agreed to a joint ultimatum asking for a reduction in prices."

Could the irony of facts go further? If the Japanese and Chinese representatives had met on the battle-field they would have attempted to kill each other. They had come to this firm to buy weapons so that their countrymen could kill each other. And what do they do? They don't even hurl words at each other. They coolly discuss the price which each is paying for the slaughter of the other's compatriots, and decide to join forces in bargaining with the armament-maker. What a bloody game it is !

The cool arrogance of the war-makers is astounding. Having defied the League of Nations, Mr. Matsuoka, the Japanese delegate, travelled to Britain. He became the special guest of the Metropolitan-Vickers Electrical Company and was taken a tour round their works. Subsequently he had an hour's interview with Sir Harry McGowan, chairman of the Imperial Chemical Industries, Ltd., the potential poison gas combine of Britain.

A DIFFERENT STORY

But there is one story of a different character which demands record. It shows that, whilst Governments will not act, a movement is beginning among the workers which may yet defeat the power of the armament-makers.

On March 5, 1933, a steamer named

Stanleyville lay in the dock at Blyth, Northumberland, loaded with a cargo of scrap metal for Japan. A Japanese boarding-house master in North Shields received instructions to procure a Japanese crew, but a meeting was held in the boarding-house by members of the Anti-War Movement and it was explained to the Japanese seamen that the scrap material would be turned into munitions, to be used in an unjust attack on China, and possibly on Russia. The Japanese seamen refused to have anything to do with the ship.

The boarding-house master then endeavoured to ship other crews, but meetings and talks were held in one boarding-house after another, among Spanish, Greek, and negro seamen, with the result that they declared that they would not take the ship out. Finally, an Arab boarding-house master accepted the job of finding the crew. He secured a mixed crew of Arabs and Malays ; but at the last moment they, too, refused to sign on. Then a crew of Somalilese and a few Maltese was obtained, but even these at the last moment declared that they would not sail if sufficient financial support were provided to maintain them.

The Congress of the Anti-War Movement was meeting in London. A telegram was despatched to it, reading as follows :

"Crew prepared to leave ship if given financial support. Otherwise homeless and penniless. All coloured."

A collection was taken among the delegates. Over £105 was collected, with promise of a further £15. Then a workman offered his life-time savings by agreeing to double what another collection would realise. The second collection amounted to £32.

Immediately two of the delegates left with the money by car for Blyth, a distance of over 250 miles. They arrived between three and four o'clock, to find a police cordon guarding every approach. The river was patrolled. The crew were threatened by officials and officers and were told that their friends had been arrested at the dock gates. They gave way. In the morning the ship sailed.

The final scene in this drama took place in the Blyth police-court the following morning. John Davidson, docker, of North Shields, was charged with being found on enclosed premises for an unlawful purpose. " I do not believe in war," he said, " and that ship is being taken to Japan with war material. I wanted to go on board the vessel to have a meeting with the crew and get them to leave the ship."

John Davidson may yet prove more powerful than Krupp and Vickers and Schneider-Creusot and Skoda.

CHAPTER IX

HOW AMERICAN ARMAMENT FIRMS ARM OTHER COUNTRIES

" I appreciate the fact that the manufacturers of arms and ammunition are not standing very high in the estimation of the public generally. . . . We are not arguing for permission to encourage warfare. That is not our disposition, despite the statements of some writers in the Press. There are some rash statements made about the arms manufacturers fomenting war, but that is just as ridiculous as a lot of other things that are said."— SAMUEL M. STONE, *President of Colt's Patent Fire Arms Manufacturing Co.*

THE AMERICAN armament firms exported the following products in 1932 :

Ammunition to the value of		840,098	dollars
Explosives	,,	1,281,935	,,
Machine-guns	,,	49,654	,, (1931)
Firearms	,,	343,659	,,
Aircraft	,,	4,358,967	,,

This gives a total value of armament exports in one year of 6,874,313 dollars.

The principal countries to which these articles went were Mexico, Peru, China

Chile, Canada, Brazil, and (particularly in firearms) Japan. It is very noticeable how the export business of the armament firms of America improves during years of actual or threatened hostilities among her neighbours.

Since 1930, Mexico has been at peace. The exports in firearms from U.S.A. to Mexico during 1932 were valued at 15,954 dollars. In 1929, when Mexico was in a state of war, the value of the exports in firearms from the U.S.A. was 370,324 dollars, over twenty times as much.

Since 1931, Argentina has been at peace. Last year the value of the export of firearms from U.S.A. to Argentina was 40,078 dollars. In 1929 and 1930, when Argentina was in a state of war, the value of the U.S.A. exports in firearms was 299,565 dollars and 179,050 respectively.

Since 1930, Brazil has been at peace. The U.S.A. exports in firearms to Brazil in 1932 were valued at 59,490 dollars. In 1929 they were valued at 618,135 dollars.

In 1931 there was a revolt in Chile. The

value of the export in firearms from U.S.A. that year was 11,308 dollars. Last year they fell to 1,103 dollars.

The same point can be illustrated by the number of aircraft exported from the U.S.A. to Central and Southern American States when engaged in or threatened by hostilities. This table compares the year 1931 (comparatively peaceful) with 1929, which was a year of war and revolt in the four countries named :

Number of Aircraft Exported from U.S.A.

	1931	*1929*
Mexico	27	85
Argentina	6	25
Brazil	1	13
Chile	1	40

American armament firms evidently thrive on the wars and revolts of Central and South America.

The American firms also do well out of the wars in the Far East. The table on the following page gives particulars of some of the exports to Japan and China. Japanese are being shattered to bits by bombing aeroplanes,

AMERICAN EXPORT OF ARMS TO JAPAN AND CHINA

	1928	1929	1930	1931
Aircraft				
Japan	$63,000 (3 aircraft)	$291,767 (17)	$301,687 (14)	—
China	$102,175 (9 aircraft)	$522,741 (24)	$935,472 (41)	$644,170 (38)
Aircraft Engines				
Japan	$41,281 (10)	$75,098 (24)	$64,557 (14)	$35,161 (7)
China	$38,900 (5)	$39,000 (9)	$65,090 (11)	$100,120 (38)
Ammunition				
Japan	$13,497	$9,386	$15,025	$8,241
China	$11,938	$11,100	$45,166	$26,477
Explosives				
Japan	$6,981	$5,219	$1,044	$1,114
China	$50	$85,946	$489,879	$145,270

guns, and explosives. So are Chinese. The American armament firms profit from the slaughter on both sides.

ARMAMENT FIRMS OPPOSE AN EMBARGO

Early this year a proposal was made that the President of the United States should be given power to place an embargo, in co-operation with other Governments, on the shipment of arms or munitions of war. The proposal was submitted to the House of Representatives Committee on Foreign Affairs. To this committee representatives of a number of firms engaged in armament production (and sometimes other articles) gave evidence.

This evidence was interesting from many points of view. First, it showed how high is the proportion of exports devoted to the purposes of war. For example, one of the witnesses was Mr. Guy Vaughan, director of the Aeronautical Chamber of Commerce, Paterson, New Jersey. He stated that the annual value of exports by his company is about 2,000,000 dollars, of which eighty per cent is for war purposes. He told how his company has five representatives in foreign countries soliciting orders, and that the Curtiss-Wright Company had considerably more. " I will say that we have shipped eighty per cent of our total shipments for war purposes," he said. " They are distinctly military aeroplanes or convertible into such."

The total export business of American aircraft firms was put at nearly eight million dollars. These exports go to forty-six foreign countries, including Central and South America, Scandinavia, Holland, Belgium, Japan, and Turkey. Mr. Thomas A. Morgan the president of the All-American Aeronautical Chamber of Commerce (which represents ninety-five per cent of the American aviation firms) estimated that from seventy to seventy-five per cent of the total exports, including both engines and planes, is classified as war equipment.

Mr. F. J. Monahan, representing the Remington Arms Company, reported that the average value of its export of ammunition is 1,000,000 dollars a year. After deducting the production of cartridges for hunting and target-practice, no less than forty per cent of the firm's business is for export. The exports include cartridges for revolvers, pistols, rifles, and machine-guns.

A second noteworthy feature of the evidence is the repeatedly expressed justification of the provision of arms to other countries on the ground that it maintains the American armament industry in a condition of efficiency, so that it is ready to meet any national emergency. This point was put clearly by Mr. Thomas Morgan :

" The aircraft industry is a vital factor in the national defence of this country. Military experts have agreed that the first battles in the next war will be in the air. The capacity of the civil air lines of the country will have to be greatly expanded in time of emergency to fulfil their transportation function alone,

and private aircraft will be commandeered
for emergency use in the same way as private
automobiles in the past. The industry therefore must be maintained on a scale which
renders it possible of effective emergency use.
Factories must be kept in operating condition, and engineering and technical personnel maintained.

" To do this requires every item of production in peace-time which can possibly be
found. Because of this, the export business
which the industry has built up, though small
as compared to that of other industries, is of
great importance. A few years ago, export
business in American aircraft was negligible.
In the last few years, however, the industry
has gone after export business systematically,
has sought and received excellent trade
assistance along these lines from the United
States Government, and has fought its way
to a place at the top group of aircraft and
equipment exporting nations of the world."

The logic of this position is that other
countries must be armed in order that your
own country may be prepared to resist their
arms !

The same point was made by Mr. Samuel M. Stone, president of the Colt's Patent Fire Arms Manufacturing Company, manufacturers of machine-guns. " That company has for a great many years maintained a qualified personnel," he said, " prepared at any emergency, upon the demand of the Government, to speedily engage in the manufacture of machine-guns in considerable quantity." To maintain this personnel, he argued, exports of machine-guns must be maintained.

Mr. Monahan, of the Remington Arms Company, used almost identical words. " The men are kept trained," he said, " and therefore ready for the emergency when it exists or when it occurs ; and we have a nucleus on which to build to take care of any of the needs of the Government."

The cross-examination which followed is worth quoting :

MR. HULL : You say they are kept in training on this foreign business ?
MR. MONAHAN : Yes, sir.

MR. HULL : That is arms and ammunition for war purposes ?

MR. MONAHAN : We never know what part of the exports, of what we call these metallic cartridges, are going to be used for war purposes and what part for protection, policing, and sport purposes.

MR. HULL : In order to keep in tune, to keep in practice, you have got to have trouble going on in some part of the world ?

MR. MONAHAN : Yes, sir.

In other words, to be prepared for war in your own country you must hope for continuous wars in other countries.

HELPING GOVERNMENTS SUPPRESS REVOLUTION

A third point of interest in this evidence is the justification made for the export of armaments on the ground that they are used to suppress revolutions. In his verbal evidence, Mr. Thomas A. Morgan instanced the insurrection in Cuba, which was suppressed with twelve American aeroplanes, and the mutiny of " practically all of the Chilean Navy," which was also suppressed with American aircraft. In his written statement he supplemented this reference :

" A good part of the export trade in aircraft equipment is with foreign Governments. The smaller countries have found an air force to be an inexpensive means of defence against revolutionary movements and against outside Powers. These air forces are effective means of keeping the peace. As illustrations we have only to recall the revolution of the Chilean Navy involving warships costing millions to build ; the uprising was suppressed by the Chilean Government flying airplanes over the ships and threatening to bomb them. A more recent instance has just occurred when the crew of a Dutch warship in the Dutch East Indies revolted and surrendered after one bomb was dropped from a Dutch Government airplane."

Later Mr. Morgan added :

" A great deal of the export trade in these products is of an emergency nature. The Government of the United States finds it is

IB

confronted with an uprising and wants aircraft. It wants them in a hurry. It wants to
know that, if it buys them, it can be certain
of delivery. It wants to know that these
deliveries will not be held up as a result of
pressure brought to bear on United States
Government officials by well-meaning but
impractical peace societies perhaps inspired
by our European competitors."

A final point revealing the methods of
armament firms may be noted. Mr. Morgan
complained that, whilst American firms had
refrained from supplying aircraft to the
Canton Government, because it is not recognised by the United States, European firms
have done so by a subterfuge. They have
supplied high-class fighting aircraft, and,
" simply leaving off the machine-guns,"
have called them commercial planes !

Mr. Morgan may or may not have justification for this allegation ; but subsequent
evidence showed that American firms have
been guilty of similar practices. One of
the leading State Department officials, Mr.

Joseph C. Green, reported that in 1931 an American company was " planning to export commercial airplanes to certain Chinese rebels, and at the same time providing them with blue-prints indicating the manner in which these planes could be converted into military planes."

Armament firms are apparently much of a muchness.

CHAPTER X

HOW ARMAMENT FIRMS PRACTISE BRIBERY AND CORRUPTION

" We are in the hands of an organisation of crooks. They are politicians, generals, manufacturers of armaments and journalists. All of them are anxious for unlimited expenditure, and go on inventing scares to terrify the public and so terrify Ministers of the Crown."—LORD WELBY (Assistant Under-Secretary, War Office, 1900–1902), quoted by Mr. Philip (now Viscount) Snowden, House of Commons, March 17th, 1914.

AT THE annual meeting of Vickers Ltd., held in April 1933, Sir Herbert A. Lawrence, the chairman, used these words :

" I would refer to the misleading views promulgated by certain pacific societies regarding private armament firms. Drawing on very vivid imaginations, they represent such firms secretly stirring up strife in various quarters of the globe with the deliberate intent to bring about war for the sole purpose of selling armaments.

" So far as this company is concerned, there never has been, and never will be, the shadow of substance for such suggestions. The military, naval and air advisers in every country determine the extent of the armaments required, and the direction of the supply depends on the efficiency of the products offered and the price.

" It is true that Vickers-Armstrong Ltd. rely very largely on armament orders. On the other hand, the safety of the Empire in the event of aggression by some other Power also depends on the capacity of the company to increase the production of armaments at short notice.

" So long as a British Navy, a British Army and a British Air Force are necessary, so long must the technical establishments and skilled men be retained—either by Vickers-Armstrong's or some other firm.

" The existence of armament firms is the result—not the cause—of the incidence of war."

In this passage, Sir Herbert A. Lawrence attempts to ridicule the suggestion that armament firms secretly stir up strife, and seeks to give the impression that Vickers-Armstrong has only the patriotic purpose of meeting the requirements of the British Navy, Army and Air Force so that they may be in a position to maintain the safety of the Empire against the aggression of some other Power.

So far as armament firms generally are concerned, we have the judgment of the Sub-Committee of the League of Nations already reproduced in Chapter II. It will be recollected that this committee concluded that armament firms have been active in fomenting war scares and in persuading their countries to adopt warlike policies ; that they have attempted to bribe Government officials ; that they have disseminated false reports concerning military and naval programmes ; that they have sought to influence public opinion through the control of newspapers ; that through international rings they have accentuated the armament race by playing off one country against another ; and that they have organised international trusts which have increased the price of armaments.

To this indictment made by an official sub-committee representing the *Governments* of Europe it does not seem necessary for " pacific societies " to add anything. In support of these conclusions of the League committee much evidence has already been given in this book. More will be given in this chapter.

But what of Vickers-Armstrong themselves? We have already seen how Vickers armed Russia during the Russo-Japanese war, although Japan was the ally of Britain. We have seen how Vickers built the Turkish forts and cannon which massacred the Australian and British troops in the Dardanelles. We have seen how at the dockyard of a subsidiary of Vickers-Armstrong—the confiscated Fiume dockyard of Henry Whitehead & Co.—torpedoes, torpedo-boats, torpedo-boat destroyers, and mines were made for the Central Powers during the Great War. We shall see how Vickers-Armstrong has a subsidiary firm in Japan and how it has supplied Japan with

munitions for a war which the British
Government and the League of Nations
have condemned as an unjustifiable act of
aggression. We shall see how it has factories
or subsidiaries in Italy, Spain, Rumania,
Holland, France, and South America, and
how it supplies a large part of the world
with armaments, a considerable portion of
which would certainly be used to mutilate
and murder British troops if another world
war occurred. We shall see how it is part of
an international armament ring, which has
the object of developing the traffic in arms.
I now pass on to a further subject, which
will read strangely after Sir Herbert A.
Lawrence's innocent remarks.

A BRITISH CASE OF BRIBERY

Early in 1910, Rear-Admiral Fujii was
sent by the Japanese Government to Britain,
in his capacity as Officer for the Supervision
of the Construction of Warships, to report
upon estimates and specifications submitted

by Vickers and Armstrong for a battle cruiser.[1]

He examined the estimates and specifications and reported favourably on Vickers (then a firm separate from Armstrong) and recommended the Japanese Naval Stores Department to accept its specifications and estimates, the former because they were the more precise and the latter because they were lower. Accordingly the Japanese Government decided to order the ship from Vickers, and on November 17, 1910, a contract to the value of £2,367,100 was signed.

Fujii was in 1914 concerned in a case in the Japanese courts. Evidence was given that he was on intimate terms with the director of the Vickers Works at Barrow, that the director had asked the admiral to show his goodwill towards Vickers, and that, after the accused's return to Japan, the director, with a view to reciprocating his goodwill, had remitted, over a period of several years, certain large sums of money to the admiral.[2]

---

[1] See the section on this case in *The Secret International*, p. 39.

[2] *Japanese Weekly Chronicle*, June and July, 1914.

I do not wish to suggest for a moment that Vickers has been worse in this respect than other firms. The " remittances " which the director of the Vickers Works at Barrow is stated to have sent to Rear-Admiral Fujii were the biggest, but the trial revealed that other firms were using the same methods. For instance, according to the *Japanese Weekly Chronicle*, in 1911 another Japanese official was visiting British armament firms. His name was Naval Constructor Yanamoto Kaizo, and in the course of his duties he is stated to have had an interview with Mr. A. F. Yarrow (the president of the Yarrow Shipbuilding Yard), who explained to him the advantages of an oil-combustion destroyer, the latest invention of that yard, and supplied him with a plan of it, expressing hope that the Japanese Navy would give the firm an order.

The specifications of the new destroyer were sent to the Japanese Naval Stores Department, followed by " remittances " to the same Rear-Admiral Fujii. The order was in due course forthcoming. On December 27, 1912, a contract was signed between the Japanese Government and the Yarrow Yard Company for the building of two of the destroyers.

Other firms were also mentioned. Weir & Co. are stated to have sent a " remittance " of £1,000 in August 1911. Subsequently an order from the Japanese Government for machinery and pumps for a battleship was received. Arrol & Co. are stated to have made the rear-admiral a gift of £1,750, subsequent to an order for materials valued at over £33,620. The Reuter correspondent in Tokyo bought from a former employee of Siemens-Schuckert secret papers which are stated to have proved the delivery, or promise of delivery, of bribes between Siemens Bros., London, and Rear-Admiral Fujii.[1]

Nor must it be thought that Japanese officials are alone guilty of receiving bribes. The *Japanese Weekly Chronicle* (July 23, 1914)

[1] *The Secret International*, p. 39.

was quite justified in the comment which it made :

" There is no nation which can afford to throw stones at Japan in connection with the existence of bribery and corruption in State services. Only recently a series of scandals in connection with the supply of stores to the British military canteens was brought into publicity in the courts. . . . In Germany and other countries there have been cases equally unsavoury, until it has been made clear that the ' profession ' of arms has become as sordidly money-grubbing as it possibly can. It would even seem that, in some countries, it is absolutely essential to resort to practices which, if not actually criminal, are grossly immoral, if any business is to be done by contractors anxious to get orders. Even where an order is obtained, it is sometimes necessary to resort to further corruption."

A GERMAN CASE OF BRIBERY

Just prior to the exposure of the Fujii affair in Japan, Karl Liebknecht had exposed a similar affair in Germany. On April 18, 1913, he made the following charge in a speech in the Reichstag :

" For several weeks now, Krupp has employed an agent by the name of Brandt, a former artillery officer, whose business it is to approach executive officials of the Government, of the Army and Navy, and *to bribe them for access to private papers in which the firm of Krupp happens to be interested*, and, above all, to discover the plans of the Government with regard to armaments, to obtain sketches of construction for internal defence, and to ascertain what rival firms were bidding, or had bidden in the past. In order to carry out this purpose, Herr Brandt is, of course, granted a generous allowance."

This charge was made the subject of inquiry by a Government Commission. It proved true, and Brandt was brought to trial. Brandt was found guilty of bribery and was sentenced to four months' imprisonment, and one of the directors of Krupp, Herr Eccius, was fined 1,200 marks for aiding and abetting him.

A SWEDISH CASE OF BRIBERY

A recent exposure of bribery by an aircraft firm has occurred in Sweden. Allegations of irregularities led to the appointment of a Commission of Inquiry by the Government. After an investigation lasting eight months, the Commission found that bribes to the extent of 16,000 kronor had been accepted by the Chief of Staff of the Air Force in the form of " long loans." In reporting this case, *The Times* (November 11, 1931) stated :

" Some of the money, the report alleges, was received from the representative of an aircraft firm. The Commissioners pass judgment on nothing for which there is no proof, and their report has revealed an almost incredible state of affairs within the Air Force higher command."[1]

[1] *The Secret International*, p. 37.

A CHARGE AGAINST A REPRESENTATIVE
OF THE SKODA WORKS

As I am writing this chapter a report appears in the Press of the arrest at Bucharest of M. Seletzsky, an Austrian subject, who represents in Rumania the Skoda Works, which, as we shall see, is the Czecho-Slovakian branch of the powerful Schneider-Creusot combine in France. M. Seletzsky was arrested following charges of bribery by Dr. Nicholas Lupu, the leader of the Opposition in the Chamber. Dr. Lupu, by means of questions to the Government, indicated that three Ministers obtained 1,000,000,000 lei (about £120,000), while a group of interested persons received 700,000,000 lei (about £90,000), in connection with the placing of an order for guns to the value of £18,000,000.

This charge caused such a sensation that the King intervened and stopped the continuance of the proceedings in the Chamber. He commanded Dr. Lupu to visit him at

once, and during a long audience the
Opposition leader was closeted alone with
King Carol. The next day, Dr. Lupu repeated his allegations, adding that the order
for the guns was given to the Skoda Works
without serious consideration. He also
alleged that documents connected with the
National Defence Council, particulars of
the output of the Rumanian armament
works, as well as other military secrets, had
been found in M. Seletzsky's house.

Following upon Dr. Lupu's initial charges,
M. Seletzsky's house had been sealed and a
military guard placed in front of it. Later, by
some mysterious means, which suggest influential support, the guard was removed
and the seals were broken. After Dr.
Lupu's audience with the King and the
renewed attack made by the Opposition
leader in the Chamber, M. Seletzsky was
arrested.

At the time of writing, the trial has not
taken place, but further revelations have
been made. It seems that a rumour (soon

found to be baseless) was spread about that Russian troops were concentrating on the Rumanian frontier. The rumours were traced to Skoda, which succeeded in getting large orders as a result of them. The effect of this scandal was so serious that General Popolescu has committed suicide.

"KISSING GOES BY FAVOUR"

There is a subtle method adopted by armament firms for obtaining influence over Government Departments. It is their custom to appoint to their directorates, or to important posts in their service, officials of high standing in the Ministerial Departments on their retirement from Government service. The advantages of this practice have been stated frankly by the technical newspaper, *Armaments and Ammunition* (September 1913) :

" Contractors naturally are very keen to avail themselves of the services of prominent officers who have been associated with work

KB

in which the contractors are interested. The chief thing is that they know the ropes, since the retired officer who keeps in touch with his old comrades is able to lessen some of these inconveniences, either by gaining early information of coming events or by securing the ear of one who would not afford like favours to a civilian. . . . *Kissing undoubtedly goes by favour, and some of these things that happen might be characterised as corruption.*"

The directors of Vickers-Armstrong include five retired, high-placed officials in Government circles or ex-officers in the fighting services. I give their official positions.

GENERAL THE HON. SIR HERBERT LAWRENCE, Chairman of Vickers since 1926. Chief of Staff, Headquarters British Army in France, from January 1918. Left Army on retired pay, 1922.

SIR MARK WEBSTER JENKINSON. Formerly Controller of the Department of Factory Audit and Costs at the Ministry of Munitions, and Chief Liquidator of Contracts at the Ministry of Munitions after the war.

GENERAL SIR J. F. NOEL BIRCH. After a long
military career, was Artillery Adviser to
the Commander-in-Chief in France, 1916–
19. Director of Remounts, 1920–21. Director-General of the Territorial Army, 1921–
23. Master-General of the Ordnance and
Member of the Army Council, 1923–27.

SIR J. A. COOPER. Principal in Charge of
Raw Materials Finance at the War Office,
1917–19 ; then became the Director of
Raw Materials Finance at the Ministry
of Munitions, 1919–21.

SIR A. G. HADCOCK. Formerly an Associate
Member of the Ordnance Committee.

Directors with military or naval experience
also include : Commander C. W. Craven,
Colonel J. B. Neilson, and Major-General
G. P. Dawnay.

A recent case was that of the late Sir
Arthur Trevor Dawson, who was a director
of Vickers-Armstrong at the time of his
death in May 1931. He was formerly
Experimental Officer at Woolwich Arsenal,
and afterwards became superintendent of

ordnance to Vickers and chairman of their Artillery and Shipbuilding Management Board.

AN ARMAMENT MAKER SCARES THE CABINET

But sometimes armament firms succeed in getting behind the permanent officials of the War Departments to the Cabinet itself. The most remarkable case of this is that of Mr. Mulliner, the creator of the war-scare of 1909. The story must be told in some detail.

The economy policy of the Liberal Government from 1908 onwards had given the armament firms a severe blow. From 1908 to 1910 the dividends of Vickers and Armstrong fell from fifteen per cent to ten per cent. The *Naval Annual* published at the beginning of 1909 recorded that " the shipbuilding industry has passed through one of the worst years ever known." Unless Government orders could be increased, there was every prospect of the dividends falling still further.

Orders for warships would not come unless a feeling of insecurity were created. A feeling of insecurity would not come without a war-scare. The war-scare was started.

On March 3, 1909, Mr. Mulliner, manager of the Coventry Ordnance Works, convinced the Admiralty that he had private information of such importance that the Cabinet was justified in taking the unprecedented step of receiving him to hear his story. He told the Cabinet that he had reliable information that the German Government was secretly accelerating her naval programme. The Cabinet accepted his story.

Mr. Asquith and Mr. McKenna hurried to the House of Commons and announced that Germany would have seventeen Dread-noughts by March 1912, instead of the nine publicly announced in her naval programme. Mr. Balfour, who had also been admitted into Mr. Mulliner's confidence, went further. He declared that Germany would have twenty-five, or at the lowest estimate twenty-one, Dreadnoughts by that date. The House became panic-stricken.

It immediately voted an increase of naval expenditure of £4,603,002. Of this, £4,409,502 went to the private armament firms. But even this was not regarded as enough. The war-scare, once started, was fanned to flame by the nationalist and patriotic Press, and by politicians who demanded still more Dreadnoughts. The Conservatives won a by-election at Peckham by a sensational majority on the cry " We want eight, and we won't wait." Before the end of the year the Government responded to the popular clamour and ordered four more Dreadnoughts.

When March 1912 came, Mr. Mulliner's story proved to be without justification. Germany had only the nine Dreadnoughts which she had foreshadowed. But the scare had secured large contracts for the British armament firms. Naval rivalries had been revived. The dividends of Vickers and

Armstrong had shot up again. " I find, in the year before the scare, Messrs. Vickers' profits amounting to £424,000," said Mr. Philip Snowden (now Viscount Snowden) in a speech delivered in the House of Commons on March 17, 1914. " Two years after that they were nearly double the amount. Every year since the success of their intrigue their profits have gone up—£474,000 ; £544,000 ; £745,000 ; £872,000."

Mr. Mulliner, however, deserves some sympathy. He was treated most ungenerously by the Government. The firm of which he was manager, the Coventry Ordnance Company, received none of the orders which he was so instrumental in inspiring, although its parent firm, Cammell Laird, got one of the first contracts. It was Mr. Mulliner's indignation against the Government for overlooking his firm which led him to give away the secret of the scare. Shortly afterwards he was pensioned off from the management of his company.

CHAPTER XI

HOW ARMAMENT FIRMS MANIPULATE THE NEWSPAPERS

" The pens which write against disarmament are made of the same steel as that from which the guns are made."— M. BRIAND.

BEFORE the World War the Ambassador of Russia in Paris was M. Raffalovitch. He used to write picturesque, amusing, and cynical letters to his Ministerial colleagues in St. Petersburg. The letter quoted below was written in April 1913 to M. Kokovtzev, the Minister of Finance :

" The affairs of men are similar in all latitudes.

" In Brazil, according to Vickers-Maxim, the President of the Republic takes upon himself to raise the price of battleships by several million francs. In Europe, the chiefs of State, their Ministers and principal subordinates, are for the most part quite honest.

" But the merchants of armaments, armoured plate, and munitions have recourse to indirect methods in influencing public opinion by the intermediary of the Press.

" They possess newspapers, acquire others, they buy journalists—those writers who sound the patriotic note, who proclaim the military preparations of neighbouring States, who talk of the German and French menace, believe themselves to be heroes.

" The corruption takes all forms, from a good dinner with choice wines in the company of pretty women (paid in advance to finish up the night), with the general seated on their right, up to the more delicate attentions, such as the promise of a well-paid situation.

" That there should be leakages (communication of military secrets) which benefit the dealers in shells and guns is very probable."[1]

M. Raffalovitch was not indulging in idle gossip. There is much evidence to prove the truth of his charges.

[1] *The Secret International*, p. 22.

HOW KRUPP USED FRENCH PAPERS

Perhaps the most sensational instances of the use of newspapers by armament firms is the case of the German Arms and Munitions Factories, quoted by Karl Liebknecht in the Reichstag in April 1913. Liebknecht was able to read the exact terms of an instruction sent by this firm, in the year 1907, to its agents in Paris to get news in the French Press which would stimulate German fear of French arms and consequently bring orders for German arms. The letter read as follows :

" We have just wired you as follows : ' Please await our letter mailed to-day.'

" The reason for our despatch is that we should like to publish an article in the most widely read of French newspapers, probably in *Figaro*, which is to run thus :

" ' The Chief of Staff of the French Army has resolved to hasten considerably the re-equipment of the army with machine-guns, and to order double the amount that had been originally contemplated.'

" We beg you to use all your power to see that such an article appears."

The authenticity of this letter was not denied, and five days later Herr Erzberger attempted to justify it in the Reichstag. His justification only served to confirm the interpretation that the purpose of the letter was to encourage the German Ministry of War to buy machine-guns by causing it to fear France's equipment in this respect.

Herr Erzberger explained that at the time the letter was written the superiority of machine-guns was not recognised. By the German Government they were regarded as " weapons to be used against Herero and Hottentot " but not against the armies of civilised nations. Then France began to order them. " When you thus conjure up the actual situation," remarked Herr Erzberger, " the letter of the German Arms and Munitions Factory takes on quite another aspect." What the different aspect was he did not indicate. Perhaps he meant to imply that the German armament firm was really doing a patriotic duty in frightening the German Government into the adoption of modern forms of armament !

We are fortunate in having a French description of this same incident. A Paris editor has anonymously written a book of his reminiscences in which, with evident knowledge, he tells how the Press story, inspired by the German Arms and Munitions Factories, failed because it was too obvious. The French War Office immediately denied it. The editor proceeds :

" However, within a few days—naturally, quite accidentally—there appeared in *Figaro*, in the *Matin*, and in the *Echo de Paris* a number of articles on the superiority of the French machine-guns, and consequently it was assumed that the French Army was far better equipped.

" With these newspapers in hand, the Prussian Deputy Schmidt, associated with the chief metal industries of Germany, interpellated the Imperial Chancellor and asked what the Government proposed to do

to offset these French threats. Bewildered
and apprehensive, the Reichstag, by a large
majority and without any discussion, gave
its consent to measures calling for an
increase of machine-guns."

HOW FRENCH ARMAMENT FIRMS USE
THE PRESS

We have already seen how Sir Basil
Zaharoff utilised newspapers to extend his
armament orders. He became part owner of
the *Quotidiens Illustrés*, the publisher of the
influential Paris paper *Excelsior*, in order to
develop his Press support. The story has also
been told how at the psychological moment
when Sir Basil, as the agent of Vickers, was
wanting to secure a French loan for the
Russian Putiloff Works, the *Echo de Paris*
published a false report that Krupp was
planning to acquire the works. The French
loan was raised ; Vickers got an order for
the largest part of Russia's new fleet.

The French armament combine,

Schneider-Creusot, can always count upon the support of a powerful section of the French Press. It is the dominant firm in the Comité des Forges, whose President, M. François Wendel, has a controlling interest in the most prominent Nationalist newspaper in France, the *Journal des Débats*, and also in the popular *Le Temps*. These papers voiced the demand of the Comité des Forges, at the time of the Versailles Conference, for the annexation of the left bank of the Rhine and the occupation of the Ruhr and the Saar Basin. Recently the *Journal des Débats* has been urging that France should give up trying to persuade Germany to disarm, and that France should be left free to arm in order to maintain the Versailles Treaty.[1]

In *The Secret International* a summary is given of an article which appeared in *La Lumière* exposing the campaign against disarmament in the French Press. The case is instanced of the *Echo de Paris*, which, in

[1] *Observer*, May 27, 1933.

addition to conducting a vigorous campaign against disarmament, opened its columns for subscriptions to intensify its propaganda. Among the contributions were anonymous gifts of 25,000, 50,000, and even 100,000 francs. " It is quite evident," commented *La Lumière*, " that these anonymous gifts hide the big interests which would lose by disarmament." The service of the *Echo de Paris* was also acknowledged by a full page advertisement from the Société d'Outillage Méchanique et d'Usinage d'Artillerie. Like the *Journal des Débats*, the *Echo de Paris* has recently been urging the policy of the super-armament of France rather than the disarmament of Germany.

HOW AMERICAN FIRMS EMPLOY PUBLICITY MEN

A recent instance of the manner in which armament firms seek to use publicity in newspapers to prevent disarmament was revealed in the Shearer Case. Again I follow the convenient summary included in *The Secret International*.

Mr. Shearer is an American publicity man. He has had an adventurous career. At one time he was a lobbyist in Washington for the interests demanding a big navy and merchant marine ; that is to say, his job was to interview Congressmen and Senators and urge them to support the cause he was serving. At another time he was a promoter of night-clubs and theatres. At another, he was an ally of bootleggers.

The publicity activities of the American armament firms would probably never have been revealed had it not been for a legal case which Mr. Shearer started in 1929 against the largest shipbuilding corporations in America for 255,655 dollars (about £73,000) which he claimed were due to him for services rendered at the Naval Conference in Geneva in 1927 in successfully preventing any effective disarmament form being realised. The three firms were the

Bethlehem Shipbuilding Corporation, the Newport News Shipbuilding and Drydock Co., and the American Brown Boveri Corporation.

Mr. Shearer admitted that he had already been paid 51,230 dollars (about £14,600), but insisted upon his right to the balance on account of influencing orders for battleships which would never have been required if the Disarmament Conference had proved successful.

This case caused such a sensation that President Hoover instructed the Attorney-General to make an inquiry. Faced by this prospect, Mr. Eugene Grace wrote, in his capacity as president of the Bethlehem Shipbuilding Corporation, to President Hoover, acknowledging that he and Mr. C. M. Schwartz, chairman of the Board of Directors of the Bethlehem Steel Corporation, had engaged Mr. Shearer as an " observer " at the Naval Disarmament Conference at a fee of 25,000 dollars (about £7,000).

The activities of Mr. Shearer have been

LB

described by Mr. Charles A. Beard, in *The Navy : Defence or Portent*, in detail. They may be summarised in this way :

1. Whatever the terms of the " oral contract " under which he was hired, he was notoriously engaged at the Geneva Arms Conference in violent anti-British propaganda, in doing his best to defeat arms limitation, in entertaining naval officers and American newspaper correspondents, in stimulating " the marine industry, both for the navy and the merchant marine " (to use his own words), in sending out literature designed to discredit American advocates of peace, and in inserting his " publicity " in reputable American newspapers, such as the *New York Times*, under the guise of news.

2. He maintained a lobby in Washington for the purpose of influencing support for cruiser and merchant-marine Bills coming before Congress.

3. He prepared political articles for publication in newspapers and magazines.

4. He lectured before patriotic societies and other civic organisations.

5. He employed " experts " and other workers, whose exact duties remain unknown.

6. He addressed the American Legion, Chambers of Commerce, and similar organisations.

It may be that Mr. Shearer was worth his £7,000 as a publicity agent for the American armament firms. But how else can his employment be described than as a conspiracy against the peace of the world ?

HOW ARMAMENT FIRMS ADVERTISE THEIR WARES

Armament firms employ the more legitimate business method of advertising their wares. Sometimes their advertisements are ingenuous. M. Francis Delaisi reproduces this advertisement from an official publication of the French Ministry of Commerce :

ARMS AND MUNITIONS
FOR SPORT AND WAR
(*Former G—— factories*)
*Shells of all calibres—torpedoes
of all makes—French and foreign, etc.*

This advertiser is evidently a kind of retail trader for all makes of armaments. " Since the big firms manufacture at their own risk," remarks M. Delaisi, " it has been impossible to forbid them to have recourse to middlemen for the marketing of their goods, and if the same factories make the machinery for both peace and war, why should they not sell the one in the same way as the other ?

" Now if anybody who likes can sell arms," he adds, " anybody who likes can buy them. Thus a private individual can take delivery of a consignment of shells in Paris and despatch them to Rotterdam or Lisbon. And if these shells finally reach the camp of Abd-el-Krim, French soldiers may have the satisfaction of being killed by the products of the national industry."[1]

HOW ARMAMENT FIRMS USE THE CINEMA

The armament firms have adapted the cinema for advertising purposes. The Barrow works of Vickers-Armstrong have their own cinema theatre, where to prospective purchasers exhibitions are given of films depicting their constructional work.

Such advertising films are also taken round the world to exhibit to rulers and representatives of Governments. The following paragraph which appeared in the *North Mail* (December 5, 1931) indicates some of these activities :

" A special exhibition of British films was given to the King and Queen of Yugo-Slavia in their new palace at Dedinje. The films were productions made by a British firm of armament-makers. There were tanks

What Would be the Character of a New War ? pp. 193, 194.

of all kinds, as well as field-guns of all calibres and tractors.

" A firm of shipbuilders also showed a film of the launching of a Yugo-Slav warship. . . . Vickers-Armstrong Ltd. are principally interested in Yugo-Slavia's pending naval contracts, and the film referred to is probably one from Barrow-in-Furness.

" The Barrow works and shipyards of Vickers-Armstrong possess their own cinema theatre, where films are exhibited dealing with constructional works. A representative of the firm is in Yugo-Slavia at present. The firm of Yarrow & Co. Ltd., on the River Clyde, were also interested in Yugo-Slavia, and are reported to have a warship under construction for the Government of that country at the present time."

Readers will agree, I think, that the evidence in this chapter is sufficient to endorse the view of the Sub-Committee of the League of Nations that " armament firms have sought to influence public opinion through the control of newspapers in their own and foreign countries." This committee adopted the following resolution : " That the

holders of shares in private munitions factories and members of their Boards of Directors should be forbidden to assume ownership or control or to exert any influence upon
newspapers." But, like many good aspira-
tions of the League, this resolution remains
a dead letter.

CHAPTER XII

HOW ARMAMENT FIRMS PROFITEER OUT OF WAR

(1) IN EUROPE AND BRITAIN

A Fool stands by the side of the road and watches the
 approach of a body of armed troops.
" Where do these men come from ? " he asks.
" From Peace."
" Where are they going ? "
" To War."
" What do they do in the War ? "
" They kill the enemy and burn their cities."
" Why do they do that ? "
" To make Peace."
" I cannot understand," says the Fool. " To come from
 Peace and to go into War, in order to make Peace !
 Why don't they stay at Peace in the first place ? "
—From a German Legend.

ONE OF the charges brought against armament firms by the League Commission of
1921 was that they exploited their nations
by forming rings to raise prices. Evidence to
justify this charge could be cited from almost
every country.

There is the early case of the French

armament firms. In 1898 two combines were established : " Des Constructeurs de Navires et de Machines Marines " and " Des Fabricants et Constructeurs de Matériel de Guerre." At least, they were the two combines in name. In effect they were one. They had the same offices and the same managing director, and, when they were both invited to submit estimates for battleships, one would withdraw in favour of the other.

The formation of these combines immediately sent up prices. For example, the price of armour-plate was 2.27 francs per kilo before the combines came into existence. After they were established the price went up to 2.96 francs per kilo. A fraction of a franc may not seem much, but in the building of a Dreadnought five million of kilos of armour-plate are required. Therefore on one battleship alone the combine would pocket an additional 3,450,000 francs for armour-plate.

Before the war the German armament firms had the completest arrangements to maintain prices. Dr. Erzberger, of the Centre

Party, declared in the Reichstag on April 23, 1913, that from the most expert sources in Germany he had learned that armour-plate could be sold at fifty per cent of the price charged to the Ministry of Marine and still yield a large profit. The armament firms were able to make their exorbitant charges, he said, owing to their systematic co-operation in international cartels and trusts.

Dr. Erzberger quoted the cases of the Nobel Dynamite Trust and the United Harvey Steel Company, of which particulars will be given later. But he gave certain instances of price-raising by German combines which are illuminating.

He told, for example, how a Marine Trust had its headquarters at Dortmund. The firms which belonged to the trust arranged with each other which should bid for contracts, and at what prices they should bid. On every contract obtained the firms were required to pay to the trust ten per cent, which was, of course, collected from the Ministry of Marine. This ten per cent was used for two purposes : first, to meet the overhead charges of the trust ; and second, to provide a fund divided between the firms which by arrangement had not entered for the contract. " By this means," commented Dr. Erzberger, " millions are amassed ; these concerns are all playing into each other's hands."

A second instance included Belgian and Austrian companies in an arrangement with German firms. The firms concerned were the German Arms and Munitions Factories of Berlin and Karlsruhe, the Arms Factories in Oberndorf, on the Neckar, the Belgian National Factory of War Material at Herstal, and the Austrian Arms Company. It will be noticed that this ring extended to both sides in the World War. Its object was to maintain prices in foreign trade. The principal clauses in the agreement signed by these five firms read as follows :

" The traffic of arms, respecting the deliveries of remodelled machine-guns or carbine rifles for Russia, Japan, China, and Abyssinia, will be carried on for mutual benefit, and the estimated earnings will be distributed to the various groups according to a predetermined scale. The two groups of factories will give each other as much mutual help as possible, in order that every factory may be able to manufacture the required arms in the cheapest and quickest manner.

" To this end, figures and dimension tables of the desired model under production, the required measuring instruments and calibres, shall be handed over at their respective cost price, in so far as possible, or lent gratis. The price of the arms to be delivered is to be at all times determined mutually by the groups.

" In order to carry out the fundamental views expressed earlier, a common chest will be established in which every factory, which manufactures, markets, or delivers rifles and carbines on its own initiative, shall be obliged to pay a fee of fifteen francs per weapon."

The advantages of this agreement to the armament firms are obvious. It was, in effect, a conspiracy which placed the Governments of Russia, Japan, China, and

Abyssinia at their mercy. Whilst apparently competing for orders, they were in fact one combine. The amounts received on their contracts were distributed between them all. They gave each other the fullest technical assistance, so that orders could be carried out economically and expeditiously, and the prices charged were mutually fixed. Any of the co-operating firms which manufactured articles on their own initiative were required to pay a fee on each weapon, to go into the common fund of the combine.

HOW BRITISH FIRMS PROFITEERED IN THE WORLD WAR

But the World War was the golden time of the armament firms. Europe was turned into a sea of blood, and the Bloody Traffic profited. In the early stages of the war the armament firms could charge what they liked, and they did. Later, the Governments passed legislation restricting the profits, but even then high profits were permitted. In Britain, for instance, the profit fixed was twenty per cent, selected because it represented the pre-war profit. Men were conscripted. They had to face death or mutilation for life. They had to surrender their future prospects by devoting the creative years of young manhood to the wasted existence of the trenches. But profits on the weapons of war were allowed to remain at their pre-war figure. On every shell that shattered young limbs to bits there was a profit of twenty per cent.

During the first year of the World War—before the restriction of twenty per cent was imposed—enormous profits were made.[1] In his book, *Practical Socialism*, Dr. Addison, who was Minister of Munitions, has given instance after instance of shameless overcharging and profiteering. Here is one :

" Up to the spring of 1916 certain main types of cordite had cost 2s. 3d. per lb., but the accountants reported, in the case of a

[1] *The Secret International*, pp. 32–5.

propellant factory—to the provision of which the firm had contributed £464,000—that *the price being obtained represented a dividend of 105.7 per cent per annum on this capital.*

" It was further pointed out that if the money being obtained were used to write off the whole cost of the factory to a scrap value of £16,000, the firm would still have been sufficient to pay dividends of 33.8 per cent per annum. . . .

" The end result was that the cordite was reduced to 1s. 7¾d. per lb., and *the savings on the year's supply of cordite* on that basis, as compared with the former price, *amounted to £3,900,000.*"

Dr. Addison gives tables showing the gross overcharging of which the armament firms were guilty. For example :

Process	Original Price	Price after investigation
Filling Fuses (per 100)	£1 4s. 0d.	12s. 0d.
Filling 4.5 lyddite shells (per 100)	£18 16s. 8d.	£7 18s. 4d.

When considering these figures, the mass amount of the articles produced must be kept in mind. In the case of T.N.T., for

example, a weekly saving of no less than
£9,000 was achieved by the reduction in
price of 1*d*. per lb. Dr. Addison indicates the
profiteering on the provision of T.N.T. thus :

" The capital cost of the six T.N.T.
factories was £1,473,000, but by April 1917
they had already produced T.N.T. which,
as against contract prices, had given a
surplus of £2,404,318. *They had, therefore,
completely wiped out their total cost of provision
and had left a balance over of 38 per cent.*"

The profiteering of the armament firms
was checked in three ways—first, by a
system of costings and investigation ; second,
by the establishment of competing national
factories ; and third, by the Excess Profits
Duty. In a speech which Mr. Lloyd George
delivered in the House of Commons in
August 1919, when surveying the work of the
Ministry of Munitions, he revealed that the
huge sum of £440 millions had been saved
by these means. He began by referring to the
original " profiteering " price made by the
armament firms for a shell :

" The 18-pounder, when the Ministry was started, cost 22s. 6d. a shell. A system of costing and investigation was introduced, and national factories were set up which checked the prices, and a shell for which the War Office, at the time the Ministry was formed, paid 22s. 6d. was reduced to 12s. 0d. When you have 85,000,000 of shells, *that saved £35,000,000.*

" There was a reduction in the price of all other shells, and there was a reduction in the Lewis gun. *When we took them in hand they cost £165, and we reduced them to £35 each.* There was a saving of £14,000,000, and, through the costing system and the checking of the national factories we set up, before the end of the war there was a saving of £440,000,000."

Before the Governments stepped in and checked and limited their profiteering, the armament firms were able to pocket the surplus which they made on their exorbitant charges. Even after the introduction of the lower prices, large profits were maintained. The armament firms were compelled to contribute to the State the following sums,

MB

subsequent to the introduction of the Munitions Levy, because their profits totalled
more than the twenty per cent allowed :

1916–17	£4,788,636
1917–18	£20,974,177
1918–19	£22,365,865
1919–20	£5,435,840

Similar profiteering took place in all the
belligerent countries during the World War.
The armament firms have discovered the
secret of how to turn blood into gold.

CHAPTER XIII

HOW ARMAMENT FIRMS PROFITEER OUT OF WAR

(2) IN AMERICA

" During the war, hundreds of people were prosecuted by the vigilant Attorney-General for violation of the Espionage Act, but who has heard of the prosecution of a war profiteer ? "—Mr. GRAHAM, *Chairman of the Committee on Expenditures of the War Department.*

THE RECORDS of Commissions appointed by the Congress and Senate of the United States of America provide voluminous evidence of how armament firms profit, callously and cruelly, through their Bloody Traffic.

HOW AN ARMAMENT FIRM RISKED THE LIVES OF SAILORS

Before examining the astonishing facts of the World War, let us look back for a brief space to an earlier inquiry in which the Carnegie Steel Company was involved. Following charges of fraud against this company, the House of Representatives, in 1894, instructed its Committee on Naval Affairs to investigate. Rarely has condemnation been expressed in stronger terms by an official body than those used in the report of this committee :

" The servants of the Carnegie Steel Co. (whether with or without the knowledge of the company), *to increase their gains*, deliberately continued for many months to commit acts whose natural and probable consequence would be *the sacrifice of the lives of our seamen in time of war, and with them, perhaps, the dearest interests of the nation.* . . .
" No fine or mere money compensation is adequate atonement for such wrongs. The commission of such frauds is a moral crime of the gravest character."

The fraud committed by the Carnegie Steel Company was to supply armour-plate which contained " blow-holes," as fit for

use. The head of the department, Mr.
William E. Corey, acknowledged that the
general superintendent of the company,
Mr. Charles M. Schwab, was also aware of
what was being done, and Mr. Schwab
himself acknowledged that he gave orders
that the occurrence of " blow-holes " should
not mean the rejection of the armour-plate.
He thought it was " likely " that his company concealed the fact of these defects in
their supplies. The President of the United
States imposed damages of 140,000 dollars
on the company.

Despite this scandal, Mr. Charles M.
Schwab retained his prominence in the
American armament industry, and in the
World War was actually appointed by the
Government as Director-General of the Ship-
ping Board Emergency Fleet Corporation.
The duty of this body was to superintend the
making of contracts between the Govern-
ment and the armament firms for ship-
building.

Mr. Schwab, whose firm was found guilty

of increasing its gains at the risk of sacrificing the lives of seamen and the " dearest interests of the nation," is a great patriot. He is one of the founders of the American Navy League, which always wants a larger fleet (which Mr. Schwab is always ready obligingly to build). At the same time he is a great lover of peace ; he assured the Sub-Committee of the U.S. Senate which inquired into the " Shearer case " in 1930 that he was interested in the Geneva Disarmament Conference because :

" I wanted to see peace come to the world, and especially to this own great country of ours."

He is profiteer, patriot, pacifist—all three !

Mr. William E. Corey, the head of the department of the Carnegie Steel Company responsible for supplying the faulty armour-plate, is also a distinguished patriot. He is president of the Midvale Steel and Ordnance Company and a director of the International Nickel Company. The *Navy League*

Journal lists these companies, with **Mr.** Schwab, as among the nineteen founders of the league.

With this glance into the past, let us turn to more recent history. We shall see that to " increase their gains " has been the dominant motive of the American armament firms in time of war as well as peace.

AN AMERICAN SCANDAL

Three years after the Armistice a Select Committee of the American House of Representatives reported on War Department expenditures. It examined the terms under which unused war materials and equipment were sold back to the great industrialists at the end of the war. The War Department, it remarked, has frequently " sold back for a song articles produced under Government contract." Here is one instance reported by the committee :

" Airplanes   costing   the   Government

20,000,000 dollars were re-sold to the Curtiss Factory for 2,700,000 dollars, or about thirteen per cent of the cost. *Thousands of American aviators* were compelled to buy at full price from the Curtiss Co., if they wanted these machines."[1]

Note that *thousands* of aeroplanes are stated to have been bought back in this way. The Curtiss Company made its original profit on their manufacture for the Government. Then the Government sold them back at thirteen per cent of the price paid, which meant the company made a further profit of 17,300,000 dollars. And finally the company sold them again to private purchasers at the original price of 20,000,000 dollars. Thus, in addition to the initial profit, the Curtiss Company made a profit of 37,000,000 dollars on the deal !

But there was a worse American aeroplane scandal, revealing, not only profiteering, but a callous inhumanity parallel to the armour-plate case already recorded.

[1] *War Policies Commission Hearings*, p. 786.

AEROPLANES WHICH WERE
"FLAMING COFFINS"

One of the remarkable facts about the armaments used in the World War is this : although America entered the war in the spring of 1917, and although its Government spent over one thousand million dollars on aviation, not one American-built pursuit or combat or bombing plane reached the front before the Armistice in November 1918. The only American aeroplanes which reached the front were 213 De Havilland 4s. These aeroplanes, known, ironically enough, as " Liberty " machines, were so faulty that, according to General Menoher, Chief of the Air Service, the battle fatalities for hours flown were *three times as great* for American aviators as for British or Belgian.

The story was told fully before the Committee on Expenditures in the War Department. Captain Eddie Rickenbacker, one of the experts called to give evidence, made this statement :

" From every side, Fokkers were piquing upon the clumsy ' Liberty ' machines [the De Havillands] which, with their criminally constructed fuel-tanks, offered so easy a target to the incendiary bullets of the enemy that their unfortunate pilots called this boasted achievement of our Aviation Department their ' flaming coffins.' During that one brief flight over Grand Pre, I saw three of these crude machines go down in flames, an American pilot and an American gunner in each ' flaming coffin ' dying this frightful and needless death."[1]

During the course of the proceedings of the committee it was revealed that the aircraft firm concerned continued to produce these machines after their defects were known, and that the American War Department continued to order them and despatch them to the front. The committee reported : " In spite of wanton waste of lives, these D.H.4s, the only American-made planes that reached the front, were kept in production after their dangerous and clumsy

[1] Committee's Report, p. 10.

construction was a matter of common knowledge."

The committee quotes this surprising conversation in a Senate Committee which sat during the war itself. Mr. John D. Ryan, who was Director of Aviation, is being examined :

SENATOR REED : You know that the best and most experienced flyers, a number of them in this country, have testified before this committee that they regard the De Havilland machine as utterly unsafe and that they would refuse to go up in it or send subordinates up in it ?

MR. RYAN : I understand that some have testified that they have refused to go up in it or let subordinates go up in it.

SENATOR REED : You propose to go on making the De Havilland 4 machines ?

MR. RYAN : Until we can put the De Havilland 9 in production.

SENATOR REED : Do you intend to do that regardless of any testimony that may be given by experienced flyers that the machine is utterly unsafe ?

MR. RYAN : I am not convinced that the burden of testimony of the flyers through-out the country is that the De Havilland 4 is an unsafe machine.

The best comment upon Mr. Ryan's final reply is a statement made by Senator New in the course of a question to Mr. Baker, the Secretary to the War Department, in the same committee :

SENATOR NEW : It is a fact that every flyer that we have had before this committee as a witness, including several who have seen long service abroad, both with our own forces, the British forces, and the French forces, have testified that the De Havilland 4 machine, with the defects appearing in it as it has been produced at the Dayton-Wright factory, is highly dangerous and ought not under any circumstances be used : and at least one officer has testified that he would no longer send men up from his field in a machine of the type until after these defects had been remedied.

Mr. Baker acknowledged that, after a talk

with Mr. Ryan, he had approved the decision not to suspend making the De Havilland 4 machine.

This is the story so far as it affects prominent Government officials. Now let us carry it a little further.

A certain Colonel Edward A. Deeds was placed in charge of the Equipment Division of Aviation in 1917. No one appears to know why. He knew nothing of aircraft and had not proved his efficiency in any previous Government activity. Four years before his appointment he had been prosecuted for alleged bribery. Upon this incident the American Attorney-General subsequently reported as follows :

" It is proper to say that, about four years before his appointment to produce aircraft, Deeds achieved considerable notoriety in Ohio, where he was prosecuted in the Federal Court for alleged bribery and criminal methods in driving his competitors out of the cash-register business, and was convicted by a jury, after a trial lasting over a month, and sentenced to imprisonment for one year.

" An appeal was taken, with fifty assignments of error, and the case was reversed and no retrial was ever had. Deeds' innocence may be conceded, for the sake of argument, though no second trial occurred, but the charge, conviction, and court record were enough to put any responsible official on inquiry before giving Deeds a place of transcendent importance in charge of matters about which he knew nothing."

JUDGE FINDS THAT CONTRACTS WERE GIVEN TO BUSINESS ASSOCIATES

From still another official report the story can be continued. In 1910, President Wilson appointed Justice Charles Evans Hughes to investigate the matter. Justice Hughes reported that Deeds began his activities by centring aircraft operations at Dayton, Ohio ; that he gave large contracts to his business associates, although they had no previous experience in such matters ; and that he was largely interested in companies controlling the Delco ignition system used in the projected " Liberty " motor.[1] The following is a quotation from Justice Hughes' report :

" At the inception of the Government's aviation activity in connection with the war and within the spheres of Colonel Deeds' important if not commanding influence, his former business associates were placed at once, through Government contracts, in a position where they had assurance of very large profits upon a comparatively small investment of their own money, and in addition were able to secure generous salaries which they charged against the Government as part .of the costs of manufacture."

Justice Hughes recommended that Colonel Deeds should be tried by court martial. He was not tried. Instead he was banqueted in Washington and praised by General Squier, who had been in chief control of aircraft matters.

Following upon the report of Justice

[1] *Death and Profits*, by Seymour Waldmen, pp. 74–86.

Hughes and the Attorney-General (who found Colonel Deeds' conduct " inexcusable, reprehensible, and censurable," and who recommended that all the facts should be submitted to the Secretary of War), Mr. Baker, the Secretary, requested the Judge-Advocate-General's office to hear other witnesses so that the report could be reconsidered. Two business associates of Colonel Deeds, connected with the same Government contracts, were then heard, and a new report was issued exonerating Colonel Deeds. The Committee on Expenditures in the War Department made this comment upon this conclusion :

" With a record that affected the lives of men, and charges of inordinate selfishness supported by specific facts, Deeds should have been placed on trial, to be convicted if guilty, to be vindicated if innocent. According to the testimony, Secretary Baker prevented such action."

So much for the inefficiency, corruption,

and profiteering of American aircraft production. Now let us look at another part of
America's armament materials—copper.

HUGE PROFITS MADE ON WAR MATERIALS

During the war the American Government appointed a " Co-operative Committee on Copper " to assist the Council of
National Defence Advisory Commission.
Every member of this body, according to the
Committee on Expenditures in the War
Department, was " deeply interested in the
copper industry and in the success of various
properties owned or controlled in part of
them." The function of this committee was
" to assist in or advise as to the purchase of
copper for the Government."

This arrangement worked out as one
would expect. After examining what happened, the Committee on War Expenditures
stated :

NB

" A fair and candid *résumé* of the whole situation cannot fail to convince the reader that the arrangement thus entered into was one extremely favourable to at least a few of the copper producers, and that from this arrangement, and because of the necessity and demands of the Government during the war, those who operated these copper-producing properties were enabled to make, and did make, extravagant and extraordinary profits."[1]

The committee gives instances of the profiteering :

" The Utah Copper Company (whose president, Mr. Charles MacNeill, was on the Government committee) made in 1917 a profit of 32,000,000 dollars, *which was 200 per cent of its capital stock*, and in 1918 a profit of 24,750,000 dollars, *which was 150 per cent of its capital stock*.

" The Calumet and Hecla Mining Company, in 1917, made a profit of 9,500,000 dollars, or *800 per cent of its capital stock*, and, in 1918, 3,500,000 dollars, or *300 per cent of its capital stock*.

[1] Report, p. 95.

" The Inspiration Consolidated Copper Company, in 1917, made a profit of 12,260,000 dollars, or 55 *per cent of its capital stock*, and, in 1918, 9,250,000 dollars, or 40 *per cent of its capital stock*.

" The Kennecott Copper Company, in 1917, made a profit of 11,826,000 dollars, or 70 *per cent of its capital stock*, and, in 1918, 9,390,136 dollars, or 60 *per cent of its capital stock*."

Two of the largest firms supplying armaments to the American Government during the war were the United States Steel Corporation and the Bethlehem Shipbuilding Corporation. The latter firm made profits of twenty-one per cent. The Government brought a legal case against it for 11,000,000 dollars alleged excess profits. And its justification was that its profits were much less than those of the United States Steel Corporation, which amounted to fifty per cent ![1]

Instance after instance of such profiteering in American war materials could be given. Here is one more glaring example.

New York Times, April 5, 1931.

Mr. Colver, the chairman of the Federal Trade Commission and a member of the Price-fixing Committee of the War Industries Board, reported that everybody in the American Metal Company, " from the chairman of the Board of Trustees down," had been paid bonuses for the purpose of hiding the profits. Quoting this case to the War Policies Commission, Mr. McSwain, a member of the Congress, said :

" The president of the company received a bonus, over and above his salary, of 364,000 dollars in one year, and it went all the way down to the foremen of the shops. The chief engineer got 23,500 dollars bonus, the manager of gas operation got 7,000 dollars bonus, and here is a list of about twenty different officers and clerks of the corporation that got a total of nearly 2,000,000 dollars bonus for the purpose of hiding as overhead expenses a part of these very war profits. Now, it seems to me, if our boys had known that such as that was going on, it would have affected very seriously their morale."

WHEN THE SOLDIERS GOT HOME

It certainly would ; and when the war
was over and the " boys " got back to
America they agitated through the American
Legion for the distribution of " equal burdens " in any future war in order to stop
profiteering. The agitation was so successful
that both the Democratic and Republican
Parties adopted a proposal to this end in
their election programme in 1924.

The Democratic Party declared that, " in
the event of war in which the man-power of
the nation is drafted, all other resources
should likewise be drafted." It added that
" this will tend to discourage war by
depriving it of its profits "—an admission
that the prospect of profiteering encourages
war ! The Republican Party declared that
" we believe that in time of war the nation
should draft for its defence, not only its
citizens, but also every resource which may
contribute to success."

In 1930 the American Congress appointed

a Commission to report on this matter. Its conclusion was that the President should be empowered, in the event of war, to stabilise prices so as to prevent *extra* profits due to the war, and that individuals and companies should be taxed *95 per cent* (not even 100 per cent) of all incomes above the previous three-year average. In addition, the Commission recommended that Congress should not consider any constitutional amendment permitting " the taking of private property in time of war *without compensation.*"

In other words, " equal burdens " was interpreted as meaning the conscription of life, but continued profits and compensation for wealth !

INTRODUCING MR. SHEARER AGAIN

Curiously enough, the representatives of the American Legion before the Commission modified the legion's demand to a limitation of war profits to seven per cent. Apparently Mr. William B. Shearer, whose service to the American armament firms at the Geneva Disarmament Conference has already been noted, had some influence over the American Legion's representatives. One of their spokesmen was Mr. Paul V. McNutt, ex-commander of the legion. Mr. Shearer, giving evidence to the Senate Committee, which investigated his activities as a paid representative of the armament firms, told how he had been asked to " post " Mr. McNutt before he made a speech at the Mayflower Hotel, Washington.

" I came down to Washington, and I entered Commander McNutt's apartment and was with him until three in the morning, educating him, we will say, or posting him, or whatever you wish. . . . Therefore I was pronounced by the National Commander of the American Legion as the best-posted man in the United States on national defence. I have the letter. . . . The next night, Commander McNutt made his famous speech. I had given him all the data that I thought was necessary. . . . When I returned to New York, I called up Mr. Willicomb,

Mr. Hearst's private secretary, and said I had received a letter from Commander McNutt expressing himself, not only for the Navy, but opposed to the World Court."[1]

Evidently Mr. Shearer served the armament firms no less well in Washington than in Geneva.

[1] Report of Hearings, p. 539.

CHAPTER XIV

THE ARMAMENT FIRMS AND
THE BANKS

" Sir Montague Threadneedle, the Banker, was very much
surprised when he found himself in Hell. He said as
much to the Devil, who met him courteously at the
entrance in morning coat and striped trousers.
" The Devil was used to this. For thousands of years, day
and night, the world's most respectable citizens had
arrived and said, ' But there must be some mistake ! '
The Devil was too much of a gentleman to laugh, but a
good joke is immortal and he still got a kick out of it.
" ' But . . .' began Sir Montague. The Devil patted him
kindly on the shoulder. ' I know, old man,' he said
kindly, ' it is a little unexpected. But you will soon feel
at home. You'll find all your friends here sooner or
later.' "—B. J. BOOTHROYD.

A subject which requires more investigation than has yet been given to it is the
relationship of the armament firms to the
banks. There is a closer relationship than is
usual with ordinary industrial concerns ;
first, because Governments are the buyers of
armaments and less wealthy nations frequently require loans for the purpose, and

second, because the Governments of the wealthier nations often wish, for political reasons, to direct and facilitate the purchase of arms by smaller nations and guarantee loans for this purpose.

This four-party arrangement between the armament firm, the bank, the small purchasing nation, and the sympathetic Power has great advantages, especially for the armament firm. Let us see how it works out.

The armament salesman convinces the Government of a small nation that it should buy arms. It has no funds for the purpose. The armament firm therefore approaches the bank. The bank wishes to be certain that the interest on the loan will be paid, so it approaches its Government. The Government sees an opportunity of bringing the small nation within its sphere of political and economic influence. The guarantee is given.

Thus the armament firm gets its order, the small nation gets its armaments, the bank gets its interest guaranteed, and the Great Power gets an ally which is useful immediately as a sphere for economic development and which, as a political supporter, may be exceedingly useful in time of war for military purposes.

Sometimes the initiative is taken, not by the armament firm, but by the Government of the Great Power ; sometimes by the Government of the small nation. In either case the benefits are mutual.

HOW THE FRENCH FIRMS USE THE BANKS

This technique has been developed most fully by the French Government, and the French armament combine, Schneider-Creusot, and its powerful subsidiary, the Skoda Works in Czecho-Slovakia.[1] The power of the French Government over the smaller nations of Europe is largely the power of loans and armaments. France has made loans through its banks to Greece, Hungary, Yugo-Slavia, Rumania, and

[1] *The Secret International*, pp. 20 and 21.

Poland, and these loans have been duly expended on orders to the French armament firms. Indeed, the French are extraordinarily catholic in their provision of loans for this purpose. Turkey, Japan, Bulgaria (outside the French sphere of political influence), and the South American States have also had loans for armament purposes.

Schneider-Creusot are well in with the banks. M. Wendel, the president of the Comité des Forges, of which Schneider-Creusot is the most important partner, is a director of the National Bank of France. M. Eugene Schneider, chairman of Schneider-Creusot, is a director of Banque de l'Union Parisienne. This is the bank through which Schneider-Creusot controls the Skoda Works and carries through most of its international transactions. The Banque de l'Union Parisienne also finances the Banque Générale de la Crédit Hongrois, which has been the Hungarian medium for French loans for armament orders.

Two of the directors of Schneider-Creusot

—M. de Neuflize and M. Villars—are
on the Board of Directors of the Banque
Hypothécaire d'Argentine, through which
the Argentine orders for armaments have
been facilitated. M. de Neuflize is also a
director of the Ottoman Bank. A relative of
M. Schneider—M. Saint-Sauveur—sits on
the Board of the Franco-Japanese Bank, and
its president is M. Charles Dumont, who
was French Minister of Marine and who,
incidentally, is one of the French representatives at the Geneva Disarmament Conference, where he ecstatically defends the
submarine as " the weapon of the poor "
which introduces " an element of mystery,
the unknown, at sea " !

In many of the countries to which
Schneider-Creusot supply armaments it has
taken the initiative in establishing banks, with
part control by French directors, in order to
facilitate the purchase of its armaments.

Sometimes the banks, as well as the armament firms, ride over all political considerations in their desire for business. We have

already seen how Schneider-Creusot and the Banque de l'Union Parisienne enabled Hungary to arm secretly, in violation of the Treaty of Versailles, and even succeeded in getting the French Government to make a loan for the purpose.

Another remarkable instance is the case of the French banking firm of Perrier, which supplied the Turkish Government with money for the purpose of building a Dreadnought, and in return for which the Turkish Government conceded Perrier the right to build and operate a tramway line from Jerusalem to Bethlehem. The pilgrims to the Holy Land who go to see the birthplace of the Prince of Peace now enjoy the privilege of travelling by a tram bargained for a Dreadnought !

During the World War, China sided with the Allies against Germany and Hungary. Nevertheless, the Lower Austrian Banking Company and Agricultural Loan Corporation concluded in the war years three separate loans with the Chinese Government.

A condition of these loans was that the Chinese Government should return a large part of the money to Austria by the purchase of cruisers and their equipment through the Cantiere Naval Triestino and the Skoda plant (then still under Austrian Control).

THE BRITISH FIRMS AND THE BANKS

We shall see how closely linked the directorate of Vickers-Armstrong is with banking concerns. General Sir Herbert Lawrence, its chairman, is also the chairman of the Anglo-International Bank Ltd., and managing partner of Glynn Mills & Co., the important bankers, and a director of the Bank of Rumania Ltd. and a member of the London Committee of the Ottoman Bank (we shall see that the activities of Vickers-Armstrong in Rumania and Turkey are considerable). Sir O. H. Nemeyer, another director, is one of the most influential figures connected with the Bank of England, and is also a director of the Anglo-International

Bank Ltd., and a member of the London Committee of the National Bank of Egypt. The directors of Vickers-Armstrong have connections with banking concerns in America, China, India, Australia, Rumania, Turkey, and Egypt, in addition to the international connections of the large London banks.

Moreover, the banks have a large share in the ownership of armament firms. This is particularly the case with the new aviation firms which have been developed in recent years in Britain.

It is not possible to penetrate fully behind the veil which hides the intimacy of the relationship of the Money Trust and the Munitions Trust. But the veil has been lifted enough for us to realise that the Bloody Traffic is closely wedded to the Banking Traffic.

CHAPTER XV

THE ARMAMENT FIRMS IN
BRITAIN

(I) FROM GUNS TO BATTLESHIPS

" We cannot live alone. No nation in the world can live
by itself. The prosperity of one is the prosperity of all,
and we have to aim at something of that kind. I believe
that the turn of the tide will come, and, when we come
back to our own concerns, I believe honestly that we are
ready for the occasion when it comes.

" We have spent freely in making our works and our equipment ready to meet any world situation. We have pre-
served our financial resources and are perfectly free to
do what we want to do. We can give credit terms, and
I believe that the time is not far distant when these
factors will have their effect and that prosperity will
come again.

" It will only come by facing the facts as they really exist
and by doing what the English Army did in the Great
War—their backs to the wall and the famous address of
Lord Haig to stand firm. I have sufficient confidence
in my race and the people of this country to believe
that they will fight it out successfully in due time."—
GENERAL THE HON. SIR HERBERT A. LAWRENCE
(*Chairman of Vickers-Armstrong*).

WE HAVE now taken a general survey of
of the methods of the armaments industry.
It is important that we should know which
OB

are the firms engaged in the Bloody Traffic
and who are their directors.

War preparations become continually
more complicated. The primitive bow and
arrow have developed into guns, tanks, submarines, battleships, aeroplanes, and poison
gas. The next development, already approached, will be disease germs. The modern
industry of war has already extended from
engineering to chemistry. It is now moving
towards biology. That will surely be the
final irony—that medical knowledge of
germs, acquired to save life, should be used
to destroy life.

The organisation of the traffic has three
main aspects : (1) armament of the older
type—from guns to battleships ; (2) aeroplanes for war use ; and (3) poison gases and
explosives.

In future warfare the second and third
aspects will probably be the most important.
In peace-time it is the first which requires
the greatest industrial activity. Poisonous
gases and explosives can be rapidly produced

on demand by industries which in peace-time are devoted to the production of other chemicals. Works which produce aeroplanes for civilian purposes can easily produce military aeroplanes and naval aeroplanes.

But the production of guns, tanks, sub-marines, and warships on a large scale con-tinues in peace-time as well as in war-time. Whilst a large part of the works used in war for such armaments are used in peace for the production of typewriters, sewing-machines, railway carriages, and speed-boats, the specialised production of vast armament supplies proceeds without inter-ruption. It is this aspect of armaments, therefore, which is dominant industrially.

THE BRITISH ARMAMENTS TRUST

Before the World War the chemical aspect of war preparations had been developed hardly at all, and military aviation was com-paratively undeveloped. The armaments industry was almost entirely concerned with guns, munitions, and warships. Even then the British firms engaged in this traffic had become linked for all practical purposes in one ring.

The four principal firms were : Vickers, Armstrong-Whitworth, John Brown, and Cammell Laird. All four were connected closely with one another, and all were connected with subsidiary companies. Vickers had taken over successively William Beardmore of Glasgow, the Naval Construction and Armaments Co. of Barrow, and the Maxim-Nordenfeldt Co. Vickers and Armstrong-Whitworth together owned the firm of Henry Whitehead & Co., torpedo makers. John Brown and Cammell Laird shared directors, and together owned the Coventry Ordnance Co. All four firms were associated in the international armaments trust, the Harvey United Steel Co.

Since the World War the process of trustification has gone still further. The two largest British firms—Vickers and

Armstrong-Whitworth—have amalgamated. Their armament, shipbuilding, and steel interests are now completely under one control. The new Vickers-Armstrong company has taken over the Vickers works at Barrow, Sheffield, Erith, and Dartford, and the Armstrong-Whitworth works at Manchester and Elswick and its naval yard at Newcastle-on-Tyne. It has also absorbed the Thames Ammunition Works, the Whitehead Torpedo Company, and Vickers (Ireland) Ltd. Finally, through the English Steel Corporation, Vickers-Armstrong company has amalgamated the steel interests of Cammell Laird and of the Metropolitan Carriage Wagon Finance Co. with its own. Apart from the Government works and docks, Vickers-Armstrong now has in its hands virtually the whole heavy armament production of the British Isles.[1]

---

[1] There are certain companies still outside the Vickers combine. They include the B.S.A. Guns Ltd., the Palmer Shipbuilding and Iron Co., John Thornycroft, the Fairfield Shipbuilding and Engineering Co., Yarrow & Co., Ltd., and Parsons Marine Turbine Co. Most of these firms are connected with shipbuilding, and only occasionally do armament work.

The amalgamation of Vickers and Armstrong-Whitworth followed a financial crisis
in the latter firm. Armstrong-Whitworth had
become heavily over-capitalised, and had to
reduce the value of its shares substantially.
It is alleged that Sir Basil Zaharoff took advantage of these financial difficulties to com-
pel a merger with Vickers, using his influence over the British Government and
the Bank of England to prevent the
latter from lending money to Armstrong-
Whitworth.[1]

As already indicated, the manufacture of
aeroplanes for military and naval purposes is
for the most part carried on separately from
the manufacture of guns, munitions, and
heavy armaments ; but Vickers are challeng-
ing this position. They have established two
subsidiary companies for this purpose : the
Vickers (Aviation) Ltd., and the Supermarine Aviation Works (Vickers) Ltd. The
former, *The Secret International* informs us,
manufactures aircraft for military and civil

[1] *War for Profits*, by O. Lehmann-Russbüldt. p. 56.

purposes ; the latter manufactures " flying-
boats, seaplanes, aircraft carriers, and the
equipment of naval aviation."

Vickers-Armstrong do considerable peace
work, but to a very large extent their purpose remains armament manufacture. At
the general meeting of Vickers Ltd., held on
April 4, 1932, General Sir Herbert Lawrence, the chairman, said : " Vickers-Armstrong depends very largely on armaments
orders for its existence, while the capacity of
its works for armament production is an
important factor in the defence of the
country."

UNIVERSAL DEATH PROVIDERS

General Sir Herbert Lawrence might have
added, " and of other countries," for the
international interests of Vickers-Armstrong
are almost as great as its British interests.

In the Far East, for example, it is associated with Mitsui, the most powerful armament combine in Japan. Vickers-Armstrong

controls one of the units of this combine, a company with the rhythmic name of Kabu-shiki Kwaisha Nihon Seiko-Sho, but known in Britain prosaically as the Japanese Steel Works.

In Italy, Vickers-Armstrong has a subsid-iary firm entitled the Societa Vickers-Terni. In Spain it controls the Sociedad Espanola de Construccion Naval and the Placencia de las Armas company. It has factories in Rumania. It has holdings in the Polish Société de Matériel de Guerre. Through its Aviation Company it holds valuable shares in the Dutch Fokker firm and in the Junkers Company of Dessau.

In Holland, Vickers-Armstrong has a grenade factory at van Heyst. At the time of the Vickers-Armstrong amalgamation, sub-sidiary companies were absorbed in France and South America. One of the French subsidiaries was called Vickers-Schneider, which links up the British combine with the great French combine, Schneider-Creusot.

The British Empire has Vickers-Armstrong

works in Canada, New Zealand, Ireland, and India (in process of formation).

Later I shall show how Vickers-Armstrong is linked with an international ring of armament firms. But in fact it will be seen that Vickers-Armstrong is itself an international ring. It controls works in at least ten countries. If a war broke over Europe to-morrow, these works would be supplying both sides with armaments. Its products would be used by Britishers, Italians, Frenchmen, Poles, Rumanians, and Dutchmen to blow each other to bits.

SHAREHOLDERS AND DIRECTORS

Vickers-Armstrong is a name. Who control this vast industry of death ? Who are behind it ? Who profit by it ?

No fewer than six of the directors of Vickers and Vickers-Armstrong are ex-officers of high position in the Army and Navy. The chairman of both companies is General the Hon. Sir Herbert A. Lawrence,

who was the Chief of Staff at the headquarters of the British Army in France from
January 1918, and who left the Army on
retired pay in 1922. Sir J. F. Noel Birch,
Artillery Adviser to the Commander-in-
Chief in France from 1916 to 1919, is another
director, and Major-General C. P. Dawnay
another (incidentally his brother, Colonel
A. G. C. Dawnay, is a member of the Land
Commission of the Disarmament Conference). The Navy is represented by Commander C. W. Craven, and there are a
colonel and lieutenant-colonel among the
directors.

But even these do not exhaust the military
and naval connections in the list. Sir Mark
Webster Jenkinson was the controller of the
Factory Audit and Costs at the Ministry of
Munitions during the World War, and subse-
quently the Chief Liquidator of Contracts.
Sir J. A. Cooper was the Principal in Charge
of Raw Materials Finance at the War
Office from 1917 to 1919, and was Director
of Raw Materials Finance at the Ministry of

Munitions until 1921. Sir A. G. Hadcock was an Associate Member of the Ordnance Committee.

Secondly, it is worthy of notice how many of the directors are connected with banking and financial institutions.

General Sir Herbert Lawrence, the chairman, is also chairman of the Anglo-International Bank Ltd., the Bank of Rumania Ltd., and the London Committee of the Ottoman Bank. He is also managing partner of Glynn Mills & Co., the influential bankers, and a director of the Sun Insurance Office Ltd., and of the Sun Life Assurance Society. Lieutenant-Colonel J. Beaumont Neilson is chairman of the English and Scottish Investors Ltd. Commander Craven is a director of the World Auxiliary Insurance Corporation. Mr. A. J. A. Jamieson is a member of the London Committee of the Ottoman Bank, and a director of the Chartered Bank of India, Australia, and China, the Union Discount Company of London, and the English & New York Trust Co., Ltd. Sir

Mark Webster Jenkinson is a director of the Broadway Finance & Investment Co., Ltd., and the Car & General Insurance Corporation. Mr. G. R. T. Taylor is a director of the Bankers' Commercial Security Ltd. Sir O. H. Nemeyer is a director of the Anglo-International Bank Ltd., and a member of the London Committee of the National Bank of Egypt. Major-General C. P. Dawnay is a director of the Central Insurance Co., Ltd., and a member of the London Board of the Liverpool and London & Globe Insurance Co., Ltd. Sir J. A. Cooper is a director of the Securities Management Trust Ltd.

It will be seen that there is scarcely a director who is not also a director of a banking, insurance, or investment company, so closely are the interests of armaments and finance linked.

Finally, it should be noted how wide and important is the scope of the interests represented by the directors.

The total number of directorates held by the fifteen men on the Boards of Vickers and

Vickers-Armstrong is 127. That gives an average of more than seven each. They include directorates covering, in addition to finance, interests in steel, electricity, railways, coal, shipbuilding, shipping, nickel, newspapers, etc. One cannot read the list without being impressed by the intimate connection between armament manufacture and the general control of industry.

Vickers had a bad time in the years following the World War, but now prosperity is returning. This year the company made a profit of £811,593, which, after deducting £282,555 for income tax, debenture interest, etc., left a balance of £529,038, from which £418,190 was distributed in dividends on preference shares. The previous year £234,329 had been brought forward, which, with this year's profits, enabled a dividend of 4 per cent (less income tax) to be paid on the ordinary shares, still leaving £222,022 to be carried forward to next year.

Under present conditions this result was evidently very satisfactory to the chairman.

" It is really almost incredible to me," he told a staff meeting at Elswick on March 3, 1933, " that the works as a whole have made a profit. This is extraordinary. I think that nothing but the great organisation and marvellous staff work and the high capacity of our workpeople have enabled this to be done." After this tribute to his workers, it must have been a little difficult for Sir Herbert Lawrence to face in the same speech the duty of justifying a reduction in wages. " It was applied to everybody from top to bottom," he said, " and we all suffered the same reduction." Equality of sacrifice again ! The directors perhaps have had to sacrifice luxuries. The labourers certainly have had to sacrifice essentials.

The quotation from Sir Herbert Lawrence which heads this chapter is also taken from this utterance. It is an amazing revelation of the mentality of the armament-maker. He begins by insisting that no nation can live by itself, and that the prosperity of one is the prosperity of all. He proceeds to boast of how Vickers is prepared to meet any world situation, and that prosperity will return to the firm.

But the prosperity of armament firms depends not upon nations living for each other, but upon them slaughtering each other. That is the world situation which Vickers is prepared to face. That is its greatest hope of prosperity.

CHAPTER XVI

THE ARMAMENT FIRMS IN BRITAIN

(2) MILITARY AND NAVAL AVIATION

" Man wins the realm of air and might have been
An eagle with a soul ; you make him harpy,
More murderous than dragons of the ooze."
—ISRAEL ZANGWILL.

IT IS GENERALLY recognised that air-fleets will be the decisive factor in the next great war. There have been varying prophecies as to their destructive power. I go for my description to a technician—Lieutenant-General von Metzsch, author of *A Change in Armaments* ? and a war-time member of the German General Staff. Writing of the function of air-fleets in war, he says :

" Their destructive power is enormous. It is a hundred times greater than it was during the World War. Also large-scale air-attacks can now be carried out in a fraction of the time needed in the World War to drop a few tons of explosives here and there. No passive system of defence will be sufficient to protect industrial, economic, and, least of all, administrative centres. Something may, perhaps, escape destruction like safes when a bank is burnt down. In some cases air-attacks may be rendered less disastrous by means of a carefully prepared system of decentralisation combined with well-organised transport facilities. Certain countries have built extensive habitable constructions which provide good protection from air-raids upon a large scale. But in every country, even the best armed, plenty of vulnerable points are still to be found, upon which explosives can be dropped, completely disorganising the country and demoralising the people."[1]

This technical description of the function of the air-fleet shows how vital is the aeroplane in war preparations. But aeroplanes will be used not only in bombing operations; they will also form an important part of the

[1] *What Would be the Character of a New War?* p. 25.
PB

military transport system in future wars. In recent manœuvres in America a complete battery of artillery was transported twenty-five miles by air. Three bombing aeroplanes were employed. They were loaded with guns, ammunition, and crew ; and the loading, transport, and the reassembling of the guns was all done in half an hour. By that time the guns were engaging the " enemy."

Incidentally it may be remarked that the " enemy " was intended to be Japan. The American War Office evidently has no doubt about its prospective enemy ! Later we shall see that one of the largest American military aviation firms has an arrangement with the largest Japanese armament firm for the manufacture of aeroplane engines.

As soon as hostilities broke out, civilian aeroplanes would no doubt be transformed into military aeroplanes on a wide scale ; but no Great Power relying upon her arms can afford to depend on these. Aeroplanes have been highly specialised for the specific purpose of war, and the manufacture of these

types is an important activity of the firms
engaged in aircraft construction.

The long-distance communications of the
British Empire, both by land and sea, have
encouraged British firms, *The Secret International* points out, to concentrate upon the
production of highly developed military
aeroplanes and naval seaplanes. In recent
years, also, the British Government has
relied chiefly upon bombing aeroplanes as
the final instrument for maintaining " law
and order " in outlying parts of the Empire.
Thus it has come about that, although the
British Air Force is not so large as that of
certain other countries, Britain leads the
world in the diversity and destructive power
of its military aviation.

As in the case of heavy armaments, the
British manufacturers of military aeroplanes
supply many other Governments and have
factories in other countries. It doesn't
seem to matter whom the planes are destined to destroy, so long as the price is
paid.

For example, the most important British firm—the Fairey Aviation Company—whilst restricting its directorate to British citizens, supplies military aeroplanes to the Governments of Holland, Belgium, Portugal, Japan, Greece, Argentina, Chile, Australia, and Ireland, and has works at Gossillies in Belgium as well as at Hayes in Middlesex. Apparently the British Air Ministry encourages this company to do work for other Governments, for its annual report concludes with an expression of thanks to the Ministry for its great assistance in obtaining overseas orders. From the Government point of view the explanation of this policy is that it is desirable for firms to have the equipment to make aeroplanes on a large scale in peacetime, because it could immediately be concentrated on making aeroplanes for Britain if war occurred.

The Fairey Company has a large experimental establishment and a skilled technical staff to enable it to develop land and sea planes to the highest point of efficiency—

that is to say, to the highest point of destructive power. Among its recent achievements is the production, to meet the requirements of the Air Ministry, of all-metal aeroplanes.

The chairman of this company is Mr. C. R. Fairey, who is president of the Royal Aeronautical Society. He is also a member of the council of the Federation of British Industries (there won't be many industries to federate after Mr. Fairey's bombers are let loose !), and of the council of the Society of British Aircraft Constructors.

Making military aeroplanes is a profitable business. The dividends for 1931 were increased from seven per cent to ten per cent (tax free), and the reserves were increased to £60,000. Apparently the total profit on the year was over £184,000—the highest in the company's history.

Another famous British firm—the De Havilland Aircraft Co., Ltd.—is also catholic in the distribution of its products. De Havillands are the makers of the famous " Moth " series. Their orders from the British Empire are so heavy that they cannot meet them from their British factories. They have had to form subsidiary companies in Australia, Canada, India, and South Africa. The company does a large trade in the United States of America and it is now developing its connections with South America. Its business is also highly profitable. Between 1927 and 1930 its capital quadrupled.

Handley Page Ltd. is another well-known firm ; it specialises in large twin-engined bombers of the " Hinaidi " type. Among its shareholders are the trustees of a religious order. Does religion countenance shattering human beings to bits ?

Another company which demands notice is the Armstrong-Siddeley Development Company, the makers of the fastest aircraft in the world. Its " Hawker Fury "—an interceptor fighter—has a speed of over 200 miles per hour and can climb 20,000 feet in eleven minutes. This company owns practically all the shares of Sir W. G.

Armstrong-Whitworth Aircraft Ltd., A. V. Roe & Co., Ltd., and the Armstrong-Siddeley Motors Ltd. Its directors include, Mr. J. D. Siddeley, Lord Southborough, and Air Marshal Sir John F. A. Higgins, described in *Who's Who* as K.C.B., K.B.E., C.B., D.S.O., A.F.C., R.A.F. (I cannot help remarking how much more impressive this reads than just plain John Higgins !) The Siddeley Company has also shown consistently high profits.

Other firms important in military aviation are the Blackburn Aeroplane & Motor Co., Ltd. (the makers of the " Lincock Fighters "), Boulton & Paul, and the Bristol Aeroplane Company.

I have already recorded how Vickers have extended their enterprise to military and naval aviation by establishing two subsidiary companies—Vickers (Aviation) Ltd. and the Supermarine Aviation Works (Vickers) Ltd. Important also are the firms which construct the engines for military and naval aeroplanes. Napier & Sons, Ltd., and Rolls-Royce

Ltd. both do a considerable trade in this direction.

These, then, are the firms which provide Britain, and many parts of the world, with the air-fleets which will hurl down death and destruction upon men, women, and children in the next great war. I turn now to the industrial organisation which will provide the explosives and poison gases with which they will do their bloody work.

CHAPTER XVII

THE ARMAMENT FIRMS IN BRITAIN

(3) EXPLOSIVES AND POISON GAS

" Poison gases, the slightest breath of which can destroy a human life, have become an essential, if not the most important, part of the armaments of the Great Powers."
—COLONEL GERTSCH.

THE LEAGUE OF NATIONS has proscribed chemical warfare. Poison gases have been put outside the pale of civilised war, as it is to be conducted in future by humane and Christian Governments. The leading Powers have solemnly sworn an oath to this effect.

In the Treaty of Versailles, Article 171 prohibited in general terms the use of chemical warfare in the future. In the Washington Treaty (Article 5) of 1922 the prohibition was made detailed and specific. The Governments of the United States of

America, the British Empire, France, Italy, and Japan then declared :

" The use in war of asphyxiating, poisonous, or other gases, and of analogous liquids, materials, or devices, having been justly condemned by the opinion of the civilised world, and the prohibition of such use having been declared in treaties to which the majority of the civilised Powers are parties, the signatory Powers, to the end that this prohibition shall be universally accepted as part of International Law, binding alike the practice and conscience of nations, declare their assent to such prohibition, agree to be bound thereby as between themselves, and invite all other civilised nations to adhere thereto."

In the Draft Convention of The Hague in the same year, in the Geneva Protocol of 1925, and in Article 39 of the Draft Convention drawn up by the Preparatory Commission for the Disarmament Conference (1930), this declaration was repeated in more or less definite terms.

These solemn declarations are in practice a dead letter, in Britain and everywhere else. Despite these pronouncements, the British Government, like other Governments, maintains its Chemical Warfare Research Laboratories, employing expert scientists for the purpose of discovering deadlier gases and explosives, and the completest arrangements have been made to convert the British chemical industry at a day's notice into a vast concern for war purposes.

In considering the chemical aspect of the Bloody Traffic, let us have clearly in mind for what its products will be used. We have no excuse for ignorance ; there are many authoritative descriptions of the future of chemical warfare. The following is from the Report of the Preparatory Disarmament Commission of the League of Nations :

" There is every reason to believe that, in a future war, aircraft would be much more numerous than in the last, and they would be able to carry much heavier weights. However reprehensible such an action might be, there would be nothing technically to prevent them dropping large bombs filled with some heavy poison gas over localities essential to the political or economic life of an enemy country.

" The gas to be employed would not necessarily be one which only disables human beings for a time, since the object would be to hamper or destroy some continuous activity aimed at by the attack. Mustard gas, for instance, dropped in large quantities, would be likely to hang about the cities and slowly penetrate the houses. Heavy poison gases linger, even in the open country, for quite a long time. In a city it is difficult to say how long they might remain, and during all the time the danger would continue.

" It may be said that such a development of warfare would be too horrible for use and that the conscience of mankind would revolt at it. It may be so, but, in view of the fact that in modern wars such as the last one the whole population of a country is more or less directly engaged, it may well be that an unscrupulous belligerent may not see much difference between the use of poison gas against troops in the field and its use against the centres from which those troops draw the sinews of war."[1]

This League report suggests that it would be " reprehensible " for Governments to adopt such means of warfare, and that only an " unscrupulous belligerent " would do so. But every War Office is preparing to do this " reprehensible " thing. The official excuse is that the preparations are defensive. When the Minister of War was once reporting on this matter in the House of Commons I asked him : " Has not the League of Nations prohibited chemical warfare ? " The answer was : " The purpose of our preparations is defensive in the event of another Power using chemical warfare against us." All the War Offices say that, but all the War Offices know very well that immediately war is declared their air-fleets will sweep out over enemy countries with bombs stocked with poison gas.

The British Government spends approximately £150,000 a year on experimental research on the effectiveness of various types

[1] League of Nations Document, A.16, 1924, IX., p. 30.

of poison gases. Twelve years ago the expenditure was only a little more than £50,000 a year. The gases are tried out on animals. During the twelve months ending October 1930, experiments were made on 731 animals, of which 366 died as the result of the experiment. During the period January 1921 to March 1931, no fewer than 4,908 animals were subjected to poison gas experiments. Of these, 1,511 died. They included 25 horses, which were declared by the Ministry to be unfit for further service.

The main experimental station is at Porton. The animals used include most of the familiar domestic pets, as this return for the period November 1, 1926, to July 8, 1929, indicates :

Animal	No. Used	No. which Died
Rabbits	410	79
Goats	47	1
Guinea-pigs	989	148
Cats	39	8
Monkeys	1	—
Mice	153	108
Canaries	40	40
Pigeons	46	30

Experiments to a considerable number are also conducted at the Physiological Laboratory at Cambridge. The time will come when the human race will look back with disgust upon a generation which made animals the victims of its viciousness and stupidity in failing to manage its affairs without the use of poison gas.

A veil of secrecy hides many of the chemical preparations for the next war. The formulas are pigeon-holed, the stocks of necessary substances noted, the plant equipped, the technicians listed—all this is going on in the dark. But the experts have revealed some of the chemicals which will be used.[1]

There is the gas known as Lewisite, sometimes called " Death Dew." It was made in the American laboratories towards the end of the World War, and the Allies intended to use it in air-attacks upon Berlin in the spring of 1919 if the war had continued.

---

[1] See " Chemical and Bacteriological Warfare," by Dr. G. Woker, included in *What Would be the Character of a New War ?*

Three drops of this gas, states Professor Noel Baker, the British expert, are enough to kill a man if they come into contact with any part of the skin. The bombs which had been prepared for Berlin, he adds, are said to have been so deadly that they could kill every person in the open within from 600 to 800 metres from the spot where they exploded.

Electric incendiary bombs have been prepared. They weigh only one kilogramme. As soon as they strike an object, the thermite (a magnesium alloy) with which they are filled develops a heat of 3,000 degrees. It burns through the cover of the bomb, and the glowing mass which is released can burn even through steel. No appliance to extinguish these bombs has yet been discovered ; water merely increases the incendiary effect. Ludendorff, the former Field Marshal of the German Army, states that preparations were being made, at the end of the World War, to set fire to London and Paris by bombs filled with magnesium powder and ferric oxide. Apparently if the war had continued the population of Berlin would have been destroyed by Lewisite and the population of London by thermite !

One of the gases actually used in the World War was diphenylcyanarsine. Lord Halsbury, Chief of the Explosives Department of the War Office during the War, stated in the House of Lords, July 14, 1928, that 40 tons of this gas would be enough to destroy the whole population of London.

Both chlorine and phosgene were used in the World War. Chlorine was replaced by other gases, partly because it is an irritant and thus quickly reveals its presence and partly because it is not so deadly as other gases. One per cent of chlorine in the air is generally fatal. At the battle of Ypres, April 1915, it caused the death of 6,000 men, but experiment provided gases which were still deadlier and which also had the advantage of not being noticeable until they had done their murderous work.

Phosgene is one of them. Trichlormethyl-chloroformate is another. The latter is known

Q B

as " Green Cross," because in the World War the shells containing it were so marked. This gas fills the lungs of the victim with blood and literally causes him to be drowned in his own blood. It is terribly painful ; the torture generally lasts for several hours.

Another gas used in the World War, and ready for use on a large scale in future wars, is chloropicrin. It causes dropsy of the lungs, followed frequently by apoplectic attacks and paralysis.

Mustard gas—sometimes called " Yellow Cross " in contrast to " Green Cross "—is better known. It is really a liquid, and is scattered through the air in a fine spray at a high boiling-point. Its weight causes it to fall to the ground, covering everything with an invisible layer. In the warmth of a room or dug-out the poison is vaporised, and mixes unnoticed with the air, one part in five million of air being enough to cause the disease. The first symptoms do not show themselves for six hours or more. Then blisters appear on the body, changing to open wounds ; purulent inflammation occurs in the eyes ; and the lungs are eaten away. The disease may last for months, the victim being gradually strangled for want of air and often dying in violent convulsions.

The masks used in the World War lessened the destructive effects of " Green Cross " and " Yellow Cross." " Blue Cross " was therefore prepared. Its special value as a death-dealer was its property of penetration. In the form of fine dust it entered the masks and caused violent sneezing and nausea. The victim then removed his mask, only to be exposed to the deadly effects of " Green Cross."

The scientists who devote themselves to war purposes have greatly " improved " " Blue Cross " since the war. They have made it still more penetrative, and have made it deadly in itself.

These are some of the preparations for chemical warfare of which we have knowledge. There are many others, and the chemists are continually at work producing still more.

The relationship between the Governments and the industries which are scheduled to prepare poison gas is, of course, close. During the World War Germany had an initial advantage in chemical warfare, because she was able to utilise the highly developed dyestuffs industry to apply secret processes which her scientists had discovered. After the war the Allies sent a Military Commission to Germany to find out these secret processes, and in 1919 the British Government established the British Dyestuffs Corporation in order to be prepared for any future war emergency. To speed the new concern on its way the Government subscribed for 850,000 preferred shares and 850,001 preference shares, " to include one share with special voting powers issued to His Majesty's Government." The Articles of Association required the company " to keep in touch with His Majesty's Government in all matters of technical information and research."

There has never been any secret about the motive for the establishment of the Dyestuffs Corporation. " The fundamental argument for the establishment of a British dyestuffs industry was national safety," wrote *The Chemical Age* (November 22, 1924), " —in other words, the existence of chemical plant and processes which could easily, in case of emergency, be switched over from peace to war purposes."

Sometimes the names of the firms which are destined to produce poison gas are most innocent. For example, the I.C.S. (Fertilisers and Synthetic Products) Ltd. How admirable its purpose—to manufacture fertilisers which will facilitate the production of food ! But in the event of a threatened war its plant might be applied at once to the production of poison gas.

The story of this firm is interesting.[1] During the Great War the scientists on the side of the Allies never fully discovered how the plant for synthetic ammonia was utilised for

[1] *The Secret International,* p. 17.

the production of poison gas. The Allies'
Military Commission made a special point
of investigating this, and in due course the
secret was passed on to the Allied Governments.

After the war the Governments sold the
chemical works which they had established
for war purposes. Among those which the
British Government sold was a factory at
Bellingham used for synthetic ammonia
production. The price for the factory was
low, but despite this it is generally understood to have covered, in addition to the
premises and plant, particulars of the secret
German process.

This secret process is now in the keeping
of the I.C.S. (Fertilisers and Synthetic Products) Ltd., and, in return for the anticipated service which the company will per-
form in the next war, the British Government has guaranteed both the principal and
interest of its five per cent guaranteed debenture stock until the year 1945. If chemical
warfare has not destroyed us all by that date,

no doubt the Government will prove willing to extend the guarantee.

But the I.C.S. (Fertilisers and Synthetic Products) Ltd. is only a minor concern in the elaborate chemical industry which is available at a moment's notice for war purposes. Even the British Dyestuffs Corporation is only a subsidiary in the great combine which has been established. The real guarantee that Britain will be plentifully supplied with poison gas and explosives in the next war is the Imperial Chemical Industries.

The Imperial Chemical Industries is the biggest chemical concern in the world.[1] It has a practical monopoly in Britain of both supplies and potential supplies. Its capital is over £70,000,000. Its directors and shareholders include some of the most solid pillars of British business and politics.

[1] The object of the Imperial Chemical Industries is to supply chemicals for normal peace purposes. It cannot therefore be regarded as an armament firm in the ordinary sense, and there is no evidence that it has pursued the practices which have been described in the case of some armament firms. But no survey of industries utilisable in the event of war can omit to notice the I.C.I.

The names of the directors are so imposing that they must be recorded :

Lord Reading (President)
Sir H. McGowan, K.B.E. (Chairman)
Lord Ashfield
Lord Colwyn
Lord Melchett
Lord Weir
Sir Max Muspratt

What other company can boast a directorate of five peers and two baronets ?

The shareholders include names almost as substantial and distinguished. For example, the Right Hon. Neville Chamberlain, M.P. (Chancellor of the Exchequer), and Sir Austen Chamberlain, M.P. (ex-Foreign Secretary). Until the beginning of March 1932, Sir John Simon, the Foreign Secretary, was a shareholder.

This powerful combine has acquired, by exchange of shares, all the main chemical industries in Britain. They include Noble Industries Ltd. (since voluntarily liquidated), Brunner Mond & Co., Ltd., United Alkali

Ltd., and the British Dyestuffs Corporation.

A chemical industry organised on this scale can be adapted for war purposes with great speed.

The Committee of Chemical Experts in connection with the Preparatory Commission of the Disarmament Conference pointed out that "no time will be required for adaptation in the case of poison gases which are at present produced in large quantities in industry. Among these gases may be mentioned more particularly chlorine and phosgene." In the case of gases not normally produced in peace-time, or produced in quantities insufficient for war requirements, the period required for adaptation will depend "on the scientific, technical, and material resources of the country and its industrial organisation."[1]

The Imperial Chemical Industries fulfils these requirements completely. It is potentially a perfect provider of the essentials of chemical warfare.

[1] Sub-Commission B, Report No. I., p. 12.

The phenol, cresol, and toluene which it normally uses for pharmacy can be utilised immediately on demand for explosives. The benzene which is used for dyeing and painting can be used for mustard gas. The cellulose which is used for artificial silk can be used for powder. The glycerine which is used for soap can be used for dynamite. The chlorine which is used for household disinfectant can be used for phosgene. The brome which is used for photographic plates can be used for tear-gas. Other industries can also be used. The process of sugar refinement can be transformed into poison gas manufacture. The production of rayon can be transformed into the production of dynamite.

Whilst the Imperial Chemical Industries Ltd., as the main source of the country's potential poison gas and explosive supplies, is so closely associated with the British Government, it is by no means insular, or even merely imperial, in its interests and activities.

It not only has associated groups in

Australia, New Zealand, South Africa, and the Malay States, but is linked up through heavy investments with important concerns in America and Germany, as well as in China, Japan, and Canada. Let us hope that none of the shares of the Chancellor of the Exchequer have been used for this purpose. It would be unfortunate if the next war should happen to be against America or Germany.

The Imperial Chemical Industries is one of the few prosperous industries in Britain. At its sixth annual general meeting, held on April 10, 1933, a gross profit of £6,415,423 on the year's working was reported. After setting aside £1 million for depreciation and £686,351 for income tax, the net profit was £4,729,072, *an increase of 38 per cent over the previous year*. A dividend of six per cent was declared on its ordinary shares.

A remarkable feature of the annual meeting was a recommendation by the directors that the wages of the workmen should be increased. This step was the more unusual since the trade unions had not demanded any increase.

The growing Anti-War Movement in Britain is urging that the workers should declare a general strike if war threatens. The workmen of the Imperial Chemical Industries will obviously occupy a key position.

CHAPTER XVIII

THE ARMAMENTS INTER-NATIONAL

" Is it not a notorious fact that practically all the armour-plate makers in the world, except one firm, comprise a ring ? "—THE LATE LORD MELCHETT.

WE NOW have in our minds a picture of the Bloody Traffic in Britain. Let us turn to other countries. We shall find that, just as the traffic is a closely knit unit in Britain, so its national units are interlinked right round the world.

Before the war there was a world armaments ring which operated through several parallel organisations covering different aspects of the industry. One was the Harvey United Steel Company, in which all the leading armour-plate firms were associated. The company was formed to enable the firms of all countries to pool the advantages of

American, French, and German patents for making armour-plate.

The chairman was Mr. Albert Vickers, the managing director of Vickers-Maxim. Its directorate included representatives of the four main *British* armour-plate firms at that time (Charles Cammell, John Brown, Armstrong-Whitworth, and Vickers-Maxim), of the two most important *German* firms (Krupp and Dillinger Steel), the three chief *French* firms (Schneider, Chatillon Steel, and St. Chamont Steel), and the Terni Steel Works of *Italy*. The Carnegie Steel Company of *America* completed the list.

This group of firms was linked with nearly all the armour-plate companies in the world. Krupp and Schneider were then both financially interested in the *Russian* Putiloff Factories ; Krupp was a partner in the *Austrian* Skoda Works ; and Vickers owned half of the capital of the Meuteron Armour-Plate Factories in *Japan*. With John Brown, Vickers also owned the *Spanish* Drydock Naval Construction Works at Ferrol, and six

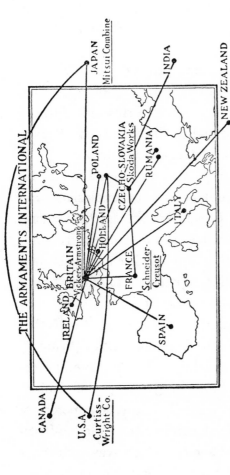

THE ARMAMENTS INTERNATIONAL

Vickers-Armstrong (Britain) has associated companies in Canada, Ireland, Spain, Italy, Rumania, New Zealand, India, Holland, Poland, Japan (part of the Mitsui Combine), and France (part of Schneider-Creusot).

Schneider-Creusot (France) is associated with Vickers (Britain) and with the Skoda Works (Czecho-Slovakia), which has associated companies in Rumania and Poland.

Curtiss-Wright (U.S.A.) is associated with a Skoda subsidiary company in Poland, and with the Mitsui Combine in Japan.

Mitsui Combine (Japan) is associated with Vickers (Britain) and Curtiss-Wright (U.S.A.).

British firms founded the *Portuguese* Ship-building Syndicate to enable Portugal to build a fleet.

Thus we see that, directly and indirectly, the Harvey United Steel Company connected up the armour-plate firms of Britain, America, Germany, France, Italy, Russia, Austria, Spain, Portugal, and Japan.

Similarly there was an international alliance of manufacturers of explosives and gunpowder. It was known as the General Cartel of Powder Manufacturers. It combined British, German, French, Austrian, Russian, Italian, Spanish, Canadian, South African, and Japanese firms.

The principal partners were the Nobel Dynamite Trust Company Ltd. (Britain), with seven branches in Britain, five in Germany, and one in Japan ; the Rhine-Siegner group in Germany, composed of three explosive factories ; the Cologne-Rottweiler Shell Factory, which was connected with British, Spanish, and Russian firms ; the German Arms and Munitions Factories, which had similar international connections ; the French Dynamite Company, the French Society for the Manufacture of Dynamite, and the French-Russian Dynamite Company. These three French firms were also linked with kindred concerns in many countries.

The nickel interests of the European armament firms were linked together in the Steel Manufacturers' Nickel Syndicate Ltd. Its shareholders were a combination of British, German, French, Austrian, and Italian firms—including : Vickers, Armstrong-Whitworth, and other important British firms ; Krupp and Dillinger of Germany ; Schneider-Creusot and other French firms ; the Witkowitzer Bergban and Ersenhutten Genurkschaft of Austria ; and the Società di Terni of Italy. Another important nickel combine was the British America Nickel Corporation, which had close connections with the important Christiana Nickel Works in Norway.

Most of these trusts dissolved into their
RB

component parts shortly before the World War or during its early months. This was not the case with the British America Nickel Corporation, which, not representing firms on the opposing sides, was free to continue, and succeeded, as we have seen, in considerably extending its business through neutral countries. But the trusts comprised of companies in enemy nations, having supplied both of the armed camps with guns and explosives and war-craft, necessarily became severed.

In their old form these trusts have not been renewed, but by other means the most important armament firms of the world have resumed their association since the war.[1]

We have seen that, in Britain, Vickers-Armstrong dominates the heavy armament industry, and that it has subsidiary companies or works in Japan, Italy, Spain, Rumania, Holland, Poland, Ireland, Canada, New Zealand, and India (in process of formation).

[1] This survey is based on *The Secret International*.

The counterpart of Vickers in France is Schneider-Creusot (with which Vickers is connected through their joint subsidiary, Vickers-Schneider). Indeed, Schneider-Creusot rivals Vickers as a universal death-provider. It has a virtual monopoly of the heavy armament industry of France, distributing its products over a great part of the world. In addition, it is now master of the vast Skoda Works, which is no longer an Austrian institution, but the armament centre of Czecho-Slovakia and of France's allies in the Little Entente. Schneider-Creusot controls the Skoda Works through the Union Européenne Banque, of which M. Eugene Schneider, chairman of the armament firm, is a director.

Through the Skoda Works, Schneider-Creusot extends its connections wide over Eastern Europe. Skoda provides every kind of war material. At Pilsen it makes cannon, munitions, and tanks ; at Prague it makes military aeroplanes as well as munitions ; at Marienberg, Asee, and Olomouc it makes gas and explosives. The growth of Skoda is illustrated by what has happened at the arsenal, Brno, in Prague. Before the war, Brno was a small repair factory ; now it employs over 10,000 men.

But Skoda is not confined to Czecho-Slovakia. Its works invade Poland and Rumania. At Warsaw it makes aeroplane engines, and it has a Polish subsidiary company which makes munitions. It has a number of factories in Rumania.

Indeed, Skoda is now a world manufacturer of armaments. It distributes its death-dealing products to Yugo-Slavia, Greece, Turkey, Bulgaria, Persia, Switzerland, Spain, Soviet Russia, China, Mexico, and Argentina.

Amidst the deepening economic gloom of Europe the financial success of the Skoda Works shines like a bright light. Its dividends have risen steadily from 5 per cent in 1920 to $28\frac{1}{2}$ per cent in 1930. The production of the instruments of death remains a paying concern when everything else fails.

Our consideration of the ramifications of the French firm, Schneider-Creusot, has taken us to other European countries, but we must not overlook other French firms. There is the firm of Hotchkiss, in whose shareholders' list British names are prominent. Since 1914 this company has repaid its capital three times over in its dividend distributions. Hotchkiss has been working overtime recently in producing armaments for the Far East.

On the side of military aviation the Société Générale Aeronautique, founded in 1930, unites seven of the most important French aircraft factories. The French military aviation works distribute their products all over the world. For example, the Société Anonyme des Ateliers d'Aviation Louis Breguet supply aircraft, not only to the Governments of Belgium, Spain, Greece, Poland, Yugo-Slavia, and Argentina, but also to Turkey—politically in the opposite camp to France—and to both China and Japan. In the Far East we may expect to see

Breguet machines in operation against each other.

The French Schneider-Creusot firm, with its powerful subsidiary, Skoda, is now the most important armament concern on the continent of Europe. It has replaced Krupp, whose work has been lately transformed into non-military production in consequence of the partial disarmament of Germany. But Germany still does a large trade in armaments, and Krupp remains connected with armament factories in Holland, Russia, and Sweden.

Holland makes a considerable contribution to the Bloody Traffic of Europe. The Fokker Aviation firm (Nederlandsche Vliegtuigenfabrik) is world famous. The Vickers Aviation Company of Britain has valuable shares in it, and, through the Fokker Aviation Corporation, it is linked with the manufacture of military aeroplanes in America.

Another firm which has attracted much attention is the Hollandsche Industrie en

Handel Maatschappij Siderius, commonly known as the H.I.H. It has a curious history. At the end of the war, large quantities of German war material were dumped into Holland. A Dutchman named Solomon Vlessing and a German industrialist named Ehrhardt seized the opportunity to establish the H.I.H. the day after the Armistice was signed. Ehrhardt brought technical knowledge, patents, and stocks left over from the war, and works were constructed at Maartenshock and connections were made with the shipbuilding yards. This firm is outside the Schneider-Creusot group and its German connections are regarded with some suspicion in France. Its manager told a special investigator of the Paris *Journal* that, whilst the firm sells material " to any Government which honours it with orders," Ehrhardt's earlier associations naturally provide Germany with special facilities.

In Russia the armament industry is nationalised. It is thus independent of the other European groups, though German firms, including Krupp, were for a time interested in a number of factories in Russia. During recent years, however, these connections have lessened.

The firm of Krupp has important share holdings in the Swedish Ordnance and Drydock Company, which operates the Krupp patents in Scandinavia. Although the Versailles Treaty prohibits Krupp from making armaments at Essen, its provisions do not prevent Krupp from being associated in the ownership of armament works in other countries.

When we turn to the continent of America we find the Bethlehem Steel Corporation dominant. It has developed on lines parallel to Vickers in Britain and Schneider-Creusot in France, and now controls a network of subsidiaries in America. Its growing power is indicated by the fact that the value of its property increased from 31 million dollars in 1905 to 502 million dollars in 1930.

America has several important aviation firms which manufacture aeroplanes for war purposes. One of the foremost is the Curtiss-Wright Corporation, which unites a large number of concerns and which specialises in experimental aircraft for the U.S.A. Army and Navy. The Curtiss-Wright Corporation has also connections with the Schneider-Creusot group in Europe. The Wright aeroplane engines are manufactured by the Polski Zaklady Skoda in Poland, a subsidiary of Skoda and Schneider-Creusot.

Another American firm which does a large trade in aeroplanes for war purposes is the United Aircraft and Transport Company Incorporated. It manufactures for the Navies of the U.S.A., Cuba, Peru, Brazil, and China. The Consolidated Aircraft Corporation has supplied the U.S.A. Army and Navy with over 1,000 training aeroplanes. The Fokker Aviation Corporation of America, associated with the Dutch firm, is also closely linked with the powerful General Motors Corporation Ltd., which holds forty-one per cent of its common stock.

Finally, let us glance at Japan, where a

large armament trust, the Mitsui, has greatly extended its power, since the World War. Mitsui is, in the Far East, the equivalent of Vickers and Schneider-Creusot and the Bethlehem Steel Company. In addition to armament manufacture it has interests in aircraft, steel, petroleum, mining, electricity —and marine and fire insurance (war risks not covered !). It is a gigantic combine. Through one of its subsidiaries—the Japanese Steel Works—it is linked with Vickers, and it is linked with the Curtiss-Wright Corporation of America, whose aeroplane engines it manufactures for the Far East.

This rapid survey of the armament industry shows that Vickers of Britain, Schneider-Creusot of France, the Bethlehem Steel Company of America, and the Mitsui of Japan, are the dominant combines in the world.

We have seen how Vickers has subsidiary and associated firms in Italy, Spain, Rumania, Poland, Holland, Japan, Ireland, Canada, and New Zealand. We have seen

how Schneider-Creusot has subsidiary concerns in Czecho-Slovakia, Poland, and
Rumania. We have seen how these two
groups supply armaments to the greater part
of the world.

The Bethlehem Steel Company Ltd. and
the Mitsui specialise in the war requirements
of the continent of America and the Far
East respectively. In Mexico and South
America the products of the Bethlehem Steel
Company are to be found. In China the
products of Mitsui are to be found.

Between three of these four large combines there is definite association. Vickers
acts as the link. It is associated with Schneider-Creusot through Vickers-Schneider and
with Mitsui through the Japanese Steel
Works.

Before the war, as we have seen, the Bethlehem Steel Company was associated with
the European armaments firms through the
Harvey United Steel Trust. I am without
evidence of any direct association now.
America is, however, linked up both with

the Japanese and European combines. The Curtiss-Wright Corporation is associated with the Japanese combine, Mitsui, which manufactures its aeroplane engines in the Far East, and with the French combine, Schneider-Creusot, whose subsidiary, Skoda, manufactures its aeroplane engines in Eastern Europe.

Thus the Armament International encircles the earth. The peoples of the world have not yet learned to unite for the purposes of life ; but the armament combines have formed a chain which unites them for the purposes of death.

" PATENTS IN EIGHT COUNTRIES "

The international traffic in armaments means that as soon as one of them discovers a more deadly weapon of destruction it can be placed at the disposal of all the Governments. For example, the British firm, Hadfield Ltd., has recently produced a new type of shell which will penetrate the finest armour-plate. Sir Robert Hadfield proudly proclaimed, at the annual meeting of the company in April 1933, that it is " the best in the world." At a distance of nine miles the shell perforates hard-faced armour-plate over one foot thick in one two-hundredth part of a second. Its large internal capacity enables it to be loaded with a very heavy charge of high explosive.

Sir Robert has reason to be proud of it. To produce a shell which can go hurtling through the air for nine miles, cut through a foot of armour-plate as though it were butter, and then explode with devastating effects—this is no small achievement. And he is very patriotic about it.

" If a time for larger employment comes," he says (a nice way, this, of saying " if war comes " !)—" If a time for larger employ-ment comes, we are ready to meet the re-quirements of the Army and Navy with projectiles capable, at long ranges, of carry-ing their charges through the armoured protection of the enemy ship with disastrous effect."

No doubt British citizens when they read this slept more comfortably at night. With such a weapon in the hands of the British Army and Navy there need be no fear of foreign fleets.

But Sir Robert Hadfield said something else. His firm has taken out patents for this shell *in eight countries* ! The British Army and Navy may enjoy the privilege of using it, but so will other Armies and Navies. In time it will become available to any Government which will pay for it.

And in due course we shall pass to the next stage in armament production. Some firm will invent a type of armour-plate which even Sir Robert Hadfield's " best shell in the world " will not penetrate, and then all the Governments will rush to spend money on it in order that they may protect their populations from the shell which Sir Robert has now presented to them.

Thus we proceed from improvement to improvement, and on all of them the armament firms make their profit.

This chapter has dealt with armaments, but armaments themselves depend upon supplies of raw materials, and in modern war supplies of oil for transport and other purposes are as important as armaments. These supplies are also controlled by international rings. In 1926 an International Raw Steel Corporation was formed, linking up the metal industries of Germany, France, Belgium, and Luxembourg, prepared to supply either side with minerals for armaments. Before this the potash industries of France and Germany had become linked.

The oil supplies of the world are controlled by the Standard Oil Company of America, the Royal Dutch Shell combine of London, and the Russian State monopoly. The American and British combines have reached an understanding. The British Government has a controlling interest in the Anglo-Persian Oil Company, which by the provisions of the San Remo Treaty places twenty-five per cent of its products at the disposal of France.

The capitalists and financiers of the world have gone far towards unity to make profit out of the madness of war. When will the peoples of the world unite to make an end of the madness?

CHAPTER XIX

THE POISON GAS INTERNATIONAL

" The World War opened the eyes of Great Britain, France, and Japan, as well as the United States. Each of these countries is busy building up a mammoth chemical industry, as a solid basis for a successful war."—MAJOR-GENERAL AMOS A. FRIES.

CHEMICAL warfare is less than twenty years old. I remember visiting a distinguished scientist in his laboratory at Oxford at the end of the World War. He had been engaged on chemical research for the Government. He emphasised that science had only been called upon to co-operate fully in the last two years of the war. Before that the character of the armaments had been determined by admirals and generals who were, in his view, stupidly conservative. They had opposed the adoption of every new development in armaments since the time of

SB

Queen Elizabeth ; it was only in the dire necessity of the World War that the contribution of chemists was seriously invited.

The scientists had co-operated so effectively that they had revolutionised warfare. I remember a graphic phrase he used : " We have discovered a gas," he said, " which could wipe out the population of a city as easily as a child wipes off the sums from his slate at school." He was referring to Lewisite, which the Allies proposed to use on Berlin had the war lasted into the spring of 1919.

As we have seen, the nations have solemnly adjured the use of poison gas in future wars, but they are, nevertheless, engaged in developing more deadly gases, and have complete preparations for mobilising the services of all the industries which would be of use in manufacturing poison gas.

The Governments of Britain, France, Italy, Poland, Japan, and the United States of America all have Chemical Warfare Research Committees which closely associate

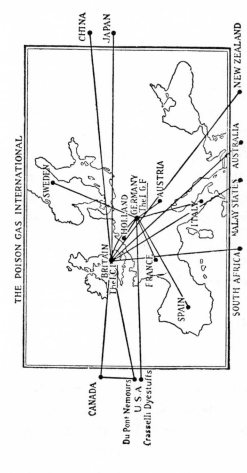

THE POISON GAS INTERNATIONAL

The Imperial Chemical Industries (Britain) is associated with companies in Canada, South Africa, Australia, New Zealand, Malay States, China, Japan and U.S.A., and with the I.G.F. Combine in Germany.

The I.G. Farbenindustrie (Germany) is associated with companies in Spain, France, Italy, Austria, Holland, Sweden and America, and with the I.C.I. (Britain).

Du Pont Nemours (U.S.A.) is part owner of the I.C.I. (Canada) and is associated with the I.C.I. (Britain).

Grasselli Dyestuffs (U.S.A.) is associated with the I.G.F. (Germany).

their chemical industries with the researches carried on continually at the universities. They also have their own Government experimental stations. In Britain the Chemical Warfare Committee links the National Physical Laboratory, the Imperial College of Science and Technology, and the Department of Scientific and Industrial Research, in a chain of research. The committee includes amongst its members most of the prominent chemical manufacturers. The Research Committees of the other Governments have been developed on similar lines.

We have seen how Imperial Chemical Industries has an almost complete monopoly of the British chemical industry and how admirably it is adapted for war-time service as a national arsenal for the production of poison gas and other essentials of chemical warfare. We have also observed that Imperial Chemical Industries is associated with similar concerns in other countries. Let us commence our survey of the Poison Gas International by noting these in greater detail.

In his speech as chairman of directors at the annual general meeting last year, Sir Harry McGowan, after noting that the company had holdings in the Imperial Chemical Industries Ltd. of Australia and New Zealand, proceeded thus :

" The marketable and other investments standing at £9,540,677 mainly represent investments in large industrial companies with which we have, directly or indirectly, trade connections.

" The chief items are investments in the General Motors Corporation, Du Pont & Co., and the Allied Chemical Company in the United States, the International Nickel Company in Canada, the I. G. Farbenindustrie in Germany, and Joseph Lucal & Sons in this country."

This statement definitely links up the potential poison gas provider of Britain with the main potential poison gas providers of the United States and Germany. The E. L. Du Pont de Nemours Company is the most important chemical concern responsible for poison gas manufacture in America. The I. G. Farbenindustrie is the great chemical combine of Germany, the father and founder of poison gas for warfare.

Incidentally, Sir Harry McGowan's statement associates the I.C.I. with another side of armaments production. The General Motors Corporation, as we have already remarked, holds forty-one per cent of the common stock of the Fokker Aviation Corporation of America, which is associated with the Dutch Fokker firm, and which in its turn carries us back to Britain by its association with Vickers-Armstrong.

In this year's speech to the annual general meeting of the I.C.I., Sir Harry McGowan revealed further international connections of the combine. He stated that (jointly with Du Pont de Nemours, of the U.S.A.) it is largely interested in the I.C.I. of Canada, and (jointly with the De Beers Consolidated Mines Ltd.) in the African Explosives and Industries Ltd. He also referred to a conference he had had in Calcutta with " the staff of our Chinese, Japanese, Malayan, and other companies." The I.C.I. is evidently well represented in all the five continents.

So much for the international connections of the potential British poison gas makers, the I.C.I. Now let us explore the international connections of the German combine, the I.G.F.

The Germans were, of course, the pioneers in poison gas manufacture. Their magnificent dyeing industry gave them both unique technical knowledge and plant during the World War. Since the war the importance of the industry has been fully maintained. Mr. Lehmann-Russbüldt remarks that the head office of the I.G.F. is " housed in a structure that is as imposing as a Government building."

The French Government may regard Germany as an enemy, but it is composed of realists. No sooner had the Allied Mission of inquiry into the German poison gas equipment returned after the war, than the French Government entered into a working

agreement with the German combine. On
November 11, 1919, the first anniversary of
the Armistice, whilst the population of
France stood in silence to vow " Never
again," representatives of the French
Government and the French chemical interests (for whom the Société de l'Azote acted)
signed an agreement with representatives
of the German I.G.F.

The French Government acknowledged
that the successful operation of the German
patents could only be secured " with the
active co-operation of the patent-holders."
Therefore it entered into a contract with the
German combine, under which the latter
agreed " to furnish the necessary facilities
for the purpose of manufacture and to take
charge of the construction of competitive
works in France or in the French Colonies
within the next fifteen years." The Germans
were promised compensation in accordance
with the number and size of the poison gas
factories built. This agreement was at first
opposed in the French Chamber of Deputies,

owing to anti-German feeling, but it was endorsed in February 1923, and was given the force of law in April 1924.

The German I.G.F. has links over a great part of the world. It is associated with companies in Britain, United States, France, Spain, Italy, Sweden, Austria, and Holland. Internationally it is on the chemical side what Vickers is on the heavy armament side.

In the manufacture of poison gas it is openly associated with the Norsk-Hydro Elektrsk Kvaelstof of A. S. & Alfred Nobel & Co., of Patsch, near Innsbruck.

In dye materials and auxiliaries it is associated with the Grasselli Dyestuffs Corporation, Cleveland, U.S.A. It holds fifty per cent of the shares in the Frabricacion Nacional de Colorantes y Explosivos of Madrid. It is connected with the Soc. Chim. Lombarda A. E. Bianchi e Co., Milan.

In the supply of inorganic products and organic by-products it is linked with the Sociedad Electroquimica de Flix, Barcelona (which it owns), and through the Dynamit

A.G. Company it has close associations
with three Austrian firms—the Carbidwerk
Deutsch Matrei A.G., Vienna ; the Stick-
stoffwerk Ruse ; and the Bosnische Elektri-
zitäts, Vienna.

On the side of oil and motor materials it
is associated with the Maatschappij Voor
Kolen en Olie Techniek (Makot) of The
Hague, which is a subsidiary of Evag, Berlin,
and with the British Bergius Syndicate Ltd.,
established in Britain to produce oil from
coal—for, among other purposes, the British
Navy.

Thus, through the international ramifications of the British I.C.I. and the German
I.G.F., we see that the potential poison gas
makers of the larger part of the world are
intimately associated. The links are as close
here as in the case of heavy armaments. In
the next great war all nations can count
upon having the most up-to-date chemicals
for mass death and destruction that the
pooled research and experience of the world
can provide.

CHAPTER XX

HOW TO END THE BLOODY TRAFFIC

" The King :
 Then where's the hope this trade in death will die ?
" Frithiof :
 There *IS* none while this social order lives.
 The man of business is the God of War,
 And gold pulls all the strings and all the triggers.
 —Israel Zangwill.

WE HAVE reviewed the Bloody Traffic. We have seen how armament firms create a demand for their goods by fomenting war scares, how they lie and bribe and profiteer, how they supply arms to ally and enemy alike. The question now arises : How are we to end the Bloody Traffic ?

The conclusion generally drawn from an examination of the nature and methods of the armament industry is that it should be nationalised. If I were a member of any legislative assembly before which came a

proposal to nationalise armament production, I should vote in favour of it ; but I
should do so recognising that it was no solution of the problem. This, for two reasons.

In the first place, the nationalisation of
the industry would mean that the Bloody
Traffic would be pursued by Governments
instead of private companies, and it might
prove a very dangerous instrument in their
hands. The wealthiest and most powerful
Governments would undoubtedly use their
ability to produce armaments as a weapon
in their foreign policy.

The smaller nations would either establish
their own armament works, which really
would be the property of the banks or the
Governments which made them loans, or
they would be dependent on one of the
Great Powers for the supply of their arms.
In either case they would become even more
subservient to the Great Powers.

Between the Powers themselves, rivalry
for armament domination over the smaller
nations would develop. The evils of the

Bloody Traffic would be transferred from trusts to Governments.

The prohibition of international traffic in arms would not remove these evils. It would only lead to the establishment of armament works in all countries. Whilst nominally such works might be nationalised in the various States, in actual fact they would be owned by those who loaned the capital.

Secondly, it is not possible now to place limitations upon the armament industry. The manufacture of guns and battleships might be nationalised ; but what of the chemical industry, which would be utilised in war-time to produce poison gas, or the metal industries and oil industries, which provide the raw materials ? If we set out to nationalise all industries which are potential war industries, we should end by nationalising practically every industry.

And that brings one to the central issue of this problem. The armament industries are only doing what all industries do. All lie and bribe and profiteer and use newspaper publicity and take every possible step to create a market for their goods. The armament industries directly encourage war by the use of these methods ; but indirectly all industries encourage war by the same methods. The struggle for markets is the underlying cause of the rivalries in the foreign policies of Governments and of the rivalries in armaments themselves. War and armaments have their roots in the economic system ; and it is only by a fundamental change in the economic system that the Bloody Traffic will be ended. That is my first conclusion.

My second conclusion is that if war is let loose on the world before this transformation of the economic system takes place, the only hope lies in the organised resistance of the peoples of the world to the Governments which call them to war.

There is no doubt that the determination to resist war is growing. The attitude of the students in the British universities is significant. Following the lead of the Oxford

University Union, the students of Glasgow, Manchester, Cardiff, Leicester, Aberystwyth, and the London School of Economics, through their associations, have all declared their decision never to fight for " King and country."

But such individual resistance must be extended to mass resistance by the organised workers if it is to be effective. In 1920, every section of the British Labour Movement was represented in a great national conference which decided that, if war were declared against Russia, not a train should run, not a wheel in an engineering shed should turn, no coal should be dug in the pits—industry would stop dead. Faced by such action on the part of the workers, no Government could conduct a war.

But it must be foreseen that, if resistance of this kind commenced, whilst the struggle might begin as war resistance, it would inevitably develop into a struggle between the organised workers on the one side, and the Government on the other. If the workers were successful, their victory might lead to the end, not only of a particular war, but of the economic system from which wars come.

To end the Bloody Traffic we must do much more than nationalise armaments. We must bring about a revolution—a complete transformation—in the basis of the present system of civilisation.

(Communiqué au Conseil,
aux Membres de la Société
et aux Délégués à l'Assemblée)

A 81. 1921
C. 321. 1921.

Genève,
le 15 septembre 1921.

SOCIÉTÉ DES NATIONS

———

RAPPORT

de la Commission Temporaire Mixte pour la Réduction des Armements.

———

LEAGUE OF NATIONS

———

REPORT

of the Temporary Mixed Commission on Armaments.

RAPPORT DE LA COMMISSION TEMPORAIRE MIXTE
POUR LA RÉDUCTION DES ARMEMENTS

La Commission temporaire mixte pour la Réduction des Armements a été nommée conformément à une résolution de l'Assemblée de 1920, afin d'étudier les problèmes du désarmement non seulement du point de vue militaire technique mais aussi dans leurs relations avec des questions politiques et économiques. Dans le temps relativement court dont elle a pu disposer, la Commission n'a pu réussir à déposer des conclusions définitives sur toutes les questions qui avaient été soumises à son examen. Elle a toutefois procédé à une exploration préliminaire du terrain et a l'honneur de présenter aujourd'hui à l'Assemblée une série de rapports qui permettront aux Membres de la Société des Nations de juger de la nature générale des recherches qui ont déjà été entreprises et de l'œuvre qui reste encore à accomplir.

Avant de soumettre ces rapports à l'Assemblée, la Commission se permet de présenter quelques brèves observations sur le problème du désarmement tel que le pose la situation politique actuelle du monde.

* * *

De tous les problèmes auxquels la Société des Nations doit faire face, il n'en est pas de plus difficile que celui du désarmement, car les armements dépendent de la politique, la politique des circonstances, et les circonstances varient d'une année à l'autre et de pays à pays.

Lorsqu'il a été élaboré, le Pacte supposait une situation dans laquelle toutes les nations se trouveraient membres d'une seule société et liées les unes et les autres par le dessein commun de maintenir la paix d'un bout à l'autre du globe. Il partait de cette idée que toutes les nations seraient en paix les unes avec les autres, et que le monde serait revenu à une position stable après les convulsions de la grande guerre. Il n'est pas besoin de dire que ces conditions n'ont été jusqu'ici réalisées qu'en partie. Trois grandes Puissances, dont la force militaire actuelle pour l'une et potentielle pour les deux autres est immense, restent en dehors de la Société: et, tant que les Etats-Unis, l'Allemagne et la Russie ne feront pas partie de notre Société, il y aura de grandes difficultés à ce que ses Membres adoptent en commun un plan de réduction systématique et progressive de désarmement, ou échangent d'une manière complète et sans réserve des renseignements militaires.

Nous ne saurions prétendre avoir atteint une période de stabilité. Les Etats limitrophes de la République des Soviets ont des appréhensions très naturelles sur les intentions de leur immense et peu sûr voisin. La situation intérieure de la République allemande est encore très loin d'être stable. Une grave tension existe entre la Lithuanie et la Pologne, et les nouveaux Etats qui ont été formés par le démembrement de l'Empire d'Autriche ne sont pas encore entièrement adaptés à la situation difficile qui a été créée par les Traités de Paix. La guerre sévit toujours entre la Grèce et la Turquie. Le Traité de Sèvres n'a pas été ratifié et un malaise grave règne dans tout le monde musulman.

Les réponses faites par les gouvernements à la lettre du Secrétaire général en date du 8 mars 1921, au sujet des dépenses nationales pour les armements, suffisent à montrer l'incertitude de la situation politique générale et la prudence avec laquelle les Membres de la Société se sentent tenus d'examiner des propositions concrètes de désarmement.

Néanmoins, il importe d'enregistrer le fait que des progrès considérables ont été déjà réalisés dans le sens désiré. Les Traités de Paix ont imposé à certains Etats des stipulations précises concernant leur désarmement. L'exécution de ces stipulations est en bonne voie de réalisation; elle devra, nous voulons l'espérer, être confirmée par l'établissement d'un régime démocratique stable en Allemagne. Par là sera offerte une garantie substantielle du maintien de la paix. En vérité, dans tout le cours de l'Histoire, on n'a jamais vu prendre de mesure aussi importante, avec des conséquences probables d'une si grande portée, que la suppression de la conscription en Allemagne et la réduction des forces militaires régulières de ce pays à une

IMPORTANT.

(Communiqué au Conseil, aux
Membres de la Société, et
aux Délégués à l'Assemblée.)

A. 81. 1921.
(C.321) ERRATUM.

SOCIÉTÉ DES NATIONS.

Errata au Rapport de la Commission Temporaire Mixte
pour la Réduction des Armements. (A.81. 1921.)

Pour remplacer le premier alinéa du Rapport sur la "Fabrication privée", page 11:

"Le règlement des deux questions qui précèdent: droit d'investigation, droit de contrôle mutuel, ne peut manquer d'avoir en fait sur le désarmement d'heureuses conséquences. Parmi des autres mesures particulieres qui peuvent faciliter et hâter la solution générale du problème, il n'en est pas de plus importants que la réglementation de la fabrication privée."

Pour remplacer le premier alinéa du Rapport sur le "Trafic des armes", page 13:

"Il convient d'examiner enfin la question du trafic des armes."

LEAGUE OF NATIONS.

Errata to the Report of the Temporary Mixed Commission
for the Reduction of Armaments. (A.81. 1921.)

To replace the first paragraph of the Report on "Private Manufacture," page 11:

"The settlement of the two preceding questions -- the right of investigation and the right of mutual control, cannot fail to have satisfactory results in the direction of disarmament. Among the special measures likely to facilitate and hasten the general solution of the problem, none is more important than the regulation of private manufacture."

To replace the first paragraph of the Report on "Traffic in Arms," page 13:

"Lastly, we have to consider the question of the Traffic in Arms."

REPORT OF THE TEMPORARY MIXED COMMISSION ON ARMAMENTS.

The Temporary Mixed Commission on Armaments was appointed in accordance with a resolution of the Assembly of 1920 to explore those aspects of the problem of disarmament which were not purely of a technical military character, but might properly be described as involving political and economical issues as well. In the comparatively brief time at its disposal, the Commission has been unable to reach final conclusions upon all the questions submitted to its consideration. It has, however, made a preliminary exploration of the ground and has the honour now to present to the Assembly a series of reports which will enable the Members of the League of Nations to estimate the general character of the enquiries which have already been undertaken, and the work which still remains to be accomplished.

Before submitting these reports to the Assembly, the Commission begs leave to offer some brief observations upon the problem of Disarmament as it is affected by the present political condition of the world.

* * *

Of all the problems confronting the League of Nations none is more difficult than the problem of Disarmament, for armaments depend upon policy, policy upon circumstance, and circumstance varies from country to country, and from year to year.

When the Covenant was framed, it contemplated a situation in which all nations were members of a single League and bound to one another by the common purpose of maintaining peace throughout the Globe. It assumed that all nations would be at peace with one another, and that the world would have settled down into a position of stability after the convulsions of the great war. It is needless to say that these conditions have so far only been realised in part. Three great Powers, one of them actually and the other potentially, of immense military importance, stand outside the League, and so long as the United States, Germany and Russia do not participate in our Society, great difficulties confront the common adoption by its members of a plan for the systematic and progressive reduction of armaments or for a full, frank and unreserved communication of military information. Neither have we reached a period of stability. The States bordering upon the Soviet Republic are naturally apprehensive of the intentions of their huge and uncertain neighbour. The internal situation of the German Republic is still far from secure. Grave tension exists between Lithuania and Poland, and the new States which have been formed out of the body of the Austrian Empire have not yet entirely accommodated themselves to the difficult situation created by the Treaties of Peace. War is still raging between Greece and Turkey. The Treaty of Sèvres has not been ratified and grave unrest prevails throughout the Moslem world.

The replies from the Governments to the letter of the Secretary-General of March 8th, 1921, with reference to the reduction of national expenditure on armaments are sufficient to exhibit the uncertainty of the general political situation, and the caution with which the Members of the League feel compelled to view comprehensive proposals for disarmament.

Nevertheless, it is important to realise that immense progress has already been made in the direction desired. The Treaties of Peace have imposed upon certain States precise stipulations concerning disarmament. The execution of these stipulations is in a fair way of being realised and will, it is to be hoped, be finally confirmed by the establishment of stable democratic institutions in Germany. Thus will a substantial guarantee be afforded for the preservation of peace. Indeed, in the whole course of history, no single step has been taken so important and far-reaching in its probable effects as the abolition of conscription in Germany and the restriction of the regular military force of that country to a voluntary army not

armée de volontaires n'excédant pas les besoins nécessaires de la défense intérieure.
Il est loisible de dire que le rigoureux maintien de cette situation non seulement faci-
litera des réductions d'armements dans les autres pays, mais devra entraîner comme
corollaire nécessaire la paix pour l'Europe occidentale.

Après le désarmement de l'Allemagne vient, en importance, la proposition
faite par le Président Harding, qu'une Conférence se réunisse à Washington pour
discuter le désarmement et le règlement des problèmes politiques du Pacifique.
La Société des Nations, dont le dessein est précisément d'assurer la concorde internationale, salue naturellement avec une grande joie l'initiative du Président
Harding.

La limitation des armements navals qui, on peut le présumer, sera l'un des
problèmes principaux discutés par la Conférence de Washington, peut en effet
être assurée de la manière la plus efficace par un accord complet entre les Puissances.
·Il faut espérer ardemment que cette Conférence portera des fruits, et que la réduction des armements terrestres sur le continent européen se verra complétée par une
entente relative à la réduction des armements navals.

En attendant, un vaste champ d'activité utile reste ouvert à la Société des
Nations. La situation financière des Etats européens exige impérieusement de
nouvelles réductions dans les budgets militaires, et, en vérité, ce n'est pas aller trop
loin que de faire dépendre, en une large mesure, de la réalisation de ces réductions la renaissance économique de l'Europe

La Commission mixte des Armements, nommée par la Société des Nations,
peut jouer un rôle utile et important en examinant soigneusement les problèmes
économiques relatifs à la question du désarmement, ainsi que les meilleures méthodes
pour obvier aux maux qui peuvent résulter de la fabrication privée du matériel
de guerre. Il ne saurait être douteux que la permanence de grandes forces militaires,
navales et aériennes, représente par elle-même une menace pour la paix, et que notre
génération manquerait à son devoir envers la postérité si, après les terribles leçons
de la récente guerre, elle ne s'attaquait pas d'une manière sérieuse et continue aux
moyens de délivrer le monde d'un fardeau pesant si lourdement sur la production
du temps de paix, et pouvant, ainsi qu'une amère expérience l'a prouvé, contribuer
à faire éclater des guerres qui n'amènent que ruines et désastres

* * *

Après l'exposé de ces considérations générales dans lesquelles la Commission
s'est efforcée de mettre en lumière l'essence des données en même temps que des
difficultés du problème du désarmement, il convient de présenter maintenant les
rapports des trois sous-commissions qui ont envisagé les solutions spécifiques à
donner à ces problèmes.

La première Assemblée de la Société des Nations. avait adopté, au cours de
sa séance du 14 décembre 1920, la résolution suivante:

« L'Assemblée propose au Conseil:

. . . .

« b) de charger, à titre temporaire, une Commission composée de personnalités
possédant la compétence voulue en matières politique, sociale et économique, de
préparer pour soumission au Conseil, dans un avenir prochain, des études et propositions sur la question de la réduction des armements prévue à l'article 8 du
Pacte. »

La Commission temporaire pour la réduction des armements, constituée en
vertu de cette résolution, a tenu sa première session à Paris du 16 au 19 juillet
1921, sous la présidence de M. Viviani.

La répartition entre plusieurs sous-commissions de l'étude des questions
inscrites à son ordre du jour, avait pour la Commission temporaire une importance
particulière: c'était pour elle définir à la fois sa compétence et ses méthodes.

M. Viviani, résumant au cours de la troisième séance plénière les discussions auxquelles cette répartition avait donné lieu, proposa de constituer trois sous-commissions.

La *première Sous-Commission* devait avoir pour objet l'étude des questions
suivantes:

a) fabrication privée des munitions et du matériel de guerre;
b) trafic des armes et des munitions.

Elle devait, en outre, à propos de la fabrication privée, se prononcer sur le
projet de résolution de M. Jouhaux en faveur de la convocation d'une Conférence
internationale chargée de réglementer la fabrication privée des armements.

exceeding the limits necessary for internal defence. It is not too much to say that the steadfast maintenance of this situation will not only enable progressive reductions to be made in the military establishments of other countries, but carries with it as a necessary corollary the peace of Western Europe.

Next in importance to the disarmament of Germany comes the proposal of President Harding that a Conference should meet at Washington to discuss Disarmament and the settlement of the political problems of the Pacific. The League of Nations which exists for the purpose of securing international concord naturally welcomes with great satisfaction the initiative of President Harding.

The limitation of Naval Armaments which will presumably be one of the principal problems discussed at the Conference at Washington (an indeed be most effectively secured by a common agreement between the Powers. It is earnestly to be hoped that this Conference will be fruitful, and that the reduction of the land armaments on the continent of Europe will be supplemented by an understanding relating to the reduction of naval armaments.

Meanwhile, a field of useful work remains open to the League of Nations. The financial position of European States imperiously demands further reductions in military expenditure, and indeed it is not too much to say that the economic revival of Europe largely depends upon such reductions being effected.

The Temporary Mixed Commission on Armaments appointed by the League of Nations can discharge a useful and important function by examining with care the economic problems connected with armaments and the best methods of averting the evils incidental to the private manufacture of munitions of war. There can be no doubt that great war establishments, naval, military, and aerial, create in themselves a menace to peace and that this generation would have failed in its duty to posterity if, after the fearful lessons of the recent war, it did not address itself seriously and continuously to the problem of ridding the world of a burden which weighs so heavily on industry in times of peace, and, as bitter experience has proved, may contribute to the outbreak of wars bringing ruin and disaster in their train.

* * *

After the statement of these general considerations, in which the Commission has striven to demonstrate the essential facts as well as the difficulties of the disarmament problem, the reports of the three Sub-Committees which have been considering the specific solutions of these problems are now submitted.

The first Assembly of the League of Nations, at its meeting held on December 14th, 1920, adopted the following resolution:—

"The Assembly proposes to the Council:—

. . . .

"(b) To instruct a Temporary Commission, composed of persons possessing the requisite competence in matters of a political, social and economic nature, to prepare for submission to the Council in the near future reports and proposals for the reduction of armaments as provided for by Article 8 of the Covenant."

The Temporary Commission on the reduction of Armaments, which was appointed by virtue of this resolution, held its first session in Paris, from July 16th to 19th, 1921, under the Chairmanship of M. Viviani.

The fact that the items on the agenda were divided amongst several Sub-Committees had a special importance for the Temporary Commission, enabling it to define both its competence and its methods.

M. Viviani, in summing up, at the third plenary meeting, the discussions which this division had occasioned, proposed to constitute three Sub-Committees.

The *first Sub-Committee* was to study the following questions:—

(a) The private manufacture of munitions and of war material.
(b) The traffic in arms and munitions.

It was, further, in the matter of private manufacture, to give its opinion on the draft resolution of M. Jouhaux in favour of convening an international Conference to regulate the private manufacture of armaments.

La *deuxième Sous-Commission* devait s'occuper:

> c) du droit d'investigation;
> d) du contrôle mutuel des renseignements fournis par les Membres de la Société.

Elle devait, en outre, examiner des projets d'amendements présentés aux articles 8 et 9 du Pacte par certains membres de la Commission.

L'étude du droit d'investigation confiée à cette Sous-Commission devait nécessairement l'amener à s'occuper de l'article 213 du Traité de Versailles et des articles correspondants des autres Traités de Paix relatifs au droit d'investigation dans les anciens Empires centraux.

La *troisième Sous-Commission* devait avoir pour tâche de recueillir tous les renseignements statistiques utiles sur l'état des armements et sur les dépenses affectées au budget militaire, naval et aérien de chaque pays. Cette question n'avait pas été inscrite à l'ordre du jour de la Commission temporaire; mais MM. Schanzer et Fisher avaient insisté pour que la Commission en entreprît l'examen.

La Commission accepta les propositions de son Président, et adopta sa conception du libre choix du président et des rapporteurs par chacune des Sous-Commissions et de l'entière indépendance de ces dernières dans la détermination de leur méthode de travail.

La Commission plénière s'est réunie de nouveau le 2 septembre, à Genève, conformément au programme de ses travaux, pour prendre connaissance des rapports de ses trois Sous-Commissions et pour présenter un rapport d'ensemble au Conseil et à l'Assemblée. Elle a décidé, après examen des rapports des trois Sous-Commissions, d'en reproduire les termes dans son rapport général.

Cependant l'ordre de présentation de ces rapports ne sera pas exactement l'ordre numérique des Sous-Commissions. La Commission croit en effet que l'exposé de ce grand problème du désarmement peut être présenté d'une manière plus logique et plus déductive ainsi qu'il suit:

> 1) Exposé de la situation actuelle sur la réduction des dépenses nationales pour les armements d'après les réponses reçues jusqu'ici des divers gouvernements. (Rapport de la seconde Sous-Commission.)
>
> 2) Statistiques à recueillir à propos des armements des différents pays. (Rapport de la troisième Sous-Commission.)
>
> 3) Droit d'investigation. (Rapport de la seconde Sous-Commission.)
>
> 4) Contrôle mutuel. (Rapport de la seconde Sous-Commission.)
>
> 5) Fabrication privée. (Rapport de la première Sous-Commission.)
>
> 6) Trafic des armes. (Rapport de la première Sous-Commission.)

1. *Exposé de la situation actuelle sur la réduction des dépenses nationales pour les armements, d'après les réponses reçues jusqu'ici des divers gouvernements.* (Rapport de la seconde Sous-Commission.)

Dans sa séance du 14 décembre, l'Assemblée a adopté le vœu suivant:

« En attendant le plein effet des mesures concernant la réduction des armements prévue à l'article 8 du Pacte, l'Assemblée émet le vœu que le Conseil soumette à l'examen des gouvernements la proposition d'accepter l'engagement de ne pas dépasser, pendant les deux années fiscales qui suivront le prochain exercice, le chiffre global des dépenses militaires, navales et aériennes prévues pour cet exercice, sous réserve qu'il sera tenu compte:

> « 1º De toute contribution d'effectifs, de matériel de guerre, d'argent, recommandée par la Société des Nations pour l'exécution des obligations prévues à l'article 16 du Pacte ou dans les Traités enregistrés par la Société;
>
> « 2º De toute situation exceptionnelle qui sera signalée au Conseil de la Société des Nations, conformément à l'esprit des paragraphes 2 et 6 de l'article 8 du Pacte. »

Ce vœu a été transmis le 8 mars, suivant les instructions du Conseil aux gouvernements de tous les Membres de la Société par le Secrétaire général.

Vingt-sept réponses ont été reçues jusqu'ici. Elles ne sont point toutes explicites et il est très difficile, sinon impossible, de les répartir dans des catégories tout à fait distinctes. Voici, néanmoins, comment on peut les classer *grosso modo:*

The *second Sub-Committee* was to deal:

    (c) with the right of investigation;
    (d) with the reciprocal control of information furnished by the Members of the League.

It was, further, to examine the draft amendments to Articles 8 and 9 of the Covenant, submitted by certain members of the Committee.

The enquiry into the right of investigation entrusted to this Committee necessarily involved the consideration of Article 213 of the Treaty of Versailles, and the corresponding Articles in other Peace Treaties, regarding the right of investigation in the former central Empires.

The *third Sub-Committee* was to collect all useful statistics regarding the state of armaments and the funds allocated to the military, naval and air budgets in each country. This item was not upon the agenda of the Temporary Commission, but both M. Schanzer and Mr. Fisher had insisted that the Committee should deal with it.

The Committee accepted the proposals of its Chairman, and adopted his view as to the free choice of the chairman and rapporteurs for each Sub-Committee, and also as to their entire independence in determining their methods of working.

The Plenary Commission met again at Geneva on September 2nd, in conformity with its programme, to receive the reports of its three Sub-Committees, and to present a general report to the Council and to the Assembly. It decided, after studying the reports of the three Sub-Committees, to embody their terms in its general report.

The order of presentation of these reports will not, however, be the numerical order of the Sub-Committees. The Commission is indeed of opinion that its statement of the great problem of disarmament may more logically and more conclusively be presented as follows:

    1. Statement of the present situation as to the reduction of national expenditure on armaments, according to the replies so far received from the various Governments. (Report of the 2nd Sub-Committee.)
    2. Statistics to be obtained as to the armaments of the different countries. (Report of the 3rd Sub-Committee.)
    3. Right of investigation. (Report of the 2nd Sub-Committee.)
    4. Reciprocal control. (Report of the 2nd Sub-Committee.)
    5. Private manufacture. (Report of the 1st Sub-Committee.)
    6. Traffic in arms. (Report of the 1st Sub-Committee.)

1. *Statement of the present situation as to the reduction of national expenditure on armaments according to the replies so far received from the various Governments.* (Report of the 2nd Sub-Committee.)

At its meeting on December 14th, the Assembly approved the following Recommendation:

"Pending the full execution of the measures for the reduction of armaments recommended by Article 8 of the Covenant, the Assembly recommends to the Council to submit for the consideration of the Governments the acceptance of an undertaking not to exceed, for the first two financial years following the next financial year, the sum total of expenditure on the military, naval and air services provided for in the latter budget, subject, however, to account being taken of the following reservations:

    " 1. Any contributions of troops, war material and money recommended by the League of Nations with a view to the fulfilment of obligations imposed by Article 16 of the Covenant or by Treaties registered by the League.
    " 2. Exceptional conditions notified as such to the Council of the League of Nations in accordance with the spirit of paragraphs 2 and 6 of Article 8 of the Covenant. "

The above Recommendation, on the Council's instructions, was forwarded by the Secretary-General to the Governments of all Members of the League on March 8th.

The replies which have been received (27 in all) are not always explicit, and therefore it is very difficult, if not impossible, to divide them into absolutely definite categories. *Grosso modo*, however, they can be grouped as follows:—

1. Deux réponses nous ont été envoyées par des pays (Autriche et Bulgarie) pour qui la question ne se pose point, les Traités de Paix ayant déjà réglé leur statut militaire;

2. Trois réponses (Suède, Brésil et Afrique du Sud) n'ont pas un caractère bien net;

3. Quinze réponses nous sont parvenues d'Etats qui, en général, acceptent le vœu. Certains s'y rallient purement et simplement (Bolivie, Guatémala, Chine); d'autres l'acceptent avec les réserves contenues dans le vœu même (Belgique, Australie, Canada), ou sous condition de son acceptation par d'autres Puissances (Grande-Bretagne, Italie, Nouvelle-Zélande, Inde). La Hollande y ajoute la condition qu'on ne regardera point une augmentation causée par l'élévation des prix, ou par des réformes sociales inévitables, comme contraire à la proposition, et que la modernisation des armements de la Hollande sera regardée comme cette « situation spéciale » prévue par le vœu. Enfin, quatre Etats (Danemark, Norvège, Roumanie et Chili) déclarent, sans prendre d'engagement précis, qu'ils n'ont pas l'intention d'augmenter leur budget militaire.

4. Sept réponses nous ont été envoyées par des Etats qui ne paraissent point disposés à accepter le vœu: certains d'entre eux (Espagne et France) donnant pour raison que les budgets ne sont point une indication convainante des forces militaires; d'autres (Finlande et Pologne) invoquant leur situation géographique et politique spéciale. La Grèce fait allusion à la guerre avec la Turquie, et l'Etat serbe-croate-slovène à la situation internationale actuelle qui interdit de prendre toute mesure immédiate. Le Japon, de son côté, ne croit pas opportun de conclure un accord tant que le Conseil n'aura pas terminé l'étude de son plan de désarmement.

Il faut d'ailleurs remarquer que même parmi les gouvernements qui ont déclaré ne pas pouvoir accéder au vœu de l'Assemblée, il y en a deux (France et Finlande) qui ont fait observer qu'ils ont néanmoins effectué déjà des réductions plus ou moins importantes dans leurs armements.

Les Puissances suivantes n'ont pas encore répondu:

Albanie	Libéria	Portugal
Argentine	Luxembourg	Salvador
Colombie	Nicaragua	Siam
Costa-Rica	Panama	Suisse
Cuba	Paraguay	Tchéco-Slovaquie
Haïti	Pérou	Uruguay
Honduras	Perse	Venezuela

Il est peut-être intéressant de jeter un coup d'œil d'ensemble sur les réponses reçues, en ce qui regarde l'Europe. Voici comment on peut, en gros, les classer:

A. — Pays dont le statut militaire a été fixé par les traités de paix: Autriche, Bulgarie.

B. — Etats qui paraissent se rallier au vœu avec des réserves plus ou moins nombreuses: Grande-Bretagne, Belgique, Hollande, Danemark, Norvège, Italie, Roumanie.

C. — Etats qui déclarent ne pas pouvoir l'accepter: Espagne, France, Finlande, Pologne, Etat serbe-croate-slovène, Grèce.

Au demeurant on peut dire, d'une manière générale, que l'enquête faite conformément aux résolutions de l'Assemblée, n'a pas donné de résultats bien concluants. La majorité des réponses, bien que favorables, en général, à l'esprit du vœu, se ressent de l'état d'incertitude qui caractérise la situation politique générale présente.

* * *

2. *Statistiques à recueillir à propos des armements des différents pays.* (Rapport de la troisième Sous-Commission.)

Le rapport de la troisième Sous-Commission, relatif aux renseignements statistiques à recueillir sur les armements des différents pays, constitue logiquement, après l'exposé qui précède, la seule base sérieuse qui permette, avec toute l'approximation actuellement possible, de trouver le critérium nécessaire pour aborder pratiquement le problème général du désarmement.

La troisième Sous-Commission de Statistiques a été constituée pour répondre à la nécessité de placer sous les yeux du Conseil et de l'Assemblée une statistique mettant en évidence la situation des armements avant la guerre et la situation

1. Replies (2) from countries (Austria and Bulgaria) for which, their military status being already determined by Peace Treaties, the question does not arise.

2. Replies (3) of not conclusive character (Sweden, Brazil and South Africa).

3. Replies (15) from States which accept the Recommendation. While some of these States signify their acceptance purely and simply (Bolivia, Guatemala and China) others accept it subject to the reservations contained in the Recommendation itself (Belgium, Austria and Canada) or to the Adoption of the Recommendation by other Powers (Great Britain, Italy, New Zealand and India). Holland further adds the proviso that an increase, due to a rise in prices or to inevitable social reforms, must not be considered in conflict with the proposal, and that the bringing of the armament of Holland up to the standard required by modern warfare shall be considered as the special situation provided for in the Recommendation. Finally, there are four States (Denmark, Norway, Roumania and Chile) which, though not giving any definitive undertaking, state that an increase of the budgets is improbable.

4. Replies (7) from States which appear to be unable to accept the Recommendation some of them (Spain and France) on the ground that budgets do not afford a fair indication of military strength, others (Finland and Poland) invoking their special geographical and political situation. Greece refers to the state of war with Turkey, and the Serb-Croat-Slovene State to the present international situation as precluding immediate action. Finally, Japan deems it inadvisable to give an undertaking pending the completion of the Council's plan for disarmament.

It should further be pointed out that even among the Governments which have declared that they cannot accede to the recommendation of the Assembly, there are two (France and Finland) which have announced that they have nevertheless already effected more or less considerable reductions in their armaments.

The following countries have not replied:—

Albania	Honduras.	Persia.
Argentine Republic.	Liberia.	Portugal.
Colombia.	Luxemburg.	Salvador.
Costa Rica.	Nicaragua.	Siam.
Cuba.	Panama.	Switzerland.
Czecho-Slovakia	Paraguay.	Uruguay.
Haiti.	Peru.	Venezuela.

A survey of the replies, as far as Europe is concerned, may perhaps be interesting and may roughly be expressed as follows:—

(A) Countries the military status of which has been determined by the Peace Treaties (Austria and Bulgaria).

(B) States which appear to accept the Recommendation with more or less numerous reservations (Great Britain, Belgium, Holland, Denmark, Norway, Italy and Roumania).

(C) States which are unable to accept (Spain, France, Finland, Poland, Serb-Croat-Slovene State and Greece).

In general, however, it may be said that the result of the enquiry, which has been conducted as a consequence of the Assembly Resolutions, has not given very conclusive results, the bulk of the replies, although generally favourable to the spirit of the recommendation, reflecting the state of uncertainty which characterises the present general political situation

. * .

2. *Statistics to be collected regarding the Armaments of the different Countries.*
(Report of the 3rd Sub-Committee.)

The report of the Sub-Committee on the statistical data required concerning the armaments of the various countries, constitutes logically, after the preceding Statement, the only sound basis on which a criterion for dealing practically with the problem of disarmament can rest.

The 3rd Sub-Committee on Statistics was formed in order to meet the necessity of placing before the Council and the Assembly statistics showing the pre-war situation as regards armaments, and also the present situation, together with the

actuelle, avec des éléments d'ordre militaire et budgétaire permettant d'apprécier, **dans une** certaine mesure, la puissance militaire des différents Etats et de contribuer **ainsi à** éclairer et à faciliter la recherche de la solution du problème de la limitation **et de la** réduction des armements, conformément à l'article 8 du Pacte.

« Un accord général sur la réduction des armements, disaient MM. Schanzer et Benini, dans leur proposition pour une enquête statistique comparée au sujet de la puissance militaire des différents Etats, devrait attribuer à chaque Etat une force militaire suffisante pour le maintien de l'ordre à l'intérieur et pour la défense de son territoire contre les dangers d'une agression extérieure, tout en tenant compte de ses conditions géographiques, de la nature de ses frontières, ainsi que de la nécessité de défendre ses colonies et ses dépendances.

« Toutefois, avant de pouvoir faire une enquête sur la puissance militaire à assigner à chaque Etat, sur les bases indiquées, il faut connaître aussi exactement que possible la puissance militaire actuelle des différents Etats, tandis que, d'autre part, il est intéressant de comparer cette puissance militaire actuelle avec celle d'avant-guerre. »

Sans doute les statistiques ne sont pas suffisantes pour résoudre la question **des armements,** cependant elles sont nécessaires pour réaliser le but que nous pour-**suivons;** en effet, si on veut établir la situation des armements dans les différents **pays,** on a besoin comme point de départ, de statistiques véridiques.

On a pensé, également, qu'il y avait lieu de ne pas perdre de vue l'élément de **sécurité** nationale, expressément prévu, d'ailleurs, par l'article 8 du Pacte :

« Il ne suffit pas, disait le Président, M. Viviani, de rapporter la preuve par écrit qu'un pays a autant de soldats qu'un autre, quoique cependant sa population soit moins nombreuse; il ne suffit pas de dire que tel pays dépense telle ou telle somme pour son budget de la guerre et de la marine, et que tel autre n'en dépense pas autant. L'égalité dans les dépenses n'est pas toujours la preuve de l'égalité de la force. Un pays qui n'a pas d'ennemis, qui par ses frontières naturelles, par son éloignement de tous les champs de bataille du monde, n'a rien à craindre, est moins en situation d'avoir une armée forte qu'un pays qui a des ennemis, qui en a eu ou qui peut en avoir. Il faudrait donc que l'élément de sécurité nationale rentre dans le cadre des recherches de la sous-commission.

« Une fois fixé le nombre des soldats, des canons, des mitrailleuses, des avions, des sous-marins, des cuirassés, étant fixée même la capacité économique du pays, au point de vue de la construction du matériel de guerre, il se poserait ensuite une suprême question : Que veut le pays où nous faisons cette constatation ? A quel destin a-t-il dû faire face dans le passé et à quel destin probable, étant donnée la situation du monde, peut-il être appelé à faire face demain ? »

Telles sont les considérations essentielles qui ont fait accueillir la proposition déterminant comme suit le travail confié à la troisième Sous-Commission :

« La Sous-Commission présentera un rapport sur :

« *a)* les forces militaires actuelles et d'avant-guerre des différents Etats;

« *b)* les charges financières actuelles et d'avant-guerre résultant des armements, pour les différents Etats;

« *c)* la mesure dans laquelle les dépenses nationales pour les armements peuvent être constatées par les budgets militaires publiés par les différents Etats.

« A tous ces éléments d'ordre statistique sera ajoutée, pour être prise en considération, la situation de chaque Etat touchant sa sécurité nationale. »

Il résulte des discussions qui ont précédé la rédaction de ce texte, que le mandat ainsi formulé doit seulement servir de « base » aux travaux de la troisième Sous-Commission à laquelle, d'ailleurs, une certaine liberté est laissée pour accomplir son œuvre.

En effet, ainsi que le déclarait le Président, M. Viviani, à la troisième séance plénière, tenue le 17 juillet dernier à Paris par la Commission temporaire pour la réduction des armements, il ne voyait aucun inconvénient à ce que « la Sous-Commission, qui est maîtresse de ses travaux, se place au point de vue analytique, c'est-à-dire se serve du travail de M. Schanzer et du Professeur Benini, et accueille toutes les suggestions qui pourront lui être envoyées par chacun des membres de la Commission, comme on le ferait dans un Parlement, quel qu'il soit. »

military and budgetary factors, so that the military power of the various States might to a certain extent be estimated, and in order by this means to help to elucidate and facilitate the endeavour to solve the problem of the limitation and reduction of armaments, in conformity with Article 8 of the Covenant.

MM. Schanzer and Benini, in their paper regarding a statistical enquiry, of a comparative character, on the subject of the military strength of the different countries, say: "A general agreement on the subject of the reduction of armaments ought to assign to each State a military force sufficient both to maintain internal order and to defend its territory against the dangers of a foreign aggression, while taking into account the geographical conditions of each State, the nature of its frontiers, and the necessity for defending its colonies and dependencies.

"However, before it is possible to carry out an enquiry as to the military power to be assigned to each State on the foregoing basis, it is necessary to have as precise information as possible with regard to the present military power of the different States, while on the other hand it is of interest to compare this present military power with that which existed before the war."

Doubtless, statistics are in themselves inadequate to solve the question of armaments, but they are necessary in order to achieve the aim which we are pursuing; indeed, if we wish to ascertain the position as regards armaments in the various countries, we need reliable statistics as a starting-point.

It was also considered that the element of national security, specially provided for in Article 8 of the Covenant, should not be lost sight of.

"It is not enough," said the President, M. Viviani, "to report in writing proofs that one country has as many soldiers as another, although its population is smaller; it is not enough to say that one country expends such and such a sum on its military and naval budget, and that another does not spend so much. Equality of expenditure is not always a proof of equality of strength. A country which has no enemies, and which, by its natural frontiers and by its distance from all the battlefields of the world, has nothing to fear, is not so likely to have a strong army as a country which has enemies, or which has had, or may have, enemies. The element of national security must therefore enter into the scope of enquiries of the Sub-Committee.

"When the number of soldiers, guns, machine-guns, aeroplanes, submarines, and armed cruisers has been fixed, and when also the economic capacity of the country from the point of view of the manufacture of war material has been determined, one supreme question then arises :— What is the aim of the country with regard to which these facts have been ascertained ? What fate has it had to meet in the past, and, in view of the present world situation, what destiny may it be called upon to face to-morrow ? "

These are the most important considerations which have led the third Sub-Committee to welcome the proposal defining the work entrusted to it as follows :—

"The Sub-Committee shall submit a report on:

"(a) the present and pre-war military forces of the various States;

"(b) the present and pre-war financial burdens of the various States in respect of armaments;

"(c) the extent to which national expenditure on armaments may be ascertained from the military budgets published by the various States.

"Besides all these factors of a statistical nature, the situation of each State in respect of its national security, will be taken into consideration."

It will be seen from the discussions which preceded the drawing up of this text, that the mandate thus worded should only serve as a basis for the work of the third Sub-Committee, to which, moreover, a certain latitude has been given for the execution of its task.

Indeed, as the President, M. Viviani, said on July 17th last at the third Plenary Meeting of the Temporary Commission on the Reduction of Armaments held in Paris, he saw no reason why the Sub-Committee, which had full powers in its own sphere, should not adopt the analytical point of view, that is to say, make use of the work of M. Schanzer and Professor Benini, and welcome all suggestions which might be submitted to it by any member of the Commission, as would be the procedure in any parliament.

Il va de soi qu'il n'est possible de présenter actuellement au Conseil et à l'Assemblée que les idées générales et les méthodes pour mener l'enquête à bonne fin.

Ces travaux seront de la plus haute importance : c'est précisément pourquoi il importe essentiellement de laisser à la Sous-Commission tout le temps nécessaire à leur exécution. Il est bien entendu, cependant, que la Sous-Commission s'efforcera de formuler ses conclusions le plus tôt possible
Une première question s'est d'abord posée : Quelle est l'étendue des renseignements qu'il convient de demander aux gouvernements ?
A l'origine, le programme se présentait avec un caractère plus étendu et comprenait notamment divers éléments importants, tels la mobilisation industrielle et le stock de munitions. Après mûre réflexion, on a cru devoir y renoncer.
D'autre part, il a été unanimement reconnu que le questionnaire élaboré par la Commission permanente consultative, et qui entre dans de nombreux détails techniques, est très complet, mais dans l'état actuel des idées et des faits, la Commission a cru devoir s'arrêter à un questionnaire plus restreint, ne comprenant que les renseignements essentiels et indispensables.

C'est dans cet esprit que la Commission soumet au Conseil et à l'Assemblée la proposition suivante :

« La Commission, ayant considéré que la connaissance exacte des forces et des charges militaires des différents Etats est une condition préalable et indispensable pour aborder le problème de la réduction des armements, d'après l'article 8 du Pacte, propose une enquête statistique qui devra relever, dans chaque Etat, pour les années 1913 et 1921, les données suivantes :

I. *Population, superficie, longueur de frontières terrestres et maritimes,* en distinguant la métropole et les colonies.

II. *Nombre de soldats en temps de paix.* C'est-à-dire les effectifs (y compris les corps spécialement affectés au maintien de l'ordre public) et le nombre d'unités pour les armées de terre et de mer, métropolitaine et coloniale, en indiquant les effectifs qui correspondent : *a)* à des obligations militaires; *b)* à la sécurité nationale.

III. *Durée du temps de service* et des obligations militaires dans l'armée active, de réserve et territoriale.

IV. *Nombre d'hommes appelés annuellement sous les armes.*

V. *Nombre d'hommes mobilisables en temps de guerre et nombre d'unités dans les armées de terre et de mer, métropolitaine et coloniale.*

Nota bene : Des données qui précèdent, on pourra déduire le pourcentage de l'effectif de paix et de guerre par rapport à la population totale.

VI. *Matériel existant en service et dans les dépôts de l'armée de terre et de mer.*

Armée de terre { Canons (lourds, de campagne, obusiers, anti-avions.)
fusils.
mitrailleuses.
chars d'assaut.
aviation terrestre.

Armée de mer { bâtiments de guerre et armements.
aviation navale.

VII. *Budget annuel ordinaire et extraordinaire.* Il y a lieu de comprendre les dépenses militaires de toutes sortes pour l'armée : les corps militaires organisés, la marine et l'aviation qui sont à la charge des budgets (états de prévision) de la guerre, de la marine, ou de tous autres budgets formant partie du budget général de l'Etat, ainsi que de toutes les dépenses qui sont à la charge des budgets locaux, en indiquant les dépenses spécialement destinées au maintien de l'ordre public à l'intérieur. Les dépenses résultant de la liquidation de la guerre 1914-1918 doivent être indiquées séparément.

VIII. *Charge du budget de la défense nationale (guerre et marine) par tête d'habitant.*

Nota bene : Vu les dépréciations très inégales des monnaies nationales il conviendra, pour permettre des comparaisons basées sur un étalon unique de valeur, de réduire les chiffres des différents budgets en dollar-or, d'après le cours des changes.

It is evidently impossible to submit to the Council and the Assembly now sitting anything more than general ideas and methods for bringing to a successful conclusion the enquiries with which they have been entrusted.

This work will be of the greatest importance; that is precisely the reason why it is essential to give the Sub-Committee all the time it desires for its execution, but it is, of course, understood that the Sub-Committee will make every effort to reach its conclusions with as little delay as possible.

A question was raised at the outset. To what extent should information be asked for from the Governments ?

The programme was originally more extensive, and included, in particular, various important items such as industrial mobilisation and stocks of munitions. After mature consideration it was thought that these should be omitted.

Moreover, it was unanimously recognised that the questionnaire which had been drawn up by the Permanent Advisory Committee, and which entered into considerable technical detail, was very complete; but, as ideas and facts were at present, the majority of the Commission considered that it should confine itself to a more limited questionnaire, which should only include essential and indispensable information.

In this spirit, the Commission submitted to the Council and the Assembly the following proposal:—

"The Commission, being of opinion that precise information on the military strength and expenditure of the various Governments is a preliminary and essential condition in approaching the problem of the reduction of armaments, as laid down in Article 8 of the Covenant, proposes to undertake a statistical enquiry on the military position in time of peace.

"The enquiry shall elicit information on the following subjects for the years 1913 and 1921."

I. *Population, area, length of territorial and maritime frontiers*, distinguishing between national territory and Colonies.

II. *Number of soldiers in time of peace.* That is to say, effectives (including corps specially employed in the maintenance of public order), and the number of units in the land and sea forces, both home and colonial, showing the effectives maintained for, (*a*) military obligations, (*b*) national defence.

III. *Period of service* and liability to military duty in the regular army, the reserve, and third line troops.

IV. *Numbers of men annually called up for service.*

V. *Numbers of soldiers in time of war, and number of units in the land and sea forces, at home and in the colonies.*

N.B. From the data given it will be possible to calculate the proportion which the peace and war strengths bear to the total population.

VI. *Material in use, or stored in the depots of the land and sea forces.*

Land Forces	Guns (heavy, field, howitzer, anti-aircraft). Rifles. Machine-guns. Tanks. Army Aircraft.
Sea Forces	Warships, with their armament. Naval Aircraft.

VII. *Annual budget (ordinary and extraordinary expenditure).* This should include military expenditure of every description for the Army, organised military units, Navy and Air Services, which are charged for in the budgets (estimates) for the Army and the Navy, and in any other budgets which form part of the general State budget, and also all expenditure which is charged against local budgets, and should indicate expenditure : pecially appropriated to the maintenance of internal order. Expenditure incurred in liquidating the War 1914-1918 should be shown separately.

VIII. *Share of the Expenditure on national defence (Army and Navy) per head of the population.*

N.B. In view of the unequal extent to which national currencies have depreciated it will be advisable, in order that comparisons may be based on a uniform standard of value, to show the totals of the various budgets in gold dollars, according to the rate of exchange.

IX. *Proportion des dépenses pour la défense nationale (guerre et marine)
dans le budget total.*

Le programme de l'enquête ainsi défini a été accepté à l'unanimité. Toutefois, quatre membres ont exprimé des réserves sur l'opportunité des points V et VI. Un membre ne les a pas acceptés.

Quant à la méthode, l'accord suivant est unanimement intervenu au sein de la Commission : on commencera par recueillir tous les renseignements possibles sur la base des traités internationaux, publications officielles, documents et discussions parlementaires, annuaires et autres sources d'informations publiques, mais en cas de besoin, on complètera l'enquête, en ce qui concerne les membres de la société, par le moyen d'un questionnaire sur la base du programme approuvé.

En conséquence, chaque gouvernement sera prié de bien vouloir fournir au Secrétariat :

1. les budgets de la guerre et de la marine pour les années 1913 et 1921 ;
2. le budget général pour l'ensemble des ministères pour les années 1913 et 1921 ;
3. les rapports et les comptes rendus des discussions parlementaires relatifs aux budgets de la guerre et de la marine en 1913 et 1921, et, en général, tous travaux législatifs ou autres publications permettant de déterminer la politique militaire de chaque Etat ;
4. le texte des lois d'organisation des armées de terre et de mer.

Au moment opportun, il sera utile de mettre chacun des gouvernements à même de pouvoir fournir un exposé des considérations qu'il croirait devoir présenter relativement aux exigences de sa sécurité nationale, de ses obligations internationales, de sa situation géographique, et de ses conditions spéciales, tous éléments expressément prévus par l'article 8 du Pacte.

La responsabilité de l'exécution de ces résolutions est laissée au Secrétariat sous la direction du Conseil. Il est entendu que le Secrétariat devra être mis en mesure d'assumer rapidement le dépouillement et la coordination des nombreux éléments statistiques et de la documentation considérable qui lui seront adressés.

Afin de réduire autant que possible les frais de l'enquête, la Commission propose de faire également appel à la coopération de correspondants compétents, dans les différents pays, dont le choix pourra être laissé à la Section des Armements, sous le contrôle du Conseil.

La question a été soulevée de savoir si l'enquête une fois exécutée pour les années 1913 et 1921, il ne serait pas opportun de la tenir à jour chaque année. La Commission a été unanimement de cet avis. en laissant au Conseil le soin d'en faire poursuivre l'exécution par les organes compétents.

Tel est le programme de l'enquête que la Commission estime devoir présenter à l'examen du Conseil et de l'Assemblée pour pouvoir procéder à une étude approfondie et documentée, qui permettra de dégager plus aisément les conclusions pratiques qu'il conviendra de préparer au sujet de la limitation et de la réduction des armements nationaux.

* * *

3. *Droit d'investigation.* (Rapport de la deuxième Sous-Commission.)

Il ne paraît guère possible d'aborder dans la pratique le problème du désarmement, si l'on ne s'assure pas d'abord que toutes les mesures prescrites par les Traités sont intégralement et loyalement exécutées. Ce n'est que grâce à la sécurité ainsi obtenue que le désarmement général peut être envisagé et progressivement résolu. L'étude du droit d'investigation, qui permet de contrôler l'exécution de ces mesures, constitue donc une des conditions essentielles de la solution du problème.

Il n'est pas nécessaire de rappeler ici le texte de l'article 213 du Traité de Versailles, de l'article 159 du Traité de Saint-Germain, de l'article 143 du Traité de Trianon, de l'article 104 du Traité de Neuilly, en vertu duquel l'Allemagne, l'Autriche, la Hongrie et la Bulgarie se sont engagées à se prêter à toute enquête que le Conseil de la Société des Nations jugerait nécessaire en vue de la mise à exécution des stipulations militaires des Traités de Paix.

1. Le Conseil a déjà adopté un rapport de la Commission consultative permanente indiquant une procédure à suivre pour le cas où le Conseil chargerait la C.C.P.

IX. *Proportion which the expenditure on national defence (Army and Navy) bears to the total budget.*

The programme of the enquiry, as thus defined, was unanimously accepted. Three members, however, expressed reservations in respect of the desirability of points V and VI; one member did not accept these points.

As regards method, the following was unanimously agreed upon by the Commission: a beginning would be made by collecting all possible information to be obtained f om international treaties, official publications, parliamentary documents and debates, year-books and other sources of public information; but, in case of need, the enquiry would be supplemented in the case of Members of the League by means of a questionnaire on the basis of the programme approved.

The Gove nments are therefore requested, when replying to this questionnaire, to furnish the Secretariat with:—

1. The budgets of the Army and Navy for the years 1913 and 1921;
2. The general budget for the whole of the Government Departments for the years 1913 and 1921;
3. The reports and minutes of the parliamentary debates on the Army and Navy budgets in 1913 and 1921, and, in general, all legislative acts or other publications which may assist in ascertaining the military policy of the State in question;
4. The texts of the laws determining the organisation of the land and sea forces.

It will be advisable in due course to give the several Governments an opportunity of furnishing a statement of the considerations which they desire to urge in regard to the requirements of their national security, their international obligations, their geographical situations, and their special circumstances — all of which factors are specifically referred to in Article 8 of the Covenant.

The Secretariat, under the control of the Council, is responsible for the carrying out of these resolutions. The Secretariat should be enabled to deal rapidly with the work of analysing and co-ordinating the numerous statistical data and the large number of documents which it will receive.

In order to reduce as far as possible the cost of this investigation, the Commission proposes, in addition, to invite voluntary co-operation by competent correspondents in the various countries, the choice of these correspondents being left to the Armaments Section subject to the approval of the Council.

The question was raised whether, when the enquiry had once been completed for the years 1913 and 1921, it would not be desirable to continue it year by year. The Commission was unanimously of this opinion, leaving it to the Council to instruct the competent organisations to carry out the enquiry.

The above is the system of investigation which the Commission desires to submit for the consideration of the Council and the Assembly; it is hoped that this will make it possible to undertake a thorough examination, based on documentary evidence, and thus to arrive more easily at the practical conclusions which are required in connection with the limitation and reduction of national armaments.

* * *

3. *Right of Investigation.* (Report of the 2nd Sub-Committee.)

It hardly seems possible to approach, in a practical fashion, the problem of disarmament unless it is ascertained at the outset that all measures laid down by the Treaties are completely and loyally carried out. It is only when this security has been obtained that general disarmament can be contemplated and gradually attained. The enquiry as to the right of investigation, which enables the execution of these measures to be controlled, is one of the essential conditions for the solution of the problem.

The terms of Article 213 of the Treaty of Versailles, of Article 159 of the Treaty of St. Germain, of Article 143 of the Treaty of Trianon, and of Article 104 of the Treaty of Neuilly, by which Germany, Austria, Hungary and Bulgaria have undertaken to give every facility for any investigation which the Council of the League of Nations may consider necessary with regard to carrying out the military regulations of the Treaties of Peace, need not be recalled here.

1. The Council has already adopted a report of the Permanent Military Commission, outlining a procedure to be followed in the event of the Council

de procéder à une investigation. D'après cette procédure, la Commission désignerait parmi ses membres une Commission composée d'un délégué de chacun des Etats représentés à la C.C.P.; à ces délégués, seraient adjoints un certain nombre d'experts choisis sur une liste qui doit être tenue à jour par les divers gouvernements.

2. Le Comité militaire interallié de Versailles a décidé, le 19 février 1921, qu'il communiquerait à la C.C.P. un rapport sur les travaux de la Commission de contrôle. Un rapport de la C.C.P. approuvé par le Conseil de la Société le 27 juin 1921, a conclu à l'acceptation de ces documents provenant du Comité militaire interallié de Versailles, ainsi que d'autres documents se rapportant aux travaux des Commissions de contrôle interalliées.

3. La C.C.P. a également attiré l'attention du Conseil sur la nécessité d'examiner quelles mesures d'ordre financier il conviendrait de prendre pour que l'organisme d'enquêtes puisse commencer ses travaux sans délai, le jour où le Conseil le désirera. Le 27 juin 1921, le Conseil a décidé que la question financière serait étudiée par la C.C.P. de concert avec les membres du Secrétariat et que, au besoin, la Commission économique et financière serait consultée.

4. Le Conseil a donc déjà pris des mesures pour assurer l'existence de moyens d'action et leur mise en œuvre immédiate, conformément aux directives du Conseil, dans le cas où l'on déciderait d'entreprendre les investigations prévues à l'article 213 et aux articles correspondants.

Etant donné le caractère général des pouvoirs conférés au Conseil aux fins d'investigation, il semble que le Conseil de la Société puisse agir à n'importe quel moment tant que le Traité de Versailles est en vigueur. Cependant, la surveillance de l'exécution des clauses militaires, navales et aériennes des Traités de Paix, pour l'exécution desquelles une limite de temps a été prévue, est confiée, pour l'instant, aux Commissions interalliées de contrôle. Le Conseil n'a jamais considéré qu'il ait à prendre l'initiative de se charger du contrôle, concurremment avec ces Commissions, tant qu'elles seront en fonctions.

5. Cette relation entre les fonctions des Commissions interalliées de contrôle et l'action éventuelle du Conseil, quand les Commissions de contrôle auront achevé leur tâche, pourrait faire naître l'impression que non seulement le Conseil succédera aux Commissions interalliées de contrôle dans le temps, mais aussi dans les pouvoirs et les attributions.

Or, dans les Traités, l'article 213 et les articles correspondants ont un caractère bien plus général.

Les Commissions interalliées de contrôle ont reçu des tâches bien définies et les enquêtes qu'elles doivent faire sont spécifiées en détail dans la Section 4 de la Partie V du Traité de Versailles, mais l'enquête envisagée par l'article 213 et que le Conseil de la Société des Nations pourra juger nécessaire, a un caractère d'ordre tout à fait général.

Il appartiendra au Conseil lui-même de définir la nature et les limites des investigations à faire, lorsque l'occasion se présentera.

* * *

4. *Contrôle mutuel.* (Rapport de la deuxième Sous-Commission.)

Le droit de contrôle mutuel représente un progrès nouveau dans la voie de la réduction des armements. Il constitue en fait la seule garantie mutuelle qui permette aux Membres de la Société, leurs armements une fois réduits, de n'être point dupes de leur bonne foi.

Le paragraphe 4 de l'article 8 du Pacte établit que, après que les divers Gouvernements auront adopté les plans proposés par le Conseil, ils ne pourront dépasser la limite des armements ainsi fixée sans le consentement du Conseil. Il pourrait être nécessaire de déterminer, à une date ultérieure, si les Membres ont dépassé ces limites sans le consentement du Conseil, mais le Pacte ne prévoit aucune procédure à suivre en ce cas.

A ce propos, il est utile de rappeler que l'Assemblée a adopté, en novembre dernier, la résolution suivante:

« De faire étudier le mécanisme en vertu duquel pourraient être vérifiées les informations militaires dont l'échange est prévu à l'article 8 du Pacte, le jour où le principe de cette vérification mutuelle entre les Membres de la Société pourrait être consacrée grâce à un amendement au Pacte. »

directing the Permanent Military Commission to conduct an investigation. Under this procedure, the Commission would appoint from among its members a Commission composed of one delegate of each of the States represented on the Permanent Commission. To these delegates would be attached a number of experts, a list of such experts to be drawn up in advance by the respective Governments.

2. The Allied Military Committee of Versailles decided on February 19th, 1921, that it would communicate to the P.A.C., a report on its work. A report of the Permanent Advisory Commission, approved by the Council of the League on June 27th, 1921, advised the acceptance of these documents from the Allied Military Committee of Versailles, together with other documents relative to the work of the Inter-Allied Commissions of Control.

3. The P.A.C. has also drawn the attention of the Council to the necessity of considering what measures of a financial nature should be taken in order that the organ of investigation should be able to commence its duties without delay whenever the Council shall so decide. On June 27th, 1921, the Council decided that the financial question should be studied by the P.A.C. with the assistance of the Members of the Secretariat, and that, if necessary, the Financial and Economic Committee should be consulted.

4. The Council has thus already taken action which would ensure that, if and when it might be decided to conduct the investigation referred to in Article 213, the agencies would be at hand and prepared to go forward without delay to carry out the Council's directions.

In view of the general nature of the power conferred upon the Council to conduct an investigation, it would seem that the Council of the League may act at any time while the Treaty of Versailles remains in force. For the time being, however, the supervision of the execution of the Military, Naval and Air clauses of the Peace Treaties, for the execution of which a time limit has been prescribed, is being handled by the Inter-Allied Commissions of Control. The Council has never considered itself called upon to take the initiative to supplement the work of these Commissions while they are still in force.

5. This relation between the work of the Inter-Allied Commissions of Control and the eventual action of the Council when the Commissions of Control have completed their work, may tend to create the impression that the Council will succeed the Inter-Allied Commissions of Control, not merely in order of time, but also as regards their powers and functions.

Article 213 of the Treaty of Versailles, however, and the corresponding Articles in the other Peace Treaties, are of a much more general character.

The Inter-Allied Commissions of Control were given very specific duties and the investigations to be made by them are detailed in Section IV of Part V of the Treaty of Versailles and in corresponding sections of the other Treaties. But the investigation contemplated by Article 213, which the Council of the League of Nations may consider necessary, is quite general.

It will be for the Council itself to determine the nature and the scope of the investigation to be undertaken as occasion arises.

* * *

4 *Reciprocal Control.* (Report of the 2nd Sub-Committee):

The right of reciprocal control represents a further step towards the reduction of armaments. It constitutes, in fact, the only reciprocal guarantee that, once their armaments have been reduced, the good faith of Members of the League will not be abused.

Paragraph 4 of Article 8 of the Covenant provides that, after the various Members of the League have adopted the plans recommended by the Council, they are obliged not to exceed the limits therein fixed without the concurrence of the Council. If might become necessary to determine at some future time whether Members had exceeded the limits without the concurrence of the Council, but the Covenant does not deal with the procedure to be followed in such a case.

In this connection it is to be remembered that the 1st Assembly adopted, last November, the following resolution:

"To consider the mechanism by means of which the military information to be exchanged under the provisions of Article 8 of the Covenant can be verified in the event of the principle of mutual verification by Members of the League being confirmed by an amendment to the Covenant."

Au cours de la première session de la Commission pour la réduction des armements, M. Jouhaux a fait allusion à l'amendement proposé et a suggéré de soumettre à la deuxième Assemblée un projet d'amendement de cette nature. M. Viviani a également proposé que les membres de la Sous-Commission soient invités à soumettre des projets d'amendements de ce genre. Il a rappelé que M. Bourgeois avait présenté le paragraphe suivant à l'adoption de la Commission de la Société des Nations à la Conférence de la Paix :

> « Les Hautes Parties Contractantes, résolues à se donner franche et pleine connaissance mutuelle de l'échelle de leurs armements et de leur programme militaire et naval, ainsi que des conditions de leurs industries susceptibles de s'adapter à la guerre, institueront une Commission chargée des constatations nécessaires. »

Le Secrétariat ayant invité les membres de la Commission à lui soumettre des projets d'amendements, a reçu les réponses suivantes :
M. Oudegeest a proposé d'amender comme suit le dernier paragraphe de l'article 8 :

> « Les Membres de la Société s'engagent à échanger *chaque année, après fixation du budget où sont votés les crédits* aux fins de guerre, de la manière la plus franche et la plus complète, tous renseignements relatifs à l'échelle de leurs armements, à leurs programmes militaires, navals et aériens, et à la condition de celles de leurs industries susceptibles d'être utilisées pour la guerre. »

et d'y ajouter les paragraphes suivants :

> « Au cas où un Membre présume que les informations données par un autre Membre sont inexactes, il peut, en exposant les considérants, adresser une demande d'enquête et de consultation à la Commission visée par l'article 9. Cette Commission dépose un rapport entre les mains du Secrétaire général de la Société des Nations avec prière de le porter à la connaissance de l'Assemblée de la Société des Nations.

> « Si un Membre refuse d'apporter des données exactes ou complètes ou si, durant deux années consécutives, il ne les a pas ou les a incomplètement fournies, un des Membres du Conseil peut demander à l'Assemblée de manifester son opinion à ce sujet. »

M. Bourgeois, au nom du Gouvernement français, a ensuite fait parvenir l'amendement suivant à l'article 9 :

> « Une Commission permanente sera constituée pour donner au Conseil son avis sur l'exécution des prescriptions des articles 1 à 8 et pour procéder, dans les formes et au moment préalablement agréés par les Gouvernements, aux constatations que le Conseil jugera nécessaires en dehors des investigations spécialement prévues dans les stipulations d'ordre militaire, naval ou aérien des différents Traités de Paix. »

> « Cette Commission sera chargée, en outre, par le Conseil, de le renseigner sur les questions militaires, navales et aériennes et notamment de prévoir et étudier les conditions de l'action commune que le Conseil pourrait, en vertu de l'article 16, être appelé à recommander aux Membres de la Société.

> « Dans les cas d'urgence, la Commission serait invitée par le Conseil à lui proposer des mesures d'efficacité immédiate. »

Il est évident qu'il ne peut être apporté aucune modification aux termes du Pacte sans qu'elle soit soumise à l'examen le plus approfondi, ce qui paraît difficile dans le peu de temps qui nous sépare de l'Assemblée. Puisqu'une Commission des Amendements a été constituée, il sera nécessaire, en tout cas, de soumettre le texte des amendements à l'examen et à l'approbation de cette Commission. La Commission ne peut donc que prendre acte des deux amendements et ajourner à un examen ultérieur, d'accord et en collaboration avec la Commission des Amendements et avec la Commission consultative permanente, le texte précis et définitif de l'amendement qui devra être soumis à l'Assemblée.

. * .

In the course of the first session of the Commission for the Reduction of Armaments, M. Jouhaux referred to the suggested amendment and proposed that a draft of such an amendment be submitted to the second Assembly, and M. Viviani suggested that the members of the sub-Committee should be invited to submit drafts. He also recalled that M. Bourgeois had proposed to the Commission of the League of Nations at the Peace Conference the following paragraph:

> "The High Contracting Parties, resolved to give each other full and frank information as to the scale of their armaments and of their military and naval programme, as well as to the condition of their industries which are adaptable to warlike purposes, shall set up a Commission whose duty it will be to collect the necessary information. ".

The Secretariat. having invited the Members of the Commission to submit drafts of amendments, has received the following answers:—

M. Oudegeest has proposed that the last paragraph of Article 8 should be amended to read as follows:

> "The Members of the League undertake to interchange *each year, after their Budgets, in which credits for war purposes are voted, have been drafted,* full and frank information as to the scale of their armaments, their military, naval and air programmes, and the condition of such of their industries as are adaptable to warlike purposes."

the following paragraphs being also added:

> "Should a Member think that the information given by another Member is not correct, it may, on submitting its reasons, address a request for an enquiry and consultation to the Commission outlined in Article 9. This Commission shall submit a report to the Secretary-General of the League of Nations, for transmission to the Assembly of the League of Nations."

> "In the event of a Member refusing to furnish precise or complete data, or if for a period of two consecutive years it fails to furnish it or furnishes it incompletely, one of the Members of the Council may ask the Assembly to express its view on the subject. "

Subsequently, M. Léon Bourgeois, on behalf of the French Government, handed in the following amendment to Article 9:

> "A permanent Commission shall be constituted to advise the Council on the execution of the provisions of Articles 1 and 8, and to proceed, at such a time and in the form previously agreed by the Governments, with such enquiries as the Council shall judge necessary in addition to the investigations especially referred to in the military, naval, and air clauses contained in the several Peace Treaties.

> "This Commission may also be charged by the Council to keep it informed on military, naval, and air questions, and in particular to study the conditions of the common action which, in virtue of Article 16, the Council may be called upon to recommend to the several Members of the League..

> "In cases of emergency, the Commission may be invited by the Council to submit to it measures of immediate efficacy. "

It is obvious that no amendment of the terms of the Covenant can be undertaken without the fullest consideration, which can hardly be given in so short a time as the interval between now and the Assembly. As a Committee on Amendments has been set up, it will, in any event, be necessary that the texts of the amendments be submitted for consideration and approval also to this Committee. The Commission therefore can only take note of the two amendments and postpone the drafting of the final text of the amendment to be submitted to the Assembly for further consideration in consultation and co-operation with the Amendments Committee and the Permanent Advisory Commission

* * *

5. *Fabrication privée.* (Rapport de la première Sous-Commission.)

Le règlement des deux questions qui précèdent: droit d'investigation, droit de contrôle mutuel, doit avoir en fait sur le désarmement général de si heureuses conséquences et permettre de réduire dans de telles proportions les armements, que le règlement de la question de la fabrication privée s'en trouvera facilité. Il y a donc avantage à aborder cette question délicate après que l'étude des problèmes précédemment posés aura déjà été entamée.

La Commission temporaire pour la réduction des armements a formé une Sous-Commission à laquelle elle a confié le soin d'examiner la question de la fabrication privée des munitions et de l'exécution des dispositions de l'article 8 du Pacte.

Cette Sous-Commission a tenu six séances et présenté le rapport préliminaire suivant:

Le Pacte reconnaît que la fabrication privée de munitions et de matériel de guerre soulève de graves objections. Quelles sont-elles ? Le Pacte ne les définit point. On ne peut, d'autre part, en trouver la trace dans les délibérations de la Commission qui a rédigé le Pacte. C'est une chose cependant bien connue que l'opinion publique est fortement prévenue contre la fabrication privée et non surveillée de munitions et de matériel de guerre et que l'on croit généralement que les guerres sont encouragées par l'esprit de compétition des grandes maisons privées d'armements, et qu'elles pourraient être rendues plus rares si l'on pouvait surveiller ou supprimer l'esprit de lucre. Les objections que l'on fait à la fabrication privée et non contrôlée des armements peuvent être classées de la manière suivante:

1. Des Sociétés qui s'occupent d'industries de guerre ont contribué à multiplier les menaces de guerre et à persuader à leurs pays respectifs d'adopter une politique belliqueuse et d'augmenter leurs armements.

2. Ces Sociétés auraient cherché à soudoyer des fonctionnaires, aussi bien dans leurs pays qu'à l'étranger.

3. Ces Sociétés ont répandu de faux rapports sur les programmes militaires et navals des différents pays afin de provoquer des augmentations de dépenses d'armements.

4. Ces Sociétés ont cherché à influencer l'opinion publique en contrôlant les journaux de leurs propres pays et de l'étranger.

5. Ces Sociétés ont organisé de véritables combinaisons internationales grâce auxquelles la course aux armements a été précipitée en jouant d'un pays contre un autre.

6. Ces Sociétés ont organisé de véritables trusts internationaux d'industries de guerre qui ont contribué à l'augmentation du prix des armements vendus aux différents gouvernements.

Une autre objection d'un ordre un peu différent a été présentée à la Commission temporaire:

Certaines de ces Sociétés ne se décidant pas à pratiquer de larges amortissements dans les installations tout à fait exceptionnelles qui avaient été motivées par les exceptionnelles nécessités de la guerre, contribuent à fausser l'économie générale de la production et à retarder le relèvement économique du monde.

La Sous-Commission n'est pas en mesure, aujourd'hui, d'apporter une conclusion définitive sur le problème délicat et compliqué qui lui avait été soumis. Elle estime ne pouvoir, dans l'état actuel de ses travaux, ni recommander la suppression de la fabrication privée, ni donner un avis sur les mesures à prendre pour contrôler cette fabrication, au cas où l'on déciderait qu'il y a avantage à autoriser le maintien de la fabrication privée. La Sous-Commission doit se contenter, pour le moment, de signaler quelques-unes des difficultés qu'entraînerait la suppression totale de la fabrication privée et quelques-uns des problèmes auxquels il faudra faire face avant que l'on puisse recommander un corps complet de règlements, si la réglementation gagne finalement la préférence sur la prohibition. En conséquence, la Commission soumet les observations suivantes sur les deux méthodes possibles de prohibition et de réglementation:

1. *Si la fabrication privée était complètement interdite,* il en résulterait que toutes les fabrications de munitions et de matériel de guerre deviendraient l'objet d'un monopole d'Etat. Au cours de la discussion de cette méthode, les difficultés suivantes ont été suggérées par quelques membres:

a) Le Pacte semble n'avoir en vue, parmi les effets fâcheux résultant de la fabrication privée, que ceux qui peuvent affecter les relations internationales. Les questions de politique intérieure, qui touchent au droit souverain, ont été laissées

5. *Private Manufacture.* (Report of the 1st Sub-Committee.)

The settlement of the two preceding questions — the right of investigation and the right of reciprocal control — ought, indeed, to have such satisfactory effects in the direction of general disarmament, and ought to render it possible to reduce armaments to such an extent, that the solution of the question of private manufacture would thereby be greatly facilitated. It would therefore be advantageous not to deal with this delicate question until the problems previously raised had been considered.

The Temporary Commission for the Reduction of Armaments has constituted a Sub-Committee to which it has referred the subject of private manufacture of munitions and the execution of the provisions of Article 8 of the Covenant.

The Sub-Committee has held six meetings and submits the following interim report :—

The Covenant recognizes that the manufacture by private enterprise of munitions and implements of war is open to grave objections. What are these objections ? They are not defined by the Covenant; they cannot be extracted from the deliberations of the Committee which drafted the Covenant. It is, however, common knowledge that the public mind is strongly prejudiced against the uncontrolled private manufacture of munitions and implements of war, and that it is a common belief that wars are promoted by the competitive zeal of private armament firms, and would be rendered less frequent were the profit-making impulse brought under control or eliminated altogether. In general, the objections that are raised to untrammelled private manufacture may be grouped under the following headings :—

1. That armament firms have been active in fomenting war-scares and in persuading their own countries to adopt warlike policies and to increase their armaments.

2. That armament firms have attempted to bribe Government officials, both at home and abroad.

3. That armament firms have disseminated false reports concerning the military and naval programmes of various countries, in order to stimulate armament expenditure.

4. That armament firms have sought to influence public opinion through the control of newspapers in their own and foreign countries.

5. That armament firms have organised international armament rings through which the armament race has been accentuated by playing off one country against another.

6. That armament firms have organised international armament trusts which have increased the price of armaments sold to Governments.

Another objection of a somewhat different kind has been submitted to the Temporary Commission :—

Some of these companies were not taking the requisite steps to provide for the amortisation on a large scale of the cost of the quite exceptional plant installed to meet the special requirements of the war, and were thus injuriously affecting the economic conditions of production, and impeding economic recovery.

The Sub-Committee is unable to-day to reach a final conclusion upon the difficult and complicated topic submitted to its consideration. It cannot at the present stage of its deliberations either recommend the abolition of private manufacture or advise upon the particular steps to be taken to control it should it be decided that on the balance of advantage private manufacture must be allowed to continue. The Sub-Committee must then content itself for the present with indicating some of the difficulties which confront the total abolition of private manufacture and some of the problems which have to be faced before a complete code of regulations can be recommended, should regulation ultimately be preferred to prohibition. Accordingly, the following observations are offered with reference to the two alternative courses of prohibition and regulation :—

1. *If private manufacture were altogether forbidden,* it would result that all manufacture of munitions and implements of war would be conducted by State enterprise. In the consideration of such a course, the following difficulties have been suggested by some Members.

(a) The Covenant seems to refer only to those evil effects attendant upon private manufacture which may affect international relations. Questions of internal policy involving domestic sovereignty are here excluded, as

de côté dans cet article du Pacte, comme d'ailleurs dans tous les autres. En d'autres termes, le Pacte ne semble viser la fabrication privée que dans la mesure où elle touche à l'augmentation des armements et aux relations entre Etats, mais non point en tant qu'elle peut avoir une répercussion sur l'économie de l'industrie nationale.

b) Une recommandation qui tendrait à supprimer la fabrication privée serait, sans aucun doute, préjudiciable aux Etats qui ne produisent pas eux-mêmes toutes les munitions dont ils ont besoin. Ces Etats ne manqueraient probablement pas de croire qu'il leur serait beaucoup plus difficile d'obtenir le matériel nécessaire de gouvernements étrangers que de maisons privées étrangères.

c) Dans l'état actuel du droit international, la fourniture de munitions ou de matériel de guerre par un gouvernement neutre à un gouvernement belligérant constitue une violation de neutralité. En temps de guerre, un Etat belligérant dépendrait donc de sa propre production et de celle de ses alliés et tous les gouvernements pourraient ainsi se croire obligés de se préparer à toutes les éventualités d'une guerre, en constituant de gros stocks de munitions et en installant eux-mêmes d'importantes usines.

d) L'abolition de la fabrication privée pourrait avoir pour effet l'établissement de nouvelles industries de guerre, par les gouvernements des Etats jusqu'ici non producteurs. Ces gouvernements n'auraient aucune difficulté à fabriquer leurs munitions pour leurs propres besoins, puisqu'il n'existe aucune restriction dans l'exportation du fer et du charbon; ainsi les Etats non producteurs pourraient devenir producteurs à leur tour.

e) Il serait plus difficile, dans certains pays, pour les gouvernements de réduire leurs fabriques d'armements à la cessation des hostilités, que pour les usines privées, en raison de la pression exercée dans les parlements par les représentants des ouvriers employés dans la fabrication des armements.

f) Peu d'entreprises industrielles travaillent exclusivement pour la fabrication du matériel de guerre. Pour la plupart, les grandes Sociétés d'armements sont des entreprises de nature très composite, dont l'activité, en temps normal, est surtout consacrée aux industries de paix.

g) Il est difficile de définir les industries de guerre. Les industries d'optique et les industries chimiques sont très importantes en temps de guerre. L'aviation représente une industrie qui est actuellement répartie entre un nombre considérable d'usines différentes. Jusqu'où doit alors s'étendre la propriété de l'Etat ? L'acceptation du principe de la propriété de l'Etat pour les industries de guerre ne conduit-elle pas logiquement à la possession par l'Etat de toutes les industries ?

h) Les arsenaux d'Etat pour la manufacture complète des armes et des munitions devraient comprendre, outre un grand nombre d'ateliers de mécanique, un outillage métallurgique complet et une usine de produits chimiques nécessaires à la fabrication des explosifs. Il est douteux que les Etats veuillent faire face aux dépenses que ces installations entraîneraient, et qu'un arsenal d'Etat de cette nature atteigne jamais un rendement équivalent à ses moyens de production.

2. *Si la fabrication privée n'était pas interdite, elle pourrait être contrôlée.* Les divers moyens de contrôler l'industrie privée, en vue d'empêcher les fâcheux effets possibles, ont été suggérés au cours de la discussion. Les suivants sont mentionnés afin d'indiquer les directives qui pourraient être suivies dans des investigations futures :

a) Possibilité d'exiger que, ni munitions ni aucun matériel de guerre, y compris les navires de guerre, ne soient exportés sans licence du gouvernement du pays exportateur, avec peut-être une disposition spéciale visant la concession de licences de la part des gouvernements neutres, pour l'exportation de munitions à des belligérants.

b) Possibilité d'exiger que, ni munitions, ni matériel de guerre, ne puissent être importés sans licence du gouvernement du pays importateur.

c) Possibilité d'exiger que toutes les licences mentionnées dans les deux premiers paragraphes soient enregistrées par la Société des Nations et publiées par elle.

d) Possibilité d'exiger que, ni munitions, ni matériel de guerre ne soient fabriqués sans une licence du gouvernement, avec peut-être obligation de faire publier ces licences par la Société des Nations.

e) Possibilité d'exiger que toutes les actions des Sociétés qui s'occupent principalement de la fabrication des munitions soient nominatives et non simplement au porteur et qu'elles ne puissent être transférées qu'après enregistrement sur les livres de chaque Société.

f) Possibilité d'exiger que les entreprises et Sociétés d'armements publient des comptes détaillés de leurs affaires en ce qui concerne les armements et que ces comptes soient publiquement apurés.

g) Possibilité d'exiger la publication des listes de détenteurs d'actions dans les Sociétés d'armements et de restreindre, pour des raisons de nationalité, par exemple, les catégories de personnes qui pourraient posséder de telles actions.

indeed elsewhere, in the Covenant. In other words, the provision in the Covenant seems to deal with private manufacture only in so far as it affects the growth of armaments and relations between States, but not in so far as it affects the domestic industrial system.

(b) A recommendation that private manufacture be abolished would doubltess be objectionable to States which do not produce all the munitions which they need. Such States would probably feel that it would be more difficult to get the necessary supplies from foreign Governments than from foreign firms.

(c) As international law stands to-day, the supply of munitions or implements of war by a neutral Government to a belligerent Government would constitute a violation of neutrality. In time of war, therefore, a belligerent would have to depend upon its own production and upon what it could get from its Allies. This might mean that all Governments would feel themselves called upon to prepare for the eventualities of war by storing up large stocks of munitions and by equipping themselves with large munition plants.

(d) The abolition of private manufacture might result in the establishment of many new armament plants by the Governments of non-producing States. Such Governments could, of course, undertake to manufacture munitions to meet their own needs, there being no restriction on the export of iron and coal. In this way, non-producing States might become producers.

(e) Governments might — in some countries — find it more difficult than private firms to reduce their armament establishments on the cessation of war, owing to the Parliamentary pressure exerted by the representatives of labour engaged in the production of armaments.

(f) Few industrial enterprises work exclusively for the manufacture of war material. For the most part, the great armament firms are establishments of a composite nature, whose activity in normal times is chiefly directed to peace industries.

(g) It is difficult to define war industries. Optical and chemical industries are all-important in war. Aviation is an industry at present distributed among a considerable number of different factories. How far, then, should State ownership extend ? Does not the acceptance of the principle of State ownership of war industries lead logically to the State ownership of all industries ?

(h) State arsenals for the complete manufacture of arms and munitions would have to include, in addition to a large number of mechanical workshops, a complete metallurgical plant and a factory for the chemical products required in the manufacture of explosives. It is doubtful whether States will face the expenditure involved. Nor would such a State arsenal ever attain to an output corresponding to its means of production.

2. *If private manufacture were not forbidden it might be subjected to control.* Various possibilities for controlling private manufacture with a view to preventing possible attendant evil effects have been suggested in the course of the discussion. The following are referred to for the purpose of indicating the lines which may be followed in future investigations:—

(a) The possibility of a requirement that no munitions or implements of war, including warships, may be exported without a licence of the Government of the exporting country, with perhaps a special provision covering the issue of licences by neutral Governments for exporting munitions to belligerents.

(b) The possibility of a requirement that no munitions or implements of war may be imported without license of the Government of the importing country.

(c) The possibility of a requirement that such licenses as those mentioned in (a) and (b) must be registered with the League of Nations and published by the League.

(d) The possibility of a requirement that no munitions or implements of war be manufactured without Government license, and possibly that such license be published by the League of Nations.

(e) The possibility of a requirement that all shares in companies devoted chiefly to the manufacture of munitions be registered, and not simply bearer shares, and should therefore be transferable only by registration on the books of the company.

(f) The possibility of a requirement that armament firms and companies should publish full accounts of their armament business, and that such accounts should be publicly audited.

(g) The possibility of requiring the publication of lists of holders of shares in armament companies, and of restricting the classes of persons who may hold such shares, *e.g.* on grounds of nationality.

h) Possibilité de prendre des mesures pour empêcher les entreprises et Sociétés d'armements ou les personnes ayant de grands intérêts ou ayant une situation responsable dans ces entreprises ou ces Sociétés d'être propriétaires de journaux ou de les contrôler ou d'exercer sur eux une influence illégitime.

i) Possibilité de réglementer la concession à des étrangers de brevets concernant l'industrie de guerre.

* * *

Pendant les discussions de la Sous-Commission, on a proposé de convoquer une Conférence internationale ayant pour objet le problème de la fabrication privée et du trafic des armes. Il a paru à la Sous-Commission qu'en tout cas il serait désirable que la Commission temporaire fût invitée par l'Assemblée à poursuivre ses travaux jusqu'à ce qu'elle fût en mesure de présenter son rapport définitif. Même si le Conseil décidait de convoquer une Conférence internationale générale sur la fabrication privée des armements, le succès complet n'en pourrait être assuré que si la matière de ces travaux était soigneusement préparée au préalable. L'Assemblée possède, dans la Sous-Commission de la Commission temporaire sur les armements, un instrument capable d'accomplir cette tâche d'enquêtes préliminaires. Si l'on devait décider la réunion d'une Conférence internationale, cette Sous-Commission rendrait à cette Conférence, une fois convoquée, les mêmes services que la Commission provisoire sur la Liberté des Communications et du Transit a rendus à la Conférence de Barcelone. On propose, en conséquence, que la Commission soit invitée à continuer en tout cas ses enquêtes

La Commission temporaire n'a pourtant pas de compétence assez étendue ou d'autorité suffisante pour exercer une influence décisive sur la politique des Membres de la Société. Les membres de la Commission ont été désignés par le Conseil, non pas en qualité de représentants des gouvernements, mais à titre de personnalités compétentes et qualifiées. Un jour viendra donc où le Conseil sera obligé d'obtenir la collaboration, non seulement des Membres de la Société, mais aussi d'Etats demeurés hors de la Société, si l'on veut donner plein effet aux recommandations que la Commission pourrait estimer devoir présenter.

Certains membres de la Sous-Commission inclinent fortement à penser que la Commission temporaire devrait recommander à l'Assemblée de 1921 d'adopter une résolution en faveur de la convocation d'une Conférence internationale sur la fabrication privée et sur le trafic des armes, invitant le Conseil à envisager la convocation de cette Conférence à une date ultérieure que celui-ci fixerait et à prendre les mesures nécessaires pour assurer la participation des Etats importants qui ne font pas partie de la Société.

D'autres membres ont estimé que cette recommandation pourrait paraître prématurée avant que la Commission n'ait terminé ses travaux, tandis que quelques autres membres ont été d'avis que cette Conférence serait tout à fait inutile.

La Commission a, en fin de compte, convenu de présenter les propositions suivantes au Conseil et à l'Assemblée :

1. Le rapport à l'Assemblée devra contenir une recommandation demandant que la Commission temporaire, par l'organe de sa Sous-Commission, poursuive l'étude de toutes les questions soulevées par l'article 8 du Pacte, au sujet de la fabrication privée et du trafic des armes.

2. Le Secrétariat fournira à la Sous-Commission toute l'assistance possible afin de lui permettre de poursuivre les enquêtes mentionnées dans son rapport et obtiendra des Membres de la Société les informations nécessaires pour permettre à la Sous-Commission de continuer ses travaux.

3. Le rapport à l'Assemblée devra contenir une recommandation pour que l'Assemblée prenne une décision en faveur du principe d'une Conférence internationale éventuelle dont l'Assemblée arrêterait l'ordre du jour, sur la fabrication privée et sur le trafic des armes, qui aurait lieu sur une invitation spéciale adressée à tous les Membres de la Société et aux Etats intéressés qui ne sont pas Membres de la Société.

* * *

6. *Trafic des armes.* (Rapport de la première Sous-Commission.)

De même que la question de la fabrication privée peut être en fait heureusement résolue, en grande partie, par le règlement du droit d'investigation et du droit de contrôle mutuel, la solution de la question du trafic des armes sera, on s'en rend compte, plus aisée à trouver, une fois résolue celle de la fabrication privée.

(*h*) The possibility of taking measures to prevent armament firms and companies or persons largely interested or holding responsible positions in such firms or companies, from owning, controlling, or unduly influencing, the newspaper press.

(*i*) The possibility of regulating the issue of patents on munitions or implements of war to non-nationals.

* * *

In the course of the discussions of the Sub-Committee, a suggestion was thrown out that an International Conference should be convoked to deal with private manufactuie and the arms traffic. It appears to the Sub-Committee that in any case it would be desirable that the Temporary Commission should be invited by the Assembly to continue its labours until it is in a position to make its final report to the·Council. Even if it should be decided to convoke a general International Conference on the private manufacture of armaments, the fullest measuie of success can only be assured to the work of the Conference if the ground is caretully prepared beforehand. In the Sub-Committee of the Temporary Commission on Armaments the Assembly has an instrument capable of performing that work of preliminaiy sciutiny, and should it be decided that an International Conference ought to be held, the Sub-Committee would serve such a Conference if and when it is convoked, as the Provisional Committee on the Freedom of Communications and Transit served the Conference at Barcelona. It is therefore suggested that in any case the Commission should be invited to continue its enquiries.

The Temporary Commission is, however, neither sufficiently general nor sufficiently authoritative to exercise a decisive influence over the policy of the Members of the League. The members of the Commission have been named by the Council of the League, not as representatives of Governments, but as competent and qualified individuals. It follows that the time must come when the Council of the League would be obliged to obtain the co-operation not only of the Members of the League, but also of States standing outside the League, if full effect is to be given to such recommendations as the Commission may feel enabled to make.

Some members of the Sub-Committee felt strongly that the Temporary Commission should recommend to the 1921 Assembly of the League, that it should adopt a resolution favouring the convocation of such an International Conference on private manufacture and trade in arms, and inviting the Council of the League to consider the convocation of such a Conference at some future date to be determined by the Council, and to take proper measures to secure the participation of important States not Members of the League.

Other Members held that such a recommendation would be premature until the Commission had finished its task, while some members were of the opinion that such a conference would be altogether useless.

The Commission accordingly concludes by making the following suggestions to the Council and the Assembly:—

1. That the Report to the Assembly should contain a iecommendation ihat the Temporary Commission, through its Sub-Committee, should continue its study and investigation of the questions raised in Article 8 of the Covenant with refeience to the private manufacture and trade in arms.

2. That the Secretariat should furnish the Sub-Committee with all possible assistance for pursuing the investigations and enquiries referred to in this Report and should procure from the Members of the League the iniormation necessary for continuing the work of the Sub-Committee.

3. That the Temporary Commission should include in their Report to the Assembly a recommendation that the Assembly should decide in favour of the principle of an eventual international conference, the Agenda of which should be drafted by the Assembly, on the private manufacture and trade in arms, to be convened by a special invitation addressed to all the Members of the League and to interested States which are not Members of the League.

* * *

6. *Traffic in Arms.* (Report of the 1st Sub-Committee.)

Just as the regulation of the right of investigation and the right of reciprocal control will materially contribute to the solution of the question of private manufacture, so also — it will be seen — the solution of the question of the traffic in arms will be more easily arrived at once the question of private manufacture has been decided.

La réglementation efficace du trafic international des armes et des munitions est d'un intérêt capital et d'une extrême urgence au point de vue de la réduction des armements. Quelle que soit l'opinion que l'on puisse avoir sur la nature et la gravité des dangers qui, selon l'article 8 du Pacte, résultent de la liberté complète laissée à la fabrication privée du matériel de guerre, il est certain que l'un des éléments essentiels d'un projet quelconque tendant à supprimer ou à diminuer ces dangers, doit être le contrôle du trafic international des armes.

Ce contrôle, ayant en vue certains buts bien définis, fait déjà l'objet d'une Convention internationale « pour le contrôle du trafic des armes et des munitions ». Cette Convention a été signée par les représentants de toutes les Puissances alliées et associées, le 10 septembre 1919, à St-Germain, mais elle n'a pas encore été ratifiée par la majorité des signataires.

Les stipulations qui y figurent et les raisons qui en ont amené la négociation ont été fort bien exposées dans un rapport de Sir Cecil Hurst et il est inutile de les reproduire ici en détail [1].

Il convient néanmoins de déclarer nettement, dès le début, que l'objet principal de cette Convention n'était pas de favoriser le désarmement des nations civilisées, mais d'empêcher les armes de parvenir entre les mains d'individus, d'organisations ou de certains peuples barbares ou demi-civilisés, chez lesquels la possession de ces armes constituerait un danger pour le monde.

Toutefois, bien que cette Convention n'ait pas en vue la restriction générale du trafic des armes, ses stipulations pourraient probablement être utilisées comme base ou point de départ des mesures de restriction que l'on pourrait décider, d'un accord unanime, d'adopter à l'avenir.

D'après les Traités de Paix, lorsque cette Convention entrera en vigueur, elle engagera l'Allemagne et ses anciens alliés.

Nous croyons savoir, en outre, que des stipulations sont prévues dans les divers projets de mandat en vue de l'application de la Convention sur le trafic des armes ou de règlements similaires, dans les territoires mandatés.

Enfin, la Convention envisage l'adhésion éventuelle d'autres Etats Membres de la Société des Nations (article 23). Il ne semble pas qu'elle renferme de stipulations précises concernant l'adhésion d'Etats qui ne sont ni Membres de la Société des Nations, ni compris dans aucune des catégories mentionnées ci-dessus, mais nous supposons que, si un de ces Etats présentait une demande d'adhésion, elle ne serait pas rejetée sans de sérieux motifs. Il est bien clair, toutefois, qu'une condition absolument essentielle pour obtenir l'adhésion des Etats non signataires et imposer l'application de la Convention à des Etats et à des territoires qui sont tenus de l'accepter aux termes d'un Traité est la mise en vigueur de la Convention entre les Etats signataires eux-mêmes.

En conséquence, nous avons soigneusement examiné les renseignements fournis par le Secrétariat sur la situation actuelle en ce qui concerne la ratification de la Convention. Nous sommes malheureusement obligés de déclarer que cette situation n'est aucunement satisfaisante. L'enquête faite récemment par le Secrétaire général a montré que les seuls Etats qui ont actuellement ratifié la Convention, ou qui y ont adhéré, sont: la Chine, la Grèce, le Siam, le Chili, le Guatémala, le Venezuela, le Brésil, le Pérou et la République de Haïti. Nous apprenons en outre que la Roumanie a décidé de ratifier la Convention et que les Pays-Bas, l'Uruguay, la Colombie, la Perse et la Finlande ont déclaré être disposés à y adhérer. Aucune des « Principales Puissances alliées et associées » n'a encore ratifié la Convention, et il est évident que tant qu'elles ne l'auront pas ratifiée, l'acceptation de cette Convention par les petits Etats ne peut exercer d'influence décisive sur le trafic des armes.

En ce qui concerne les principales Puissances alliées et associées, nous apprenons que l'Empire britannique est prêt à ratifier la Convention, dès que toutes les autres Puissances « principales » seront disposées à le faire. La France attend seulement l'approbation du Sénat pour faire une déclaration semblable, la Convention ayant déjà été votée par la Chambre des Députés. L'Italie est disposée à ratifier la Convention aussitôt que le Parlement l'aura approuvée. L'attitude du Japon est sensiblement la même que celle de l'Empire britannique et de la France.

Restent les Etats-Unis d'Amérique. En raison de l'importance de leur fabrication d'armes et de munitions, de matériel de guerre, et plus encore en raison du rendement virtuel dont est capable leur industrie, avec ses ressources si abondantes, leur attitude est d'une importance capitale au point de vue qui nous occupe.

---

[1] Voir Annexe au Rapport de la Sous-Commission A de la 6ᵐᵉ Commission de l'Assemblée 14 décembre 1920).

The effective regulation of the international traffic in Arms and Ammunition is a matter of vital and urgent importance in connection with the question of reduction of Armaments. Whatever views be held as to the nature and extent of the evils which, according to Article 8 of the Covenant, result from the unrestricted private manufacture of munitions, it is evident that an essential feature in any scheme which aims at removing or diminishing these evils must be to bring the international arms traffic under control.

The control of this traffic for certain definite purposes already forms the subject of an International Convention "for the Control of the Trade in Arms and Ammunition," which was signed by representatives of all the Allied and Associated Powers on September 10th, 1919, at St. Germain, but has not yet been ratified by the majority of the signatories.

The provisions of this Convention and the reasons which led to its negotiation have been well described in a report by Sir Cecil Hurst, and need not be repeated in detail.[1]

It should, however, be clearly understood at the outset that the main purpose of the Convention was not to promote disarmament as among civilised States, but to prevent arms from getting into the hands of private persons or organisations, or of certain barbarous or semi-civilised peoples, whose possession of those weapons would be a danger to the world.

While, however, the Convention does not purport to be a measure for the general restriction of the traffic of armaments, its machinery could presumably be used as a basis or starting-point for any measures of restriction which it may be decided hereafter by general agreement to adopt.

Under the Treaty of Peace, this Convention, when it comes into force, will be binding on Germany and its late Allies.

We understand, moreover, that provisions are included in the various draft Mandates which have the effect of applying the Arms Traffic Convention or similar regulations to "Mandated" territories.

Lastly, the Convention contemplates the eventual adhesion of other States Members of the League of Nations (Article 23). There appears to be no express provision for the adhesion of any State which is neither a Member of the League of Nations nor included in any of the categories mentioned above, but we presume that such adhesion, if applied for, would not be refused without strong reason. It is clear, however, that an essential condition for obtaining the adhesion of non-signatory States as well as for imposing the Convention on States and territories which are under a treaty obligation to accept it, is that the Convention should be brought into force as among the signatory States themselves.

We have therefore examined with care the information supplied by the Secretariat as to the present position as regards the ratification of the Convention, a position which we regret to state is by no means satisfactory. From recent inquiries made by the Secretary-General it appears that the only States which have actually ratified or adhered to the Convention are China, Greece, Siam, Chile, Guatemala, Venezuela, Brazil, Peru and Haiti. We are further informed that Roumania has decided to ratify, and the Netherlands, Uruguay, Colombia, Persia and Finland have expressed their willingness to adhere. None of the "Principal Allied and Associated Powers" have yet ratified, and it is obvious that, until they do so, no acceptance by the smaller States can have a decisive influence on the arms traffic.

As regards the position of the "Principal Allied and Associated Powers" we are informed that the British Empire is ready to ratify as soon as all the other "Principal" Powers are prepared to do so; that France is only awaiting the authority of the Senate to make a similar declaration, the Convention having been already approved by the Chamber of Deputies; that Italy is willing to ratify the Convention as soon as it is approved by Parliament; and that Japan's attitude is substantially the same as that of the British Empire and France.

There remains the case of the United States of America, which, in view of the magnitude of its production of arms and munitions, and still more of the potential output of which the vast industrial resources of the country are capable, is of capital importance from the present point of view.

---

[1] See Annex to Report of Sub-Committee A of the Sixth Committee of the Assembly (December 14th, 1920).

Les Etats-Unis figurent parmi les signataires de la Convention de Saint-Germain, mais, pour autant que nous le sachions, cette Convention n'a pas encore été soumise à la ratification du Sénat.

Une nouvelle législation serait, croit-on, nécessaire aux Etats-Unis, en vue d'assurer le contrôle de l'exportation des armes (sauf à destination de certains territoires bien délimités).

Cependant, nous sommes convaincus que si le trafic des armes n'est pas soumis à un contrôle en Amérique, la Convention de Saint-Germain restera inopérante. Toute tentative des autres Etats pour contrôler le trafic des armes n'aurait d'autre résultat, en effet, que de faire des Etats-Unis le grand fournisseur d'armes.

Nous ne prétendons pas que la Convention doive nécessairement échouer si le Gouvernement des Etats-Unis n'est pas en mesure de la ratifier sous sa forme actuelle. Les Etats-Unis pourraient, par exemple, subordonner leur ratification à certaines réserves de détail qui, ne touchant point au principe même de la Convention, pourraient être aisément acceptées par les cosignataires.[1]

Un résultat analogue pourrait peut-être être obtenu par voie de législation intérieure.

Aussi longtemps que le trafic des armes échappera à tout contrôle dans des régions étendues, on pourra toujours craindre que l'on puisse éluder toute Convention, en installant dans ces régions des usines de munitions (peut-être dirigées et soutenues financièrement par des nationaux d'Etats contractants), dont les produits seraient librement exportés dans toutes les parties du monde, sauf dans les territoires mentionnés à l'article 6. Nous ne voyons qu'un moyen d'éviter ce danger : ce serait l'adoption générale d'un protocole additionnel interdisant l'importation, en temps de paix, d'armes et de munitions provenant d'un pays où le trafic des armes demeure sans contrôle.

Un tel protocole ne peut naturellement pas s'appliquer à la situation anormale actuelle de l'Asie Mineure. Ce pays ne possède pas, en effet, de gouvernement sur lequel on puisse compter pour appliquer la Convention, et il reste ouvert en conséquence à l'importation non réglementée des armes provenant de la Russie des Soviets, pays également en dehors de la Convention. Il faut espérer que cette difficulté sera bientôt résolue par la conclusion d'une paix définitive avec la Turquie. Dans l'intervalle on pourra, s'il est nécessaire, obvier à la difficulté par une forme provisoire de réserve.

Notre attention a été attirée sur un autre point, d'importance relativement secondaire, où l'on a pu voir un obstacle à la ratification : la difficulté de distinguer entre les armes de guerre et les autres (chasse, sports, etc.). Conformément à l'article 1 de la Convention, le soin d'établir cette distinction est laissé aux Hautes Parties Contractantes, qui doivent prendre en considération l'importance, la destination et toutes autres particularités de chaque expédition.

Il est évident que les Etats contractants devraient être guidés par des principes clairs et uniformes, en établissant cette distinction ; nous recherchons en ce moment quelles indications la Commission navale et militaire permanente pourrait fournir à cet égard.

A notre avis, cette question n'a pratiquement qu'une faible importance et ne devrait, sous aucun prétexte, retarder la ratification générale de la Convention.

Nous n'avons rien dit jusqu'ici du protocole annexé à la Convention, sur les mesures à prendre par les Etats signataires en attendant la ratification. Ce protocole, quelle que soit sa valeur juridique, ne peut être considéré que comme un instrument transitoire, dont les effets cesseront dès l'entrée en vigueur de la Convention.

Nous enregistrons avec satisfaction le fait que depuis juillet 1920 un accord officieux est intervenu entre certains des principaux Etats signataires. En attendant la ratification ils s'engagent à ne prendre aucune mesure contraire aux dispositions relatives à l'exportation et au contrôle des armes dans les zones mentionnées à l'article 6 de la Convention. Nous regrettons que le Gouvernement des Etats-Unis n'ait pas été en mesure d'adhérer à cet accord.

Si, comme nous l'espérons vivement, on peut trouver le moyen de résoudre la principale difficulté sur laquelle nous avons attiré l'attention, nous avons tout lieu d'escompter pour un avenir très prochain, la ratification générale de la Convention de Saint-Germain par les principaux Etats signataires. Cette ratification sera certainement suivie de l'adhésion de certains gouvernements non-signataires et de l'extension *ipso facto* de la Convention à un certain nombre d'autres Etats. A notre avis, une étape importante vers la réduction générale des armements serait ainsi réalisée, bien que nous sachions parfaitement que la Convention ne solutionne qu'une petite partie du problème.

Nous avons déjà indiqué l'opportunité d'un protocole supplémentaire touchant un point particulier. La mise en œuvre de la Convention nécessitera, sans aucun

---

[1] Il s'agit des clauses qui confèrent à la Société des Nations certains droits de contrôle et de juridiction (article 5 et 24).

The United States was one of the signatories to the Convention of St. Germain, but, so far as we can learn, the Convention has not yet been submitted to the Senate for ratification. We understand that fresh legislation would be required in the United States in order to enable the export of arms (except to certain limited areas) to be controlled. It has, however, become clear to us that, if the American traffic in Arms is not controlled, the Convention of St. Germain is likely to remain inoperative, since any attempted control of the arms traffic by the other States might merely result in transferring the source of supply to the United States.

We do not, of course, suggest that the Convention will necessarily fail if the United States Government finds itself unable to ratify it as it stands. For example, the United States might accompany ratification by reservations with regard to certain details not touching the main principles of the Convention, which the co-signatories might be prepared to accept [1]. Or it is possible that a similar result might be achieved by domestic legislation,

While, however, the arms traffic remains uncontrolled throughout any considerable areas of the world, there will always be a danger that any Convention may be evaded by establishing in some such outside area munition factories (possibly controlled and financed by nationals of Contracting States), the products of which could be freely exported to all parts of the world except the territories referred to in Article 6. So far as we can see, this danger could only be avoided by the general adoption of an additional Protocol prohibiting imports of arms and ammunition in time of peace from any country in which the arms traffic remains uncontrolled.

Such a protocol would not, of course, deal with the present anomalous position in Asia Minor, which possesses no Government that can be relied on to administer the Convention, and which is therefore open to the unregulated import of arms from Soviet Russia, a country also outside the Convention. It is to be hoped that this difficulty will shortly be ended by the conclusion of a definite peace with Turkey, and in the meantime it could be met, if necessary, by some form of provisional reservation.

One other point, though of comparatively minor importance, has been brought to our attention as a possible obstacle to ratification, viz., the difficulty of discriminating between weapons of war and other (e. g., sporting) weapons. Under Article I of the Convention, this discrimination is left to the High Contracting Parties, which are to take into account the size, destination and other circumstances of each shipment.

It is of course *prima facie* desirable that the Contracting States should be guided by definite and uniform principles in making this discrimination, and we are ascertaining if the Permanent Naval and Military Commission can give any guidance in the matter.

We regard the point, however, as of limited importance in practice, and it should not on any account be permitted to delay the general ratification of the Convention.

Nothing has been said above as to the Protocol annexed to the Convention, which refers to the action of the signatory States pending ratification, because this Protocol, whatever its legal force may be, can be considered only as a transitory measure, the effects of which will cease when the Convention becomes operative.

It is satisfactory that since July 1920 an informal understanding has been acted on by some of the principal signatory States that, pending ratification, they will take no action contrary to the provisions relating to export and control of arms in the areas mentioned in Article 6 of the Convention, but we regret that the United States Government has not been in a position to adhere to this understanding.

If, as we earnestly hope, means can be found to clear up the main difficulty to which we have called attention, we may reasonably expect the general ratification of the Convention of St. Germain by the principal signatory States in the near future, and this will doubtless be followed by the adherence of certain non-signatory Governments, as well as by the automatic application of the Convention to a number of other States. This will, in our opinion, constitute an appreciable step towards the general restriction of armaments, although we are fully aware that the Convention covers only a small part of the whole ground.

We have already suggested one point in respect of which a supplementary Protocol may be thought desirable. Experience of the practical working of the

---

[1] Those entrusting the League of Nations with certain control and jurisdiction (Arts. 5 and 24).

doute, d'autres modifications de détail ou des définitions plus précises, par exemple, en ce qui regarde les catégories de munitions visées par la Convention ou les principes d'après lesquels les Etats contractants pourraient exercer leur faculté d'accorder des licences.

Cependant, le principal objet sur lequel doivent actuellement porter tous nos efforts, c'est d'obtenir la mise en vigueur générale de la Convention à une date aussi rapprochée que possible; tous les projets en faveur de son amélioration devraient, à notre avis, être subordonnés à cette fin essentielle.

* * *

L'inévitable conclusion qui se dégage de tout ce qui précède est que l'humanité est présentement trop éloignée encore de l'idéal pacifique dont tous les efforts, ainsi que l'objet même de la Société des Nations, doivent cependant, et au plus vite, le rapprocher. Ces retards, ces difficultés, ces angoisses même, proviennent de ce que la Société des Nations se propose avant tout de « maintenir la paix », alors que sur de trop nombreux points du globe, les sinistres feux de la guerre ne sont pas encore éteints.

Quoi qu'il en soit, la Commission croit pouvoir dès maintenant se permettre l'affirmation que ses travaux n'auront pas été inutiles à la réalisation progressive de cet idéal magnifique. Il serait cruellement injuste de lui reprocher ce que son étude a encore d'incomplet. La Société des Nations, après deux ans seulement d'existence, ne saurait avoir apporté toutes les solutions à tous les problèmes qui, depuis des siècles et des siècles, troublent le monde. Elle a le droit, cependant, de s'enorgueillir, même à ce point de vue essentiel du désarmement, d'avoir montré et ouvert à tous les hommes de bonne volonté la voie qui les rapprochera d'un idéal un peu moins sauvage que celui qu'ils ont connu depuis l'origine de l'Histoire.

Convention may, no doubt, suggest other points requiring amendment, or further definition, *e. g.*, as regards the classes of munitions included, or the principles on which the Contracting States should exercise their licensing powers.

The great object, however, on which it is desirable to concentrate at present, is to bring the Convention into general operation at the earliest possible date, and all schemes for its improvement should, in our opinion, be subordinated to this principal aim.

* * *

The inevitable conclusion to be drawn from the present report is that mankind, at the present time, is still too far removed from the ideal of Peace, towards which, however, all our efforts, and the League of Nations, whose supreme object it is, must lead it. The delays, the difficulties, the cruel anxieties which beset us, arise from the fact that, while the League of Nations aims, above all, at "maintaining peace," the fires of war are still smouldering in all too many quarters of the globe.

Nevertheless, the Commission feels justified in the confidence that its labours will not have been without value in furthering the realisation of this splendid ideal. It would be a cruel injustice to reproach it with not having yet completed its enquiry. The League of Nations, after two brief years of existence, could scarcely be expected to have solved all the problems which have perplexed the world for so many centuries! But even in this vital question of disarmament it may pride itself on having opened up to men of good-will a road which will lead them to the realisation of a less primitive ideal than that which has guided them since the dawn of History.

THE
SECRET
INTERNATIONAL

ARMAMENT FIRMS
AT WORK

Published by

THE UNION OF DEMOCRATIC CONTROL
THIRTY-FOUR VICTORIA STREET, LONDON,
SOUTH-WEST ONE

Eighth Impression
"The Secret International," October, 1934

The following points must be added to *The Secret International* to bring this Impression up-to-date.

LORD HAILSHAM

Lord Hailsham, who was a shareholder in Vickers, Ltd., has now disposed of his shares. (See page 43 of previous Impressions.)

SIR JOHN SIMON

The *Star* of March 9, 1933, carried the following paragraphs concerning Sir John Simon and the shares which, as the previous Impressions of *The Secret International* have pointed out, were held by him in Imperial Chemical Industries, Ltd.:—

" Sir John Simon has taken a step which every lover of peace will recognise as a handsome effort to clear himself of any suggested connection with armaments. It was recently pointed out to him that through his holdings in Imperial Chemical Industries he had actually become financially interested in munitions since one of its subsidiary companies was making munitions for the Far East.

" Sir John, when the point was brought home to him, immediately cleared out all his holdings in these shares. He is seriously concerned about the traffic which he said in the House of Commons many people regarded as ' horrible.'

" He has read through with careful attention the pamphlet *The Secret International* which the Union of Democratic Control published on the international activities of the armament interests, and he could not help being impressed by its cold statement of facts." (See page 17 of previous Impressions.)

WESLEYAN CHAPEL PURPOSES (LTD.), MANCHESTER

When, after reading *The Secret International*, the Trustees of the Wesleyan Chapel Purposes (Ltd.), Manchester, realised that Handley Page, Ltd., in which they held shares on behalf of their Swanage Circuit, was an armament firm which included military aircraft amongst its manufactures, they decided to advise the Swanage Circuit to sell the investment and reinvest the money in a security against which there could be no objection. (See page 19 of previous Impressions.)

ARMAMENT ORDERS

The Naval Estimates for 1933 show a net increase of £3,093,700. There is a net increase of £2,442,500 in the amount of orders placed with the private armament firms.

The Army Estimates for 1933 show a net increase of £1,462,000. The cost of the Army Contracts Directorate shows an increase of £779.

The Air Force Estimates for 1933 show a net increase of £26,000. The cost of the Air Force Directorate of Contracts shows an increase of £405. (See pages 30 and 31 of previous Impressions.)

IMPERIAL CHEMICAL INDUSTRIES, LTD.

The Report of I.C.I., Ltd., for 1932 shows an increase of £3,408,290 in its net income. Its gross profits were one-third greater than in 1931. Its net profits were 40 per cent. greater than in 1931. The accounts of I.C.I. (Metals), Ltd., the subsidiary of I.C.I., Ltd., which manufactured such considerable quantities of munitions for the Far East during the past year, are not shown separately so that it is impossible to estimate the proportion of profits due to the " war " between China and Japan. (See page 17 of previous Impressions.)

FAIREY AVIATION COMPANY

The Fairey Aviation Co., Ltd., according to the Annual Report for 1932 has increased its reserves from £60,000 to £90,000. The profits for 1932 increased from £184,000 to £198,000—the highest in the company's history. (See page 18 of previous Impressions.)

A new pamphlet " Patriotism Ltd." contains further additional information on the war danger.

PREFACE

TWO facts have again brought to the public attention the " grave objections," to use the phrase of the Covenant of the League of Nations, which are entailed in the private manufacture of arms. The first is that, while the Powers have been assembled together in an attempt to put an end to the struggle between Japan and China, private manufacturers within the territory of the Powers themselves have been actively and impartially supplying arms to both combatants. The absurdity of such a situation has led to a demand both in Europe and in America to end the manufacture of arms.

The second fact is that one observer after another of the slow and almost hopeless discussions at the Disarmament Conference has testified to the opposition to the cause of disarmament exerted through the Press and other channels by the vested interests of armament manufacturers. It is not, therefore, surprising to find Lord Cecil again saying : " There is a very sinister feature to all the disarmament discussions. I refer to the tremendous power wielded against all the proposals by armament firms . . . It is no longer safe to keep in private hands the construction of these terrible instruments of death. We must aim at getting rid of this immense instrument in the maintenance of suspicion."

The exposure of the corrupt influence of Krupps before the war and of the sinister activities of the armament rings as a whole led to the public recognition of the danger of private manufacture of arms in the Covenant of the League of Nations. Certain scandals could not be hidden and books and pamphlets like *The War Traders* (1914) by G. H. Perris ; *The International Industry of War* (1915) published by The Union of Democratic Control ; *The War Trust Exposed* and *How Europe Armed for War* (1916) by J. T. Walton Newbold gave a startling account of the pre-war position.

Since the war, however, little has been published on the subject, though useful information may be obtained from *War for Profits* (1929) by Lehmann-Russbüldt, from a League of Nations Union pamphlet *Traffic in Arms* (1928), and from the League of Nations' very inadequate publication, *The Statistical Year Book of the Trade in Arms and Ammunition*. This last deals, however, only with the export of arms and even in this restricted field omits such important items as battleships and aircraft! The most stimulating contribution to the subject since the war is the brilliant summary in Chapter 12 of *The Work, Wealth and Happiness of Mankind* by H. G. Wells. The American aspect of the problem is discussed in an interesting book entitled *Deaths and Profits* by Seymour Waldman (Brewer, Warren & Putman, 1932).

This pamphlet is an attempt to collect the available information and to state as clearly as possible the present case for the public control of the whole armament industry. Where the facts have been already published, they have been carefully checked before being repeated, and the source of every important statement and fact is indicated either in the text or in the footnotes. The conclusion seems to prove beyond all doubt that the abolition of the private manufacture of arms is a necessary element in any genuine work for international peace.

Acknowledgments to *De Notenkraker* of Amsterdam and to *Plebs* for permission to reproduce cartoon on front cover.

First Impression,	July, 1932.
Second Impression,	July, 1932.
Third Impression,	October, 1932.
Fourth Impression,	December, 1932.
Fifth Impression,	April, 1933.
Sixth Impression,	October, 1933.
Seventh Impression,	January, 1934.
Eighth Impression,	October, 1934.

More recent information on the development of EUROPEAN RE-ARMAMENT as well as on the growing WAR DANGER has been published in

"PATRIOTISM LTD."
An Exposure of
THE WAR MACHINE

DESCRIBES the re-armament of Germany.

REVEALS secrets of war research work.

EXPOSES gun-running in Central Europe.

TELLS the story of the greatest arms scandal since the war.

SHOWS the activities and the profits of the armament industry during the Disarmament Conference.

Also Price Sixpence (by post, 7d.) from

**UNION OF DEMOCRATIC CONTROL
34 Victoria Street, London, S.W.1**

Chapter I

ARMAMENT FIRMS

AND

THE LEAGUE OF NATIONS

I N 1921 a League of Nations Commission[1] which had been appointed to inquire into the problem of the private manufacture of arms came to the following conclusions :—

(1) That armament firms have been active in fomenting war scares and in persuading their own countries to adopt warlike policies and to increase their armaments.

(2) That armament firms have attempted to bribe Government officials both at home and abroad.

(8) That armament firms have disseminated false reports concerning the military and naval programmes of various countries in order to stimulate armament expenditure.

(4) That armament firms have sought to influence public opinion through the control of newspapers in their own and foreign countries.

(5) That armament firms have organised international armament rings through which the armaments race has been accentuated by playing off one country against another.

(6) That armament firms have organised international armament trusts which have increased the price of armaments to Governments.

These are definite charges and it is a pity that the evidence on which they were based has not been published.

No effort has been made to rebut them and not all the evidence of their truth is hidden. Every now and again some scandal occurs which leads to a public inquiry. Occasionally a persistent member of the House of Commons or the Chamber of Deputies or of Congress refuses to be put off by an official reply and some real information is obtained. Much too may be learnt from Blue Books, Company Reports, Trade Returns and the Records at Somerset House. In this pamphlet some of this available and publishable evidence is gathered together.

In reviewing the facts it is well to remember that the armament industry differs in several essentials from other industries. In most types of business, wares are advertised in the hope of persuading customers to buy

---

[1] The First Sub-Committee of the Temporary Mixed Commission of the League of Nations. Report A.81. 1921.

from one firm rather than from another. Within some limited market it may suit the firm to amalgamate, but in no other industry are the inducements to international combination so great and the results of competition from the manufacturers' point of view so poor. The articles supplied satisfy no real human need ; no wealth is produced by the sale of arms. On the contrary, all money spent on arms is economically pure waste; arms are only bought at the expense of other commodities and every purchaser who restricts his demand simultaneously persuades other purchasers to do the same. In the same way, if one country decides to increase its armaments, its rivals feel compelled to increase theirs. The main fact for an armament manufacturer to bear in mind, therefore, is that increased sales in the foreign market, whether supplied by his own firm or another, increases almost automatically the demand in the home market. If a British firm sells a new type of aerial bomb to the French Government, the British Government is thereby stimulated to buy bombs of the same, or of a more powerful, type. While nations compete for arms, armament firms have every inducement not to compete. They all stand to gain by each other's increase of business. Accordingly, we find that though armament firms often have national names and special connections they always tend to organise themselves into international rings and to link themselves up with other closely related industries which specialise, for instance, in chemical or explosive production. Once these rings are formed, their only interest is to increase the total world demand for armaments, and, since governments are the purchasers, the potential demand is almost unlimited. The actual size of this demand depends on the degree of fear and uncertainty in which the nations can be induced to live ; whereas the interests of ordinary men lie in peace and security, the interests of those who live by the sale of arms lie in fear, insecurity and, ultimately, in war. Therefore, the business method of increasing the sale of arms is to promote, by whatever means come to hand, open or underground, the fear of war in the world. Every armament manufacturer has a direct interest in jettisoning the League of Nations and breaking up Disarmament Conferences.

To-day almost everyone pays lip-service to the cause of disarmament. No one says in public that it would not be better if the nations spent less money and employed fewer men on the making of shells and guns, tanks and submarines, battleships and battle aeroplanes, in devising new and more deadly forms of poison gas and explosives. This pamphlet assumes general agreement about that. It also assumes that most people are bitterly disappointed that the progress towards a goal which is generally desired is so slow, and it suggests that one reason why it is so slow is that there is a very active and powerful force working nationally and internationally against disarmament.

No doubt it is true that the greatest obstacles in the way of disarmament are the " Unseen Assassins " of which Sir Norman Angell has written[1]— the unreasoning nationalism that persists side by side with the nascent internationalism of the world, the greed for power that afflicts every organised political group, the fear that others will be more powerful, the unwillingness we all show to sacrifice the desire of the moment for long-distance ends. But those who have worked for the cause of disarmament during the last twelve years, those who study the attitude of the newspapers and even sometimes of government servants at critical moments during disarmament conferences, agree that they meet in many indirect ways an opposition which is secret and powerful, an opposition which is not internal

---

[1] *The Unseen Assassins*, by Norman Angell. (Hamish Hamilton. 7s. 6d.)

but external, which does not spring from popular apathy towards disarmament but which is organised by those who have a financial interest in the upkeep of arms. This organisation and propaganda against disarmament is itself international. Those who promote it are not patriots or nationalists; they are business men whose interests are to encourage inflated patriotism and national animosities. They aim not at the triumph of any particular nation but at selling as many munitions as possible. The armament manufacturer is above patriotism. In the South African War the Boers shot British soldiers with British rifles; in the world war Australian and British troops in the Dardanelles were mown down by British guns.[1] During the last few months many of the guns with which Chinese have been defending themselves against the Japanese have been supplied by Japanese manufacturers.[2]

Those who make arms live by the fears and hatred which lead to war. When war does come, they grow fat. The follies and divisions of mankind are their daily bread; the catastrophes which impoverish the world are their banquets. They prosper most when we mourn over a generation dead.

---

[1] Mr. Hugh Dalton, speaking on the Naval Estimates in the House of Commons on March 11, 1926, described this incident as follows : " Vickers had been supplying the Turkish artillery with shells which were fired into the Australian, New Zealand and British troops as they were scrambling up Anzac Cove and Cape Helles. Did it matter to the directors of these armament firms, so long as they did business and expanded the defence expenditure of Turkey, that their weapons mashed up into bloody pulp all the morning glory that was the flower of Anzac, the youth of Australia and New Zealand, yes and of the youth of our own country ? These men, these directors of armament firms, are the highest and completest embodiment of capitalist morality."

[2] During recent years, the Far East has been the greatest market for arms. Japan has been preparing for her Manchurian adventure both in her own factories and by importing from Germany, Belgium, Great Britain, France and Spain.
China, which has practically no arms factories of her own, is the world's greatest importer of arms. Her largest supplies come from Hamburg, through which port the Skoda factories in Czechoslovakia do their overseas trade. China also imports arms from Belgium, Norway and Great Britain. But she has bought in recent years an increasing amount from Japan, which in 1930 supplied her with no less than 37·5 per cent. of her total imports. 1930, the year before the present trouble in China, was a golden year for the armament factories in Japan, in Belgium, in Germany, in the U.S.A. and to a less extent in Great Britain and Norway.
Shanghai has now become a centre of the armament industry for the whole of the Far East. It is a port of landing where armaments from the big European firms are sorted out, some for China and some for Japan.

Chapter II

THE CHARACTER AND SCOPE
OF THE
BRITISH ARMAMENT INDUSTRY

BEFORE the war, no armament firm occupied so large a place in the public mind as Krupps. The desire to show Germany as the great military menace, combined with certain notorious scandals, led to an exposure of the character of this firm and the methods which it employed. Major Lefebure has rewritten the history of this firm in his recent book *Scientific Disarmament*.[1] The essentials of the story are that this firm was built up by the ingenuity of three generations of the Krupp family who founded their fortunes by persuading a variety of governments to embark on a policy of competitive arming, each country being induced to buy a new form of gun because a rival was already equipped with it. On the basis of this international organisation Krupps were able to form a special relationship with the Hohenzollern family, to dictate to a considerable extent the foreign policy of Germany and at the same time to carry on a large export trade in arms all over the world. The compulsory disarmament of Germany has now put Krupps out of the picture as an armament firm. The question we have to ask is whether other armament firms that still flourish to-day have a similar history.

We may begin at home with the firm of Vickers-Armstrongs. The story of this firm has not been told. Even a superficial examination of its history and position before the war, and its development since 1918, suggest a close parallel with the story of Krupps.

The firm of Vickers, Ltd., goes back to the business of George Naylor, founded in 1790. In 1829 it became Naylor, Hutchinson, Vickers & Co., and later, in 1867, it was incorporated as Vickers Sons & Co., with a capital of £150,000. Four years later the capital had increased to £500,000.

In 1892 by the creation of new shares and the acquisition of interests in other companies, notably William Beardmore, Vickers, Ltd., developed into a vast concern with Ordnance Works at Glasgow, factories at Sheffield and Erith and Naval Works at Walney Island.

An important step afterwards was taken in 1897, when the directors, realising the importance of ironclads for wars of the future, bought up the Naval Construction & Armament Co., of Barrow, for the sum of £425,000.

---

[1] *Scientific Disarmament*, by Major V. Lefebure. (Gollancz. 5s.)

An even more significant step was the purchase of Maxim-Nordenfeldt Guns & Ammunition Co. for £1,353,334 in cash and shares. The combine then became known as Vickers, Sons & Maxim and it had a capital of £3,750,000.[1]

It is at this point that Mr. Basil Zaharoff, born in Greece in 1849, must be brought into the picture, for the history of Vickers is inseparably connected with that of the financial genius of this man who had begun his career as a salesman of armaments, travelling for the firm of Nordenfeldt. Mr. Zaharoff came into the armament industry in 1877 at a time when the Balkans were in a ferment against Turkey, and when Turkey and Russia were struggling for power in the Near East. Zaharoff reaped harvests from the re-equipment and enlargement of the Greek army in 1880 and the following years. It was at this time that Nordenfeldt produced an effective submarine. It was offered by Zaharoff to the great naval Powers, but they were still hesitating to employ submarines and refused to buy. But Greece eagerly accepted Zaharoff's offer " and so there arose the curious situation that Greece was the first country in the world to receive the first practical submarine."[2] Very soon afterwards Zaharoff persuaded Turkey that, if Greece had one submarine, Turkey must have two.

In 1888, mainly through the influence of Zaharoff, the Nordenfeldt Guns & Ammunition Co., Ltd., and the Maxim Gun Co. were amalgamated into one concern. Hiram Maxim was the inventor whose machine-gun revolutionised modern warfare. Nordenfeldt subsequently left the Company, and, as we have seen, in 1897 it was purchased by Vickers. Henceforth, Zaharoff became the dominating figure in the firm which was destined to become the leading armaments firm in this country.

Immediately after the Boer War they acquired the Wolseley Tool & Motor Co. for £160,000 and the Electric & Ordnance Accessories Co. for £110,000.

During the Russo-Japanese War, England, the ally of Japan, supplied armaments to both sides, and Zaharoff effected an alliance with the St. Petersburg Ironworks and the Franco-Russian Company. Through these firms he obtained orders for guns and heavy material for cruisers, whilst through the Russian Shipbuilding Co. he received an order for two first-class battleships in the Black Sea. At the same time Beardmore, the Glasgow firm which belonged to Vickers, co-operated with Schneider-Creusot and Augustin Normand in the building of a dockyard and cannon factories in Reval. The international character of the firm was thus well established, and Zaharoff held shares not only in Vickers-Maxim but also in Schneider-Creusot and in ten other British arms factories, including Armstrong-Whitworth.

The Armament Ring

But by this date it is misleading to consider Vickers as a firm by itself; it had become part of the vast international Armament Trust, the Harvey United Steel Co. This Trust was formed in 1901 and remained in being until 1913 ; Mr. Albert Vickers, the managing director of Vickers & Maxim, was its chairman, and already in 1902 it included on its directorate representatives of four British firms : Charles Cammell & Co., Ltd., John Brown & Co., Ltd., Sir W. G. Armstrong Whitworth & Co., Ltd., and Vickers, Sons & Maxim, Ltd.; the two great German firms of Krupps and the Dillengen

---

[1] *The War Traders*, by G. H. Perris. (National Peace Council, 1914.)
[2] *Sir Basil Zaharoff*, by Richard Lewinsohn. (Gollancz, 12s. 6d.)

Steel Co.; the American firm, the Carnegie Steel Co., and the French firms of Schneider, the Chatillon Steel Co., and the St. Chamont Steel Co., and the Italian Terni Steel Works.[1] Though in subsequent years there were changes in personnel and new combinations, the Harvey Steel Trust remained up to the year before the war a comprehensive ring comprising the chief armament firms of Great Britain, Germany, France, Italy and the United States. Closely associated were other rings—the Nobel Dynamite Trust and the Chilworth Gunpowder Co. which controlled the explosive and chemical side of armament manufacture.

The Chilworth Gunpowder Co., Ltd., formed in 1885, was run as a joint concern by the managing directors of the United Rhenish and the Dueneberg Powder Mills and the Armstrong firm. Its chairman was a director of Armstrongs and its international character was kept up until the war broke out, when the Germans retired.

These rings were completely international in character and were highly successful in keeping alive in each country the demand for armaments which were bought by each rival government on the plea that they could not afford to be less well armed than their neighbours. When the war came the ring itself necessarily broke up into its component parts and the people of the world whom they had jointly supplied with arms used these arms to destroy one another.

When the war broke out in 1914 the firm of Vickers, Ltd., was almost the equal of the firm of Armstrongs with whom it shared an interest in the Whitehead Torpedo factory. Together they were the leaders of the English armament industry. Vickers was even larger than Krupps if judged by the size of its share capital, whilst it had many more connections at home and abroad. It had relations with the German factory Loewe & Co., a member of that family being on the Vickers Board of Directors.[2] It had factories in Spain, Italy, Russia, Japan and Canada and was the most international armament firm in the world.

The power and influence of the armament rings, and of Vickers in particular, during the period of international unrest that preceded the war did not altogether escape notice. Viscount Snowden, who as Philip Snowden had a keen eye for such matters, made a striking statement in a speech on the Naval Estimates in 1914. He complained of the political activities of armament rings and called special attention to the part played by Vickers.[3]

---

[1] *The International Industry of War.* (Published by the Union of Democratic Control, 1915.)

[2] According to J. T. W. Newbold in *How Europe Armed for War* (Blackfriars Press, 1s. 3d.):—

> "Mr. S. Loewe early joined the directorate of the Maxim and Nordenfeldt Gun and Ammunition Co. of London, and passed on to the Board of Vickers, Sons & Maxim, Ltd., when the smaller firm was absorbed. He was with this most British of British firms until his death in 1903... Vickers afterwards maintained the Loewe tradition by continuing to act as the London agents of Paul von Gontard's concern, the Deutsche Waffenfabrik."

[3] *Hansard*, March 17, 1914:—

> "I find in the year before the scare Messrs. Vickers' profits amounting to £424,000. Two years after that they were nearly double that amount. Every year since the success of their intrigue their profits have gone up— £474,000, £544,000, £745,000, £872,000 ...
>
> The First Lord of the Admiralty ... some time ago said that the relations of the Admiralty with Vickers and another large firm in the trade are far

TEN

The following years proved that Philip Snowden accurately described the anticipation of Messrs. Vickers.

Just as an increase of capital was made before the South African War, so was the capital of Vickers, Ltd. (the name was changed in 1911), increased by £740,000 in 1913. The balance sheet for the year ending December 31, 1913, shows an item " Premium on 740,000 ordinary shares issued at £1 10s. per share," which indicates the popularity of Vickers, Ltd., and the handsome profits already made, and what profits in the opinion of those most competent to judge were probable during the ensuing trade year. This optimism was amply justified and the share capital was increased from £4,440,000 to £5,550,000 in 1914. The profits increased to £929,107.

In a review of the period preceding the war in 1914, the shares of Vickers, Ltd., could be recorded as a barometer with which to test the political storms then threatening in Europe. The fact that during the years from 1909 to 1914 the needle progressively rose till the column almost overflowed showed that at each successive international crisis there was an increasing number of persons willing to speculate heavily upon the probability of war.

The files at Somerset House show that there was a feverish anxiety to deal in armament shares in the summer of 1914, and, with the coming of war, we find a number of well-informed persons, certain prominent bankers, and Sir Basil Zaharoff himself, increasing their holdings. Amongst the shareholders at that time were various important people closely associated with the Government.[1]

The close relationship between Vickers and Government departments in this country and Government officials in a number of foreign countries was no secret before the war. Vickers had already established the practice, so usefully developed later, of placing in prominent positions on their Board and on their high-grade staff experts who had retained military and naval titles in His Majesty's Forces. The war itself, of course, made the relationship between Governments and armament firms more intimate still, and Sir Basil Zaharoff was himself a close friend and adviser of Mr. Lloyd George, Minister of Munitions and, later, Prime Minister. Just how great his international influence was no one can be sure. Much that is improbable as well as much that is certainly true has been written of this " mystery man of Europe." It is at any rate certain that he was largely responsible for bringing Greece into the war on the Allied side. The Allied propaganda in Greece which brought M. Venizelos into power was carried on largely at the personal expense of Sir Basil, who acted as the agent of France in buying a number of influential Greek newspapers. For these services he was decorated with the

---

more cordial than the ordinary relations of business. That might be one reason why the representative of these firms was received in audience at a Cabinet Council . . .

Patriotism is not one of the distinguishing features of the trade methods of this great combine. For instance, I find Messrs. Vickers have works at Barrow, Sheffield and Birmingham, but they do not confine themselves to this country. They have a yard in Placentia de las Armas in Spain ; they have another place in Spezzia in Italy. They evidently take time by the forelock. They anticipate the promise of a Mediterranean squadron."

[1] The trustee for the debenture holders of Vickers was Lord Sandhurst, formerly Under-Secretary of State for War, and at that time Lord Chamberlain. The Secretary of State for the Colonies, Rt. Hon. Lewis Harcourt, M.P., was an important shareholder. A. J. Balfour was trustee for Beardmore, whilst Col. Parks, the great conscription enthusiast, was a director.

ELEVEN

French Legion of Honour. It is also certain that by the end of the war he was one of the wealthiest men in Europe and that he had immense financial interests not only in armaments but also in oil, international banking, and in shipping, and that he was a close friend of Clemenceau and Briand and had a large interest in several Parisian, as well as Greek, newspapers.[1]

In 1917, when there was a possibility of peace negotiations through United States intervention, Zaharoff was consulted. Lord Bertie, the British Ambassador in Paris at that time, reported in his diary on June 25, 1917, that " Zaharoff is all for continuing the war *jusqu'au bout.*"

The Post-war Position of Vickers

Since the war, the situation has changed in some respects and the tendency has been in the direction of rationalisation and of grouping together all the various armament interests in this country round Vickers, Ltd. Of course, Vickers is by no means exclusively devoted to the manufacture of armaments. But here we are not concerned with the manufacture of sewing machines and speed boats, but with the fact that Vickers to-day dominates the armament manufacture in this country. Step by step the interests of Vickers, Ltd., have been combined with the interests of other companies which deal in products necessary for armament manufacture.

Before the war the firms of Vickers and Armstrongs had been the two leading firms in this country. After the boom period of the war had subsided, first Vickers, and then Armstrongs, which had become heavily over-capitalised, found it necessary to carry through far-reaching schemes of reorganisation.

Then, in 1927, the armament, shipbuilding and steel interests of Vickers, Ltd., and those of Sir W. G. Armstrong Whitworth, Ltd., were amalgamated, and thus Vickers-Armstrongs became the leading armament firm in this country and the most international armament firm in the world. This new firm took over Vickers works at Barrow, Erith, Dartford and Sheffield and the Armstrong-Whitworth works at Manchester (Openshaw), Elswick and the Naval Yard at Newcastle-on-Tyne. In its leading article of November 4, 1927, *The Times* referred to the exceptional importance of this amalgamation. It remarked that :—

> " It would be hard to name an amalgamation in industry equal in importance to the fusion which is announced to-day of the great armament firms of Vickers and Armstrongs. . . . The scope of the Armstrongs-Vickers amalgamation covers the whole of their armament making, naval shipbuilding, and heavy and special steel manufacture. These works represent about 75 per cent. of their own activities apart from those of their subsidiary companies."

At the Extraordinary General Meeting when this amalgamation took place, the chairman, the Hon. Sir Herbert Lawrence, G.C.B., said that :—

> " Vickers and Armstrongs depend very largely on armament orders to occupy their works on a profit-earning basis, but since the war such orders have been insufficient to keep the plant of the two

---

[1] Four years before the war Zaharoff took shares to the value of 250,000 francs in the Quotidiens Illustrés, a firm in Paris which issued the newspaper *Excelsior*.

In February, 1916, the Agence Radio was founded with M. Turot as the director and Zaharoff provided 1½ million francs to run it. The Agence Radio was a particularly effective medium for French propaganda. (*Vide Sir Basil Zaharoff*, by R. Lewinsohn.)

companies fully occupied, or to yield a satisfactory return to the shareholders."

He argued that it was, therefore :—

" Of national importance as well as in the interests of the share-holders that the capacity of the works to undertake armament work of the largest character should be maintained,"

and explained how the amalgamation would enable " the armament work available " to be concentrated in the most economical way. He added that an arrangement had been made with the Sun Life Assurance Office, Ltd. (of which Sir Herbert Lawrence is himself a director) :—

" whereby if the profits . . . in any year during the five years ending December 31, 1932, do not amount to £900,000, then a con-tribution not exceeding £200,000 will be made in each year."

At the same time Vickers-Armstrongs also took over those subsidiaries of the two firms which dealt in armament production : the Thames Ammuni-tion Works, the Whitehead Torpedo Co., and Vickers (Ireland), Ltd.

The next step was the formation of the English Steel Corporation which was formed by the amalgamation of the Steel Interests of Cammell Laird & Co., Ltd., and Vickers-Armstrongs and the Metropolitan Carriage, Wagon Finance Co., Ltd. The following table shows the completeness of the Vickers group and the way in which these organisations work for the production of all heavy armaments for use on land, or sea, or air.

Vickers-Armstrong Group

Armaments.
Shipbuilding.
Plant for docks, harbours, bridges, collieries, cement works, railways, steel works, &c., &c.
Non-ferrous metals.
General engineering.

English Steel Corporation Group

Steel-ingots, castings, forgings, bars, tubes, sheets and drop stampings.
Special alloys and heavy iron castings and forgings.
Water turbines and hydraulic plant.
Oil well, water and quarry drilling equipment.
Small tools, hacksaws, files, &c.
Railway and tramway materials, e.g., tyres, axles, wheels, &c.
Pumps.

Metropolitan-Cammell Group

Railway rolling stock of all descriptions.

Vickers (Aviation), Ltd.

Aircraft and accessories for military and civil purposes.

The range of activities of Vickers, and particularly of its leading company, Vickers-Armstrongs, was demonstrated in the new showroom opened at Vickers House, Westminster, on May 28, 1931. According to *The Times*, May 29, 1931 :—

" Mr. Douglas Vickers, speaking after the informal opening of the showroom, said that while, in recent years, the Vickers group had parted with certain interests considered to be too far apart from their main trades, they could yet claim to have within the groups the biggest range of interests in the world. It might have been noticed that war material played a great part in the showroom. There were two reasons for this. War material was still a large interest of the firm, and there was less difficulty in showing such productions than the specialities of civil engineering.

" Anyone who went into the history of the artillery and technical side of the war would know that of the various types introduced with success those which were supplied by the constituent firms of Vickers and Armstrongs played the largest part. He did not say this in disparagement of the Royal gun factories, but he thought a private firm had great advantages over a State factory. The private firm had to go into the world and meet competition, and they got to know in this way what was up against them and what they had to beat. This sharpened their wits.

" There were people who maintained that armaments should be taken out of private hands and who believed old stories about the influence which armament firms were said to have exercised in the past in the interests of war. There was not a shadow of truth in such stories. Armament firms were the most peaceful of people, and in their own interest did not want war, but only that we should be prepared for war. They felt it would be absolutely criminal to send out our men unless they were equipped and armed in the best possible way, and for that reason he thought the term ' a national asset,' applied to their firm during the war, could still be applied to-day. It was useless to expect the League of Nations to settle all quarrels, and a private firm making armaments was deserving of the support he claimed for it."

At the sixty-fifth annual general meeting of Vickers, Ltd., held on April 4, 1932, Sir Herbert Lawrence, the chairman, described the present position :—

" Considerable progress has been made," he said, " with the development of our land armaments, in certain branches of which until recent years we were almost unknown. To get into this market has involved the retention of special staffs and considerable expenditure on research and experimental work, but as a result orders are being obtained for anti-aircraft artillery, predictors and tanks, including the amphibious tank which Vickers-Armstrongs were the first to introduce. Had the demand for armaments been normal, there is no doubt that the expansion of the company's business in this direction would have proved very remunerative, and even now the volume of work obtained has proved distinctly helpful.

" Although every endeavour is made to develop our main products . . . Vickers-Armstrongs depends very largely on armament orders for its existence, while the capacity of its works for armament production is an important factor in the defence of the country. If, therefore, orders are not forthcoming in sufficient quantity to retain the thousands of skilled men employed, the position in case of national emergency arising which demanded an immediate increase in the output of munitions would be a serious one."[1]

Sir Herbert Lawrence then pointed out how Vickers, Ltd., is " severely prejudiced by exclusion of armaments from the British Export Credit

---

[1] *Manchester Guardian*, April 5, 1932.

Scheme " and lamented the diversion of armament work to Italy and France. He also referred to the satisfactory financial position of Vickers Aviation, Ltd.

Whilst Disarmament Conferences are meeting, Vickers-Armstrongs continue to plan ahead for the production of new and ever more effective armaments. Recent prospectuses mention the following developments : (1) the Vickers-Carden-Lloyd Light Amphibious Tank, which after many years of research and experiment has been so constructed that it will cross rivers, negotiate rough country, climb up hill at a continuous slope of 30° at a speed of about six miles per hour when fully loaded with two men, machine gun and 2,500 rounds of ammunition; (ii) the Vickers Vildebeest Bombing Machine which can be used for reconnaissance general purposes, bombing and torpedo work; and (iii) the Anti-Aircraft Predictor, which will produce mechanically the data required to hit an aeroplane flying at 200 miles per hour in less than five seconds.

Vickers Abroad

Apart from selling to the British Government, Vickers-Armstrongs, Ltd., must look for markets abroad. In this it is greatly helped by its international connections and its factories which are strategically placed in various countries.

In Italy there is the Societa Vickers-Terni ; in Canada, the Vickers Two Combustion Engine Corporation ; in Japan, Vickers-Armstrongs has a subsidiary company, Kabushiki Kwaisha Nihon Seiko-Sho (Japan Steel Works) which is part of the Mitsui concern, the dominating armament industry in that country. Thus in the preparation for the " war " in China, Japanese firms have been working under contract with Vickers, and the Japanese army has fought with the most modern armaments on land and in the air, and have transported equipment in up-to-date warships and air-craft carriers.

Vickers have their factories in Rumania. We may presume some connection with the fact that Sir Herbert Lawrence, the chairman, is a director of the Bank of Rumania. There are Vickers factories in Ireland (Vickers Ireland, Ltd.); in Spain (Sociedad Espanola de Construccion Naval and Placencia de las Armas Company, Ltd.); in New Zealand, Vickers (New Zealand), Ltd. ; in Holland they are associated with Fokkers aviation firm which also has connections in America, whilst the Neder-landsche Engelse Techniese Handelsmij in the Hague is the bureau of Vickers, and the grenade factory of van Heyst is one of their factories. In Poland Vickers have holdings in the Société Polonaise de Matériel de Guerre, in which the French firm of Schneider is also interested.

It would seem that Vickers and the French firm of Schneiders are closely linked up. In the agreement which was signed at the time of the Vickers-Armstrong amalgamation in 1927 the firm of Vickers-Schneider was included amongst the list of firms which were purchased by Vickers-Armstrongs from Vickers. Amongst other firms which were involved are : S. A. Le Nickel, S. A. Aciêres et Domines de Resita, Société des Etablissements Miniêre de Starachowice Uzinele Metalurgice din Copsa-Mica si Cugir, Experiencias Industriales S. A.

Apart from these direct connections, however, there are the important ramifications brought about by the directorships which are held by the directors of Vickers, Ltd. Sir Herbert A. Lawrence, of both Vickers, Ltd., and Vickers-Armstrongs, Ltd., is also manager of Glynn Mills, and a director of the Bank of Rumania, Ltd., of the Sun Assurance Office, Ltd., of the Sun Life Assurance Society, and is also chairman of the London Committee of the Ottoman Bank. Major-General G. P. Dawnay, another director, is also chairman of Sir W. G. Armstrong-Whitworth & Co., Ltd., and is a director of Financial Newspapers Proprietors, Ltd., and the Economist Newspaper, Ltd. (His brother, Col. A. G. C. Dawnay, C.B.E., D.S.O., is a member of the Land Commission of the Disarmament Conference.) Sir Otto Niemeyer, also a director of Vickers, Ltd., has been with the Bank of England since 1927, and is also a director of the Anglo-International Bank.

At this point we may for a moment leave the romantic story of Vickers. We have seen how, step by step, Vickers-Armstrongs has become the outstanding armament firm in this country. The great firms of William Beardmore & Co., Ltd., and of Cammell Laird & Co., Ltd., still exist, but the first, as we have mentioned, is now a subsidiary of Vickers, Ltd., and the second has become associated with them through the formation of the English Steel Corporation. Through small beginnings the Vickers combine has developed into an immense concern with many ramifications, with an issued capital of nearly £16,000,000.

Other Firms

Other firms which are of importance in connection with the manufacture of armaments include Thomas Firth & John Brown, Ltd., B.S.A. Guns, Ltd., Yarrow & Co., Ltd., specialises in torpedo boats, in destroyers, &c., whilst Tubes, Ltd., manufacture torpedoes and tubes. R. & W. Hawthorn Leslie, Messrs. Palmer Shipbuilding and Iron Co., Messrs. Swan, Hunter & Richardson, the Wallsend Slipway and Engineering Co., Messrs. John Thornycroft and the Fairfield Shipbuilding and Engineering Co., and Messrs. Parsons Marine Steam Turbine Co. are all firms associated with the naval side of armament manufacture and, as we shall mention later, are engaged at the moment on fulfilling contracts for the Admiralty.

The Industry of Chemical Warfare

The next war, according to such authorities as Major Lefebure, is likely to be predominantly a war in the air, carried out by bombing aeroplanes dropping incendiary explosives and gas bombs supported by swifter fighting planes. Supplies for munitions, poison gas and explosives are all practically in the hands of the Imperial Chemical Industries, Ltd., the biggest chemical concern in the world which, with an issued capital of over £70,000,000, controls the whole chemical industry in this country, both civil and military.

The President is Lord Reading, the chairman is Sir H. McGowan, K.B.E., and other directors are Lord Ashfield, Lord Colwyn, Lord Melchett, Lord Weir and Sir Max Muspratt. The I.C.I. was formed to acquire by exchange of shares Nobel Industries, Ltd. (since voluntarily liquidated), Brunner Mond & Co., Ltd., United Alkali, Ltd., and the British Dyestuffs Corporation. Through its subsidiary companies the I.C.I. has close connections with His Majesty's Government, to which it is a contractor. Take the example of Synthetic Ammonia and Nitrate, Ltd. The war experience showed how useful large synthetic ammonia plant can be for the manufacture of explosives. After the war, the Allies sent a military commission to Germany to obtain information concerned with the process involved in the preparation of poison gas. Following this, the British Government sold their factory for synthetic ammonia in Billingham at a very low price to Brunner Mond,

Ltd., and gave them, if report speaks truly, the secret processes which had been learnt from the Germans for the oxidation of ammonia to nitric acid. This company is now known as the I.C.I. (Fertilisers and Synthetic Products), Ltd. In peace time it converts ammonia into synthetic fertilisers. In war time, or as soon as a war is imminent, it converts ammonia into explosives. The issued capital is £5¾ millions and both the principal and the interest of its 5 per cent. guaranteed debenture stock, 1930-45, are guaranteed by His Majesty's Government.

It was the war experience, too, which showed the vital importance of dyestuffs. In the years before the war, Germany had acquired the virtual monopoly of dyestuffs manufacture as well as the biggest chemical industry in the world. In the war, poison gas came from the chemical factories and in the dyestuffs factories there was the plant for making organic chemicals used as lachrymators and vesicants. In 1919, the chief dyestuff factories in Great Britain were combined to form the British Dyestuffs Corporation, Ltd., and the Government subscribed for 850,000 preferred and 850,001 preference shares " to include one share with special voting powers issued to His Majesty's Government."

In the Articles of Association No. 88 (i) provision is made "that not more than 25 per cent. of the shares and voting power shall be held by foreigners, and the company is to keep in touch with His Majesty's Government in all matters of technical information and research, in such manner as the President of the Board of Trade may direct." Referring to the Dyestuffs Corporation, *The Chemical Age* (November 22, 1924) candidly stated: " The fundamental argument for the establishment of a British dyestuffs industry was national safety—in other words the existence of chemical plant and processes which could easily in case of emergency be switched over from peace to war purposes."

The power of Imperial Chemical Industries does not rest alone on its subsidiary companies, but also on the interlocking of directorships. I.C.I. is in effect comparable with the huge German I.G. Combine before the War.[1]

In the report of the annual meeting of the Imperial Chemical Industries, Ltd., on April 14, 1932, Sir Harry McGowan, the chairman and managing director, gave a survey of the company. He said :—

> " The shares and debentures in and advances to subsidiary companies shown in the balance sheet at £60,264,978 represent in the main the company's holdings in the eight manufacturing groups referred to in the report, namely, Alkali, General Chemical, Explosives, Fertiliser and Synthetic Products, Dyestuffs, Leathercloth, Lime and Metals, in Imperial Chemical Industries, Ltd., of Australia and New Zealand, and in our foreign merchanting companies." ...
> ... " The marketable and other investments standing at £9,540,677 mainly represent investments in large industrial companies with which we have, directly or indirectly, trade connections. The chief items are investments in the General Motors Corporation, Du Pont & Co. and the Allied Chemical Company in the United States, the International Nickel Co. in Canada, the I.G. Farbenindustrie in Germany, and Joseph Lucal & Sons in this country."

Thus we see that, in the same way that Vickers, Ltd., has become the big armament combine with interests at home and abroad, the Imperial Chemical Industries, Ltd., has become the poison gas combine with a virtual monopoly at home, and ramifications in all the leading countries of the world.

---

[1] Well-known shareholders and the number of shares held in the I.C.I., according to the annual returns, on April 28, 1932, were: Sir John Simon, M.P., 1,512; Baron Doverdale, 34,124; Earl of Dysart, 88,020; Lord Cochrane of Cults, 47,180; Rt. Hon. Neville Chamberlain, M.P., 11,747; Sir Austen Chamberlain, M.P., 666.

Military Aviation

Great Britain is not only the centre of the world's armament industries; she leads the world in military aviation. Her bombing machines are known in every quarter of the globe ; they are the modern symbol of Empire. Single-seater fighters, bombers both for day and night work and general purposes machines for long and short range reconnaisance are the main types of aircraft used by the Air Force, and the whole of these are duplicated in marine aircraft such as seaplanes and flying boats.

The Fairey Aviation Co., Ltd. [1]—now the most important firm manufacturing military aeroplanes—was formed on October 1, 1928, and supplies land planes and seaplanes to the British and other Governments. The foreign sales have been increasing as nations realise that efficiency in war preparation demands an adequate supply of the latest type of military machine.

In addition to supplying orders to the Australian, Irish, Argentine, Chilean, Dutch, Portuguese, Japanese and Greek Governments, this company has just obtained an order for as many as thirty day bombers which are among the fastest in the world. The order, worth £300,000, is the second one of its kind during the past year. Like the armament firms, the Fairey Aviation Co. has developed its factories abroad, and the work on the Belgium order will be shared by factories in Hayes, Middlesex, and those in Gossillies, Belgium.

Other firms include the de Havilland Aircraft Co., Ltd., makers of the famous " Moth " series. So great has been the foreign demand for their machines that the de Havilland Aircraft Co., Ltd., has established subsidiary companies in Australia, Canada, India and South Africa, and it has contracts in America for the production of aircraft and engines from which valuable royalties are received. It is now developing in South America. The increase in development is shown by the fact that its capital quadrupled between 1927 and 1930. Handley Page [2] which makes the large twin-engined bombers

---

[1] The Fairey Aviation Co., Ltd., has increased its dividends for 1931 from 7 per cent. to 10 per cent. (tax free) and its reserves to £60,000. From the report of the last annual meeting in December, 1931, it appears that a profit of over £184,000 was recorded—the highest in the company's history. A large experimental establishment and a highly technical staff has enabled the directors to maintain a progressive technical policy. Recently works at Hayes have been equipped to enable aircraft to be constructed in metal to meet the requirements of the Air Ministry. The report ended on a note of thanks to the Air Ministry and other Government departments for the great assistance they have rendered in obtaining overseas orders.

All the directors of the Fairey Aviation Co., Ltd., must be British subjects. The chairman of the board of directors is Mr. C. R. Fairey, who is a member of the Council of the Federation of British Industries, President of the Royal Aeronautical Society and member of the Council of the Society of British Aircraft Constructors. In scanning the long list of shareholders in this company one notices that the leading banks hold big blocks of shares for their nominees whose names, unfortunately, are not divulged. According to the annual returns on January 18, 1932, Sir Harry Hope, M.P., holds 500 shares ; Sir G. Dalrymple-White, M.P., 400 ; Mr. Oswald Lewis, M.P., 1,400 ; and Major G. Lloyd George, M.P., 500. The other shares are held by the Brunner Investment Trust, Ltd., several well-known flying men, Sir Charles C. Wakefield, an ex-Lord Mayor of London, Lord Whitborough, and many others.

[2] Handley Page, Ltd. Mr. F. Handley Page, C.V.E. (managing director), gave this very interesting information about the work of this firm in his speech at the general meeting on May 21, 1931 :—
" The last two years have seen the complete change over to all-metal construction in our works, and with this change a considerable re-equipping

of the "Hinaidi" type; the Armstrong-Siddeley Development Co., which owns practically all the shares of A. V. Roe & Co. Ltd.; the Blackburn Aeroplane & Motor Co., Ltd., makers of the "Lincock Fighters," Boulton & Paul, the Bristol Aeroplane Co., and the Armstrong-Siddeley Development Co.,[1] which make the fastest aircraft in the world [2]—all these are important firms in military aviation and, in differing degrees, in commercial aviation.

No survey of military aviation is complete without a mention of Vickers (Aviation) Ltd. Vickers is attempting to become as important an armament firm in aeroplane manufacture as it is in the making of guns, munitions and heavy armaments. Aircraft for military and civil purposes, aircraft parts, components and equipment are manufactured by Vickers (Aviation) Ltd., whilst in the Supermarine Aviation Works in Southampton there are manufactured flying-boats, seaplanes, aircraft carriers and other equipment of naval aviation.

Mention must be made too of Napier & Sons, Ltd., and Rolls Royce, Ltd., which are the two most important aero-engine manufacturers.

We have surveyed the armaments industry in this country in its three separate directions, heavy armaments, poison gas and military aviation; together they represent a more or less complete survey of our preparation for war.

We shall now pass on to a brief survey of the biggest armament ring in post-war days, which is to be seen in the Schneider-Creusot firm, and Skoda, which it controls.

---

of our plant. It is satisfactory that we have been able to carry this through without drawing upon our reserves or undue dislocation of work.

"With regard to our Air Ministry contracts, we have been engaged during the past year, and are still engaged, on the production of our Hinaidi aircraft (large twin-engined bombers). In addition we have several experimental aircraft under construction for the Air Ministry; these show great advances on previous designs, one now under trial being a replacement of the present 'Hinaidi' type."

The shareholders of this firm on June 5, 1931, included Sir Basil Mayhew, K.B.E., Sir Henry Grayson, K.B.E., many banks and investment companies, Wing Commander Louis Greig, C.V.O., Mr. C. R. Fairey, the Rt. Hon. J. Downe, C.M.G., D.S.O., the Duchess of Grafton, Lord Arthur Browne, Mr. F. Handley Page, Mr. Arthur J. Page. Smaller shareholders are taxi-drivers, municipal officers, printers, stationmasters, brass founders, boot repairers, woolsorters, carpenters, chemists, farmers, police constables, schoolmasters, fish merchants, naval officers, an Air Vice-Marshal, an occasional clergyman, a Brigadier-General, a civil servant in the Foreign Office, a professor of music, doctors, and the trustees for the Wesleyan Chapel Purposes (Ltd.), Manchester.

[1] This Company with an issued capital of £1,419,750 owns practically all the shares of A. V. Roe & Co., Ltd., Sir W. G. Armstrong-Whitworth Aircraft, Ltd., and Armstrong-Siddeley Motors, Ltd. Some of the directors are Mr. J. D. Siddeley, Lord Southborough and Air Marshal Sir Jack E. A. Higgins, K.C.B., K.B.E., D.S.O., A.F.C.
During a period which has proved notoriously difficult for many industries, this firm has showed high profits every year. Among the main preference shareholders are the Rt. Hon. Wentworth Allendale, Major the Hon. E. G. Beaumont, Sir J. R. Ellerman, whilst large blocks of shares are held by the Siddeley family, by banks and investment companies, including the A. W. Second Stock Trust, Ltd.

[2] The Hawker Fury, e.g., an interceptor fighter, has a speed of over 200 miles per hour and climbs 20,000 feet in 11 minutes.

Chapter III

ARMAMENT FIRMS ABROAD

THE firm of Schneider-Creusot is the Vickers-Armstrongs of France, and through its control of the Skoda works exercises a dominating influence in Central Europe. It is the most influential firm in the Comité des Forges, the powerful industrial union in France which played a great part in the Ruhr occupation and admittedly had a considerable influence on the Poincaré Cabinet. Its influence was behind the propaganda for the Saar Basin and the demand at the Peace Conference for the Left Bank of the Rhine. The President of the Comité des Forges is M. Francois Wendel, who is also a Deputy in the French Chamber and a director of the Bank of France. He has a controlling interest in the best known Nationalist French newspaper, the *Journal des Débats*, and recently he acquired a controlling number of shares in *Le Temps* with M. de Peyerinhoff, who is the President of the Comité des Houillères.

The Schneider Ring

Schneider-Creusot, like the English Vickers-Armstrongs, has its close association with the big European banks. M. Wendel is not the only link. Mr. Eugene Schneider, the chairman of Schneiders and another of the most important people in the French armament industry, is a director of the Banque de l'Union Parisienne, the bank which finances the Banque Générale de Crédit Hongrois. He is also the President of the Union Européene Banque which is not only interested in the Banque Générale de la Crédit Hongrois, but is the bank through which Schneiders control the Skoda Works. Thus we see that the French armament industry controls that of Czechoslovakia, and, ironically enough (as Paul Fauré, ex-M.P. [1] for the Creusot Division, in which are the Schneider headquarters, mentioned in a speech in the French Chamber), Hungary is being armed secretly by French armament capital. [2]

---

[1] Paul Fauré was defeated in the recent French Election, mainly by the skilfully organised election propaganda of the Schneider firm and their intimidation of their employees.

[2] This speech was referred to as follows in the *Manchester Guardian* of December 14, 1931 :—

"Another financial matter likely to cause difficulties to the Government is the loan to Hungary, the fact of which was unknown until it was discovered the other day by the Finance Committee of the Chamber. Investigation into the matter has shown that the Hungarian Government had originally obtained a loan from the armament firm of Schneider at Creusot, and when the firm asked to be repaid the Hungarian Government could not produce the money. Thereupon the French Government lent the Hungarian Government the amount necessary to repay the Schneider firm, which was transmitted to Hungary not by the Bank of France but by the Union Parisienne, a bank in which the Schneider firm holds a controlling interest."

During the past few years, the Schneider firm has delivered armaments to Mexico, Jugoslavia, Greece, Japan, Rumania, Turkey, Bulgaria, Montenegro, Russia, Argentina, Spain and Italy. For most of these operations banks have been founded which have interests in the country concerned as well as in France.

For instance, the Banque Hypothécaire d'Argentine has on its Board MM. de Neuflize and Villars, who are also members of the Board of directors of Schneiders, whilst M. de Neuflize is also a director of the Ottoman Bank.

Just as Vickers-Armstrongs have their contacts with Japan, so the French armament firms have their connections. On the Board of the Franco-Japanese Bank are to be found M. Saint-Sauveur (who incidentally is a relation of M. Schneider), whilst the president of this bank was Charles Dumont, who was the French Minister of Marine and has been representing France at the Disarmament Conference.[1]

Discussing the inter-relatedness of French loans and armament orders in the French Chamber on February 11, 1932, Paul Fauré pointed out that just as French loans before the war enabled Turkey to arm itself with French arms which were shortly afterwards used against France, so to-day French loans granted to Bulgaria, Mexico, Greece, Japan, Hungary, Jugoslavia, Rumania and Poland were being spent with the French armament firms.[2]

---

[1] It was M. Charles Dumont who, at the Disarmament Conference, in advocating the necessity of the submarine, said :—
"The naval supremacy of the powerful nations with large navies might become insupportable if submarines, the weapon of the poor, did not introduce an element of mystery, the unknown, at sea, so that the more powerful fleets would never be certain of success should they be tempted to use their power. The submarine is a weapon against the pride of power. It could be the support of the righteous. It must be retained."

[2] Extract from M. Paul Fauré's speech, February 11, 1982, in the French Chamber :—
"Turkey has taken fifteen loans, on thirteen of which nothing is being paid to-day. The last of these loans was in 1914 to permit Turkey to make war against France.
I want to make two or three observations on the Turkish and Bulgarian loans. One of these Bulgarian loans was in 1906 or 1907. I have in my dossier a photograph of Prince Ferdinand visiting the Creusot factories, accompanied by M. Eugene Schneider himself, and buying arms and cannons which you found later on the Eastern front for four years. What happened ? The order was so exaggerated that when King Ferdinand found himself before the Financial Commission of the Sobranje, which is probably as severe as you are, Gentlemen, it refused to ratify the credits. The French Government intervened at this point and declared that if the Sobranje did not ratify the credits the Bulgarian loan would not be authorised. The Sobranje spoke, France paid, and the armaments of Creusot were sent there.
"I have also in my dossier a photograph showing the Turkish Minister of Marine visiting the Creusot factories, preceded by all the inventors who showed him the latest developments on the side of defence. The Turkish Minister gave his order. He had already used up the last loan lent him by France. Only the war came too quickly (for this visit took place in July, 1914). Several days later war broke out, and the unfortunate Minister could not take away the French cannons. But as he had French money, he bought on the way back at Krupps in Essen and at Skoda the cannons which were used on the Eastern front.
"The French Government has lent money to the Rumanian Bank, and it is discussing at the moment the loan of three milliards of lei . . . In any case, whilst Rumania has been concerned with money a military mission from Rumania is at Creusot."
After referring to the fact that the directors of Skoda, which is controlled by

The influence of armament firms in France may provide some explanation for the militarist policy and tone of many politicians and of the Parisian press. As M. Briand once put it, " The pens which write against disarmament are made of the same steel as that from which guns are made." That this interlocking of the Press and the armament industries is no new plan is revealed by Raffalovitch whose position enabled him to state with authority in the years before the war what moneys passed between the bankers, the Governments and the armament firms in France and Russia.

In April, 1913, the Councillor Raffalovitch wrote a letter to Kokovtzev, Minister of Finance in St. Petersburg, which is not without interest to-day.

"The affairs of men are similar in all latitudes. In Brazil, according to Vickers Maxim, the President of the Republic takes upon himself to raise the price of battleships by several million francs. In Europe the chiefs of State, their Ministers and principal subordinates, are for the most part quite honest. But the merchants of armaments, armoured plate and munitions have recourse to indirect methods in influencing public opinion by the intermediary of the press ; they possess newspapers, acquire others, they buy journalists, and those writers who sound the patriotic note, who proclaim the military preparations of neighbouring states, who talk of the German or the French menace, believe themselves to be heroes. The corruption takes all forms, from a good dinner with choice wines in the company of pretty women paid in advance to finish up the night with the General seated on their right, up to the more delicate attentions, such as the promise of a well-paid situation. That there should be leakages (communication of military secrets) which benefit the dealers in shells and guns is very probable."

When one considers this relationship it is easy to understand the tone of the leading French newspapers,[1] their scathing attacks on the Disarmament

---

Schneider, have supported the electoral campaign of Mr. Hitler, Paul Fauré summed up the present situation as follows :—

"We find then M. Schneider arming Bulgaria, M. Schneider arming Turkey, Skoda supporting Hitler, Hungarian and Rumanian loans, Franco-Japanese, Franco-Argentine, and Franco-Mexican banks. This is all extremely suspicious."

[1] An article in the French paper *La Lumière* provides evidence of the way in which French armament firms have influenced the French press in their campaign against disarmament. The following is a summary of it :—

"A violent and audacious campaign is being carried out against disarmament ; it is being done through the *Echo de Paris*, and its political leader writer, M. de Kerillis. To fill at the same time the coffers of his propaganda organisation and those of the *Echo de Paris* M. de Kerillis has launched an appeal for funds, which cynically are called ' the campaign against disarmament' (*Echo de Paris*, March 10, 1932), and whilst he announces that the propaganda is going to be intensified in their district, he puts in the headlines ' The Struggle against Disarmament ' (*Echo de Paris*, March 16, 1932).

"On the subscription lists which this big reactionary paper publishes, one sees several anonymous subscriptions of 25,000, of 50,000, and even of 100,000 francs. It is quite evident that these anonymous gifts hide the big interests which would lose by disarmament."

The article subsequently describes the full page advertisements taken in the *Echo de Paris* on July 15, 1931, by " S.O.M.U.A." S.O.M.U.A. is connected with Schneider and stands for " Société d'Outillage Mécanique et d'Usinage d'Artillerie."

Thus it is the artillery manufacturers, namely, the cannon merchants, who fill the coffers of the *Echo de Paris*.

Conference, and to appreciate one at least of the reasons why the French proposals at the Disarmament Conference did not contain any proposals for disarmament.

Other French Firms

Apart from Schneider-Creusot, there is the firm of Hotchkiss which is partly owned by English people. It was of the Hotchkiss shares that the *Manchester Guardian*, in February, 1932, reported a marked rise owing to the fighting between China and Japan.

Military aviation in France, as in England, has stimulated the development of an enormous aviation industry. The Société Générale Aeronautique, founded in 1930, unites seven of the most important French aircraft factories and produces all types of aircraft and flying boats, both commercial and military. Another well-known firm is the Société anonyme des Ateliers d'Aviation Louis Breguet. The French army uses the Breguet aircraft, and it has been supplied to the Governments of Belgium, Spain, Greece, Poland, Jugoslavia, Turkey, Argentina, China and Japan.

Skoda

The Skoda Works and enterprises are found in all parts of Czechoslovakia. In Pilsen cannons, munitions, tanks and other material are manufactured; in Bolovec there is a testing ground, in Prague aeroplanes are made, and the arsenal Brno, which before the war was a small repair factory, has become an immense concern employing about 10,000 workmen. Since the war, Skoda has developed to enormous proportions in its manufacture of aeroplanes, and the aerodrome near Prague which specialises in military aeroplanes has a large output.

Poison gas is also produced in Skoda factories. Nitrogen works are at Marienberg and in Asce, whilst there are military chemical factories in Olomouc.

Skoda has found markets for her armaments in Jugoslavia, Poland, Switzerland, Greece, Turkey, Persia, China, Mexico, Argentina, Spain, Bulgaria and the U.S.S.R.

The Skoda Company also has factories in Poland (aeroplane engines are made in Warsaw, and it controls Polskie Zaklady Skoda which was formed in 1926 to take over interests acquired in Poland) and in Rumania.

It is important to remember that the Skoda Company is controlled by the French armament firm of Schneider-Creusot, through the Union Européene Banque.

Its registrar of debentures is the British and Allied Investments Corporation, whilst the trustee for the debentures is the Royal Exchange Assurance. Dividends for the past ten years [1] tell their own story. They were : 1920, 5 per cent. ; 1921, 8½ per cent. ; 1922 and 1923, 10 per cent. ; 1924, 12½ per cent. ; 1925, 13¾ per cent. ; 1926, 15¾ per cent. ; 1927, 17½ per cent. ; 1928, 21⅞ per cent. ; 1929 and 1930, 28½.

Mitsui

The Mitsui firm is the Vickers-Armstrongs of Japan, and it has corresponding ramifications in that country. It has interests in the Nippon Petroleum Co., in the Mining Co., and the Medajima Aircraft Co., in electricity works, and in the Taisho Marine and Fire Insurance Companies.

---

[1] *Stock Exchange Year Book*, 1931, page 8093.

It is linked up with the Nippon Steel Works, which are controlled by Vickers—this being the point of contact between the British and Japanese armament firms.

Krupps and Bofors

A great deal has been written about the transformation of Krupps works at Essen into factories where agricultural and other peace time machinery is manufactured, but less is known about the Bofors Munition Factory in Sweden, which seems to be the post-war translation of Krupps. In 1927 Krupps " acquired important shares in Swedish Bofors Ordnance and Dry-dock Co., which operates with the Krupps patents."[1] Krupps also have connections with armament factories in Holland where a considerable amount of armaments has been manufactured for Germany, and with factories in Russia, where a large industry with important German connections has developed in recent years. Although the Treaty of Versailles expressly prohibited the manufacture and traffic in armaments by Germany, her armament development during the past few years has not been commented upon by Members of the Council of the League of Nations, to which, since the withdrawal of the Inter-allied Commission of Control, right and duty of supervision has been transferred.

Armament Firms in Holland

In an article in the *Vredes Strijd*, a Dutch pacifist paper,[2] Hein van Wijk has made a survey of the leading firms in the Dutch armament industry. Under State control there are artillery works in Zaandam, a dye factory in Amsterdam, other factories in Muiden and Ouderkerk. Apart from these there seems to be a fairly comprehensive private armament industry, which includes the Dutch shell and metal works factory in Dordrecht, Alard Sons, a revolver factory in Maastricht, the Machine en Apparaten fabriek (M.E.A.F.) which makes torpedoes in Utrecht, the I.F.F.A. Minimax works at Amsterdam, which make poison gas, and the H.E.V.E.A. firm which specialises in gas masks at Heveadorp.

The aviation industry is represented by the Nedelandsce Vliegtuigen-fabriek, which is really Fokker, a firm with connections both with Vickers and with firms in America. There is also Aviolanda at Papendrecht.

Interesting comments on the Dutch armament industry were made by a series of special articles written by M. Edouard Helsey for the French paper *Le Journal* in January, 1932. M. Helsey visited the Siderius factories in Maartenshoef and Rotterdam, their depot at Krimpen and the offices at the Hague within a few steps of the Palace of Peace. The Hollandsche Industrie en Handel Maatschappij Siderius (the full name) manufactures cannons and other machinery used in war. It has kept up close connections with the big cannon merchants of the Ruhr. It is this firm which administers at Krimpen the German material which was suddenly thrown into Holland at the time of the Armistice. Its founder was a Dutchman, named Solomon Vlessing, who, during the war, was closely associated with some German enterprises specialising in war material. On the day after the Armistice, Vlessing in association with the German industrialist Ehrhardt brought the H.I.H. (as the firm is usually called) into being for the purpose of manufacturing war material. Ehrhardt brought his patents and his technical knowledge and stocks of material made in anticipation of the war being continued. Works were constructed at Maartenshoek and agreements were concluded with shipbuilding yards. In 1930 the firm became predominantly Dutch, although Ehrhardt held a considerable number of shares.

---

[1] *War for Profits*, by Lehmann-Russbüldt. (A. H. King, New York. $1·75.)
[2] *Vredes Strijd*. May, 1932.

The manager of this firm made it quite clear to M. Helsey that they sold their material equally to any Government which cared to give orders, including, of course, the German Government. And the close association with the German Ehrhardt would undoubtedly give Germany special facilities.

Apart from these associations between Dutch and German firms we have already mentioned that Fokkers are associated with Vickers, whilst M.E.A.F. is one of the concerns of Julius Pintsch of Berlin. In addition to these firms there are the offices of the following foreign armament manufacturing concerns in Holland : Vickers, Schneider, Skoda, Krupps, Bofors and others.

United States of America

The Bethlehem Steel Corporation, which belonged to the Harvey Steel Trust before the war and which figured largely in the Shearer case, is the leading armament firm in U.S.A. It has developed into a holding and owning company in very much the same way as Vickers has developed in Great Britain. The size of the development is shown by the increase in its net property from thirty-one million dollars in December, 1905, to 502 million dollars in 1930. Other leading firms are the Newport News Shipbuilding and Drydock Co. and Brown Boveri Electric Co., all of which were involved in the Shearer case. The E.L. de Pont Nemours Co. is an important chemical concern responsible for the production of poison gas. It is linked up with the I.C.I. in this country, which has investments in it and in the Allied Chemical Co.

As in other countries there has been a very considerable development in military as well as in commercial aviation in the U.S.A. One of the foremost companies is the Curtiss-Wright Corporation, which includes a large number of firms of importance in the manufacture of aeroplanes and aero-engines. During 1930 the Curtiss-Wright Corporation had considerable Government orders for bombers and training aeroplanes, for fighting and command planes. It specialises in experimental aircraft both for the U.S.A. Army and Navy. It is interesting, in view of what we have already seen of the international ramifications of the armament industry, that Wright engines are manufactured in Poland by the Polskie Zaklady Skoda, which are controlled by the Skoda works in Czechoslovakia. In Japan, Wright engines are made by the firm of Mitsui.

Other firms in the industry of military aviation include the Fokker Aviation Corporation of America, in which the General Motors Corporation hold 41 per cent. of the common stock, the United Aircraft & Transport Company Incorporated, which includes about fourteen of the American companies and has had large orders both from the American navy and from the navies of Cuba, Peru, Brazil and China. Lastly, there is the Consolidated Aircraft Corporation which specialises in the design and construction of training aircraft and which since its incorporation has delivered 1,000 military training aeroplanes to the Army Air Corps and the Naval Air Service.

The Present Position of the Secret International

These are the firms in the main exporting countries in the world. There is not to-day any single armaments ring which corresponds to the Harvey Steel Trust in pre-war days. There are obvious connections between the leading firms, whilst the directors of armament firms often belong to the same bank. For example, M. de Neuflize (director of Schneider) is also a director of the Ottoman Bank, the London Committee of which is presided over by Sir Herbert Lawrence, the chairman both of Vickers, Ltd., and of Vickers-Armstrongs, Ltd. The connection between banks and armament firms is frequently a very close one. This close association places armament firms in a formidable position. In France, where the connection is unusually clear, no informed person doubts that armament firms have a direct influence on foreign policy. We need not doubt in view of the facts we have given that this influence is at work in varying degrees in other countries.

We may now consider more general questions that arise from this relationship and to point to definite instances in which armament firms have in the past employed corrupt means. Nothing has been done since the war to make impossible the use of similar methods to-day, and instances have occurred which show that they are sometimes still employed.

Chapter IV

THE GOVERNMENT
AND
WAR CONTRACTORS

" The Government of your country ! I am the Government of your country, I and Lazarus. Do you suppose that you and half a dozen amateurs like you, sitting in a row in that foolish gabble shop, govern Undershaft and Lazarus ? No, my friend, you will do what pays us. You will make war when it suits us and keep peace when it doesn't. . . . When I want anything to keep my dividends up, you will discover that my want is a national need. When other people want something to keep my dividends down, you will call out the police and military. And in return you shall have the support of my newspapers, and the delight of imagining that you are a great statesman." (Undershaft, the armament maker, in Shaw's *Major Barbara*.)

A DRAMATIC overstatement, of course. Relationships in diplomacy and politics are complex not simple. It is probably nearly as untrue to say that wars are made at the dictation of armament firms as to say that armament manufacturers are governed by national policy. The relationship is subtler and varies from country to country. In preparation for war each Government to-day has a paper scheme of the whole country mapped out as a vast arsenal; every large iron and steel works and motor factory which can be converted to military use in time of war is included in the scheme. The United States Government, for instance, has even gone to the length of preparing contracts with armament firms. These contracts, which number some thousands, are locked in safes only waiting for the endorsement at the word " Go." In each country the supply of raw materials, of poison gas and of the essential chemicals is provided for and Government research goes on side by side with that of private enterprise. The most complete example of war preparation is probably that embodied in the French Act for the general organisation of the country in war-time which became law in February, 1928.

An intimate relationship, therefore, exists between Governments, armament firms and corporations like the I.C.I. But these great firms are not controlled by the governments. If they are to be ready for the necessary output in time of war they must be permitted to sell arms where they can find a market in times of peace. Since all Governments aim at the highest war efficiency they plan on the basis of a possible quick expansion at the outbreak of war. Aeroplanes and tanks quickly grow out-of-date and if production were limited to government factories it would be restricted by budgetary necessities. Every War Office and Air Ministry, therefore, supports the policy of keeping private firms as large as possible in time of peace, which means permitting them to develop as large a peace-time export industry as possible. Thus, while we do not expect to find Vickers selling arms in Germany before the war or Krupps supporting the British Government, we do find these firms both supplying the potential markets in the Near East and the Balkans. When the war came, these countries were thus supplied with both German and British armaments. These armaments no doubt proved equally efficient whether these countries came into the war on the British or German side.

During the war the export of armaments was, of course, strictly regulated. One regulation—licensing of armament exports—has remained. According to the answer given in the House of Commons by the Parliamentary Secretary of the Board of Trade, the licence is virtually a matter of form. The Board of Trade is " guided in this matter by the advice of the Foreign Office and the Service Departments."[1] In other words, all export licences have the formal endorsement of the Board of Trade, the Foreign Office, the Admiralty or War Office or Air Ministry. Questions in the House of Commons have elicited from the Board of Trade statements of the number of licences granted, but the firms to which they have been granted are never divulged.

The system of export and import licences which is in practice in this country provides no real check. As we shall show, one of the main evils in the armament industry is connected with the solicitation of orders. Presumably armament factories and governments both prefer a considerable degree of secrecy about their relationships and about the whole traffic in arms ; all that they permit us to know is the bulk of the armament exports which leave the various ports. We cannot even be sure from these figures in what country the exported armaments are made, since in some cases (as, for instance, in that of exports from Hamburg which may really have come from the Skoda factories in Czechoslovakia) the arms may be made in one country and exported from another ; nor can we do more than guess how far government direction or encouragement leads to contracts being given to one rather than to another. Sometimes the relation is obvious. Where large credits have been given by a great Power to an economically dependent Power, we find, as we should expect, that the dependent Power buys its arms from its creditor. The case of France and the Little Entente is an obvious example. In such cases all parties are well satisfied. The small State gets its arms, the armament firms get the orders and know that they will be paid for, and the creditor Power gets its money back in the form of purchases and has the satisfaction of knowing that its small ally is equipped against their joint enemies in preparation for the expected war. From the great Powers' point of view such arrangements have the special advantage that the small Power which buys its armaments from a single great Power is thereby rendered completely dependent upon it for munitions of the same type. If France, for instance, supplies guns of a certain type with a particular bore to Rumania, Jugoslavia and Poland, the policy of these countries must be subservient to France because their supply of shells and accessories and munition replacements can only come from France. In general we may summarise by saying that armaments firms sell wherever there is a market and that Government control, in so far as they control at all, simply consists in seeing to it that certain markets, which they wish to see supplied by firms of their own nationality, have the necessary credit.

---

[1] *Hansard.* November 80, 1931. Col. 776.

Governments Would Not Dare

In 1928 a special commission set up by the League of Nations Assembly to draft a Convention for the Supervision of the Private Manufacture and Publicity of the Manufacture of Arms and Ammunition and Implements of War recommended that each Government " should undertake to transmit to the Secretary-General of the League, or to publish within two months after the close of each quarter," certain information about the armament licences granted.[1] This information included " the names of all the enterprises with which the holder (of the licence) has concluded agreements or associations of any kind whatsoever, with a view to the production of the articles of war material for which the licence has been granted." (Clause 2.) One objection raised was that the countries dependent on imports of armaments from abroad would be unable to keep private the nature of their war preparations while their manufacturing neighbours would enjoy all the advantages of secrecy. The British delegate gave several very illuminating reasons for refusing to accept this clause :—

> " In the first place my Government could not give this information ; they have not got it. Secondly, it is only the manufacturers—the licensees themselves—who could furnish it, and they would certainly refuse to do so. Thirdly, we have no power to compel them to do so, and, fourthly, very few Governments would have the courage to introduce legislation to make them do so."

The British representative was undoubtedly right in suggesting that very few governments would have the courage to introduce legislation to force armament manufacturers to divulge information about their work. The association of governments with armament firms is too close for such control and the investigation which would necessarily precede such legislation would be embarrassing. The public would discover, for instance, that officials in the fighting service and other administrative departments not infrequently passed on retirement, or before, into the service of armament firms. Philip Snowden in a speech on the Naval Estimates in 1914—if we may again quote from that classic and fruitful source—referred to a paper called *Armaments and Explosives* devoted to the interest of the armament trade. In the issue of this paper in September, 1913, there was the following extract :—

> " Contractors naturally are very keen to avail themselves of the services of prominent officers who have been associated with work in which the contractors are interested. The chief thing is that they know the ropes, since the retired officer who keeps in touch with his old comrades is able to lessen some of these inconveniences, either by securing the ear of one who would not afford like favours to a civilian. . . . Kissing undoubtedly goes by favour, and some of these things that happen might be characterised as corruption. Still, judged by all fair tests, the result is good. The organisation of facilities for supply is maintained through times of peace on an efficient and economical basis. Manufacturers do not make huge

---

[1] Article 4 reads :—

" The High Contracting Parties undertake to transmit to the Secretary-General of the League of Nations, or to publish within two months after the close of each quarter . . . a list of the licences granted during that quarter, together with :—
(a) A description of the war material for which the licence is granted ;
(b) The name and address of the registered or head office of the licensees and the period for which the licence has been granted.

profits, and they are enabled to survey from year to year, and to be on hand in the case of national emergency."

Had Philip Snowden been talking on the Naval Estimates in 1932, he could, without repeating his charge of corruption of which to-day there is no evidence, have abundantly illustrated the way in which high placed officials and soldiers in the fighting services become on retirement the Directors of armament firms. He could, for instance, have taken the Board of Directors of Vickers-Armstrongs as it stood on April 14, 1932.

General the Hon. Sir HERBERT LAWRENCE has been chairman of Vickers, Ltd., since 1926. He was formerly the Chief of Staff, Headquarters British Army in France, from January, 1918. After a distinguished military career in South Africa, in Egypt, in France and in the Dardanelles, he left the army on retired pay in 1922.

Sir MARK WEBSTER JENKINSON was the controller of the Department of Factory Audit and Costs at the Ministry of Munitions, and Chief Liquidator of Contracts at the Ministry of Munitions after the war.[1]

General Sir J. F. NOEL BIRCH, after a long military career, was Artillery Adviser to the Commander-in-Chief in France from 1916-1919. He was the Director of Remounts, 1920-21, Director-General of the Territorial Army, 1921-23, Master-General of the Ordnance and Member of the Army Council, 1923-27.

Sir J. A. COOPER was the Principal in Charge of Raw Materials Finance at the War Office from 1917-19, and then became the Director of Raw Materials Finance at the Ministry of Munitions from 1919-21.

Sir A. G. HADCOCK was an Associate Member of the Ordnance Committee, and like Commander C. W. Craven, Colonel J. B. Neilson and Major-General G. P. Dawnay and other directors had previous military experience.[2]

Armament Orders and their Value

The Navy Estimates may be quoted to give some idea of the valuable orders which the Government has placed with private firms even at a time when we are told that England alone has disarmed and that the service estimates are "cut to the bone." Section 3 of Vote 8 for the years mentioned shows that the following sums have been paid for contract work, the money coming from the pockets of the British taxpayers :—

Contract Work

1927 .. £8,839,423	1928 .. £8,263,060	1929 .. £7,291,217
1930 .. £5,532,728	1931 .. £4,456,200	1932 .. £5,193,200
	(Estimate)	(Estimate)

---

[1] On March 18, 1924, less than a month before the Disposal and Liquidation Commission was wound up, Mr. W. Graham, the then President of the Board of Trade, gave a reply in the House of Commons to the effect that the total sales of war materials had amounted to £670,000,000 and that the remaining materials were worth approximately £8,000,000.

[2] Mention must also be made of one of the most important people who have been associated with Vickers and Vickers-Armstrong. The late Sir Arthur Trevor Dawson, who was a director until the time of his death in May, 1931, was at one time Experimental Officer at Woolwich Arsenal, and was afterwards Superintendent of Ordnance to Vickers, and subsequently chairman of their Artillery and Ship-building Management Board.

Whilst the First Lord of the Admiralty in presenting the Navy Estimates on March 7, 1932, was complaining that the expenses were being reduced to their lowest level, he omitted any reference to the increase of £737,000 in the value of the work given to *private firms* for that year alone. In the Navy Estimates a programme is given of the work which is being carried out at present by contract as well as in Government dockyards. Messrs. William Beardmore & Co. are making a flotilla leader; Messrs. Vickers-Armstrong are making two destroyers, the "Swordfish" and the "Sturgeon." Submarines are being manufactured by Messrs. Yarrow & Co. and Messrs. Hawthorne Leslie. The cruiser "Achilles" is being made by Messrs. Cammell Laird, whilst Messrs. Hawthorne Leslie, Messrs. John Brown & Co., Messrs. Palmers Shipbuilding & Iron Co. and the Wallsend Slipway & Engineering Co. are busy making nine destroyers; Messrs. Parsons Marine Steam Turbine Co., nine destroyers; Messrs. Vickers-Armstrong, Messrs. John Thornycroft and the Fairfield Shipbuilding & Engineering Co. are engaged on the machinery for seventeen destroyers.

No information is given in the Army Estimates concerning the firms which are engaged in contract work. We are only told that there is a separate section of the War Office called the Army Contracts Directorate and that this is costing £33,620 in 1932. Similarly, in the Air Estimates there is an item of the Air Ministry called the "Directorate of Contracts" which is costing £37,802 in 1932.

Military aviation is in a slightly different position from land and sea armaments. Aerial warfare is new and it grew up during the war when governments were controlling and utilising the whole arms production of the country. Its overwhelming importance has, therefore, been realised from the beginning and an attempt has been made to keep its development strictly under Government supervision. The same forces, however, which have made it impossible for governments to keep the makers of land and sea armaments under their control have also forced them to relax their restrictions in the case of military aviation. In presenting the Estimates in the House of Commons in 1926,[1] Sir Samuel Hoare, then Minister of Air, explained the situation in suitable terms. He said:—

> "Obviously the aircraft industry is essential to the expansion of the Force in any time of emergency. It is no good denying the fact that the aircraft industry has many difficult problems to face. It is in a peculiarly difficult position through the fact that, unlike any other great industry in this or any other country, it is almost entirely dependent on the orders of a single Government Department. In the case of other great industries, there are private customers who give orders, and the industry is not entirely dependent on one Government Department. This means that in the case of the aircraft industry a change in Government policy reacts with particular force upon the industry because it has no other customer. . . .

> "I have been considering the position with my advisers, and have come to the conclusion that it is now safe and legitimate to withdraw many of these restrictions and, by this means, to enable British firms to sell their newer types in foreign markets a great deal sooner than they would be able to do without the withdrawal of the restrictions. I hope, as a result, it will be possible for the British firms to be less exclusively dependent on a single Government Department here, and that it will help them to build up for themselves markets abroad for British machines and British engines—than which there are no better anywhere in the world."

---

[1] *Hansard.* February 25, 1926. Cols. 770-771.

Since that date military aviation has made rapid progress in this country and British firms are beginning to lead the world trade. We have already mentioned the considerable orders placed with firms like the Fairey Aviation Co., the de Havilland Aircraft Co., Vickers (Aviation), Ltd., &c., by the Governments of practically every leading country in the world which does not produce its own war requirements.

The Government and the Chemical Industry

Lastly, there is the close association of the makers of chemical materials with the Government. We have already seen in Chapter II that the principal and interest of the 5 per cent. guaranteed debenture stock, 1930-45, of the Synthetic Ammonia & Nitrate Co. are guaranteed by His Majesty's Government, whilst the Government has a very considerable number of shares in the British Dyestuffs Corporation, Ltd., with which it keeps in close touch.

As a recent pamphlet[1] has accurately put it :—

" In almost every country in the world there exists a close association between the Governments and the chemical industries for control, collaboration, research, and subsidy. Chemical Warfare Research Committees link the chemical industries with the universities. In Britain the Chemical Warfare Committee connects up the National Physical Laboratory, Imperial College of Science and Technology, and the Department of Scientific and Industrial Research (D.S.I.R.). On the Chemical Warfare Committee are many of Britain's most prominent chemical manufacturers. Similar Chemical Warfare Committees exist in France, Italy, Poland, Japan, and U.S.A. Chemical supplies for munitions, explosives, and poison gas in Britain are almost entirely in the hands of the Chemical Combine (I.C.I.) who control most of the dye works—90 per cent. explosives production, 100 per cent. of alkalis (sodas). This chemical combine stands as a menace to the peace of the peoples."

The Profits of Armaments

One of the charges brought by the League Commission against armament rings was that they had kept up the price of armaments. Clearly, they are in a very strong position to do so. They combine the advantages of international co-operation with those of a close, secret, and personal connection with national Governments. When the war itself came the international rings were necessarily broken up for the time, but the component firms could at first charge almost anything they liked both from their own Governments and from their Allies, which suddenly found themselves in need of an immense quantity of munitions. Great Britain, above all, supplied all her Allies with astronomical loans for this purpose.

The size of the profits made in these circumstances by armament firms has never been published. It is not surprising that by the terms of the Munitions Act of 1915, which temporarily carried out a part-nationalisation of the armament industry, the profits of private shareholders were limited to 20 per cent., which was the average pre-war figure. Some estimate of what this 20 per cent. represented during the war itself may be made from

---

[1] *The Menace of Chemical Warfare to Civilian Populations*, by A. J. Gillian. (Chemical Workers' Union. 2d.)

a reply given by the Chancellor of the Exchequer to a question in the House of Commons.[1]

A study of the history of the Ministry of Munitions and the contracts that were placed during the war provide abundant information on which to base some estimate of the enormous profits that are made by armament firms when all their plans and preparations have proved successful and the country is thrown into a war. Here is a specimen of an early war contract for ·303 Ammunition Mark VII, showing the position within a month of the time of the outbreak of war at the end of August, 1914.[2]

Firm	Contract	Rate for delivery	Quantity
Birmingham Metal & Munitions Co.	C/7749	per month 500,000	3 million
	C/8134	per week 2,500,000	48 million
Messrs. Greenwood & Batley	C/7749	per month 875,000	7 million
	C/8134	per week 1,000,000	18 million
King's Norton Metal Co., Ltd.	C/7749	per month 750,000	4 million
	C/8134	per week 1,800,000	32 million
Messrs. Eley Bros. ..	C/7749	per week 158,000	6 million
	C/8134	per week 375,000	8 million
Messrs Kynoch, Ltd. ..	C/7749	per mth. 2,000,000	
	C/8134	1,000,000 in 4 weeks then 2,400,000 pr. week	48 million

A further remark may be made about these profits. Dr. Addison, who was Minister of Munitions after 1916, has pointed out in his book *Practical Socialism*[3] that the cost to the State of buying munitions from private

---

[1] Statement showing for the United Kingdom the gross receipt repayments and net receipt of the Excess Profits Duty and Munitions Levy during each year they were in operation :—

Year	Gross Receipt	Repayments	Net Receipts
	Excess Profits Duty		
	£	£	£
1915–16	187,846	—	187,846
1916–17	138,008,790	1,182,494	136,826,296
1917–18	205,777,184	3,635,271	202,131,913
1918–19	268,891,916	7,280,920	261,610,996
1919–20	296,778,885	13,006,679	283,772,206
1920–21	234,724,592	17,579,212	217,145,380
1921–22	122,142,427	91,664,614	80,477,813
	Munitions Levy		
	£	£	£
1916–17	4,788,636	—	4,788,636
1917–18	21,234,065	259,888	20,974,177
1918–19	22,658,039	292,174	22,365,865
1919–20	5,617,723	181,883	5,435,840
1920–21	1,401,323	447,575	953,748
1921–22	200,468	1,007,589	−807,121

As regards the current financial year, the gross receipts of Excess Profits Duty (including Munitions Levy) from April 1, 1922, to February 28, 1923, is approximately £49,500,000 ; the net receipts during the same period amounts to slightly over £1,000,000. I regret that I am unable to forecast the amount of repayments to be made in the future.—*Hansard.* March 6, 1923. Col. 244.

[2] *History of the Ministry of Munitions.* Vol. 1, page 73.

[3] *Practical Socialism*, by C. Addison. (Labour Publishing Company. 2 vols. 1s. each.)

manufacturers was consistently greater than when it bought them from national factories.

He quotes cordite as an illustration, and bases his claim on the *Findings of the Costings Commission during the War.* He says :—

" Up to the spring of 1916 certain main types of cordite had cost 2s. 3d. per lb., but the accountants reported, in the case of a propellant factory—to the provision of which the firm had contributed £464,000 —that the price being obtained represented a dividend of 105·7 per cent. per annum on this capital. It was further pointed out that if the money being obtained were used to write off the whole cost of the factory to a scrap value of £16,000 the firm would still have received sufficient to pay dividends of 33·8 per cent. per annum.

" . . . There is no need to tell the details of the story, but the end result was that the cordite was reduced to 1s. 7¾d. per lb. and the savings on the year's supply of cordite on that basis, as compared with the former price, amounted to £3,900,000 . . ."

Dr. Addison showed that savings on typical contracts were as follows :—

	Original price	*Price after investigation*
Filling fuses	£1 4s. 0d. per 100	12s. 0d.
Filling 4·5 Lyddite shells	£18 16s. 8d. per 100	£7 18s. 4d.

Dr. Addison gives further examples, including that of the production of T.N.T. By the saving of 1d. per lb. a weekly gain was achieved of no less than £9,000 for each thousand tons.

" The capital cost of the six T.N.T. factories was £1,473,000, but by April, 1917, they had already produced T.N.T. which, as against contract prices, had given a surplus of £2,404,318. They had, therefore, completely wiped out their total cost of provision and had left a balance over of 83 per cent. . . . Extending our summary to all the national factories provided up to April, 1917, and comparing the prices—not with the inflated prices obtained as the result of the application of the costing methods—we could already record a gain of £10,000,000. It appears that all the capital costs had been repaid by the end of 1918, whilst many of the individual factories had repaid theirs long before that date."

Mr. Lloyd George himself summarised the situation in a speech in the House of Commons on August 18, 1919. He said :—

" The 18-pounder, when the Ministry " (of Munitions) " was started, cost 22s. 6d. a shell. A system of costing and investigation was introduced, and national factories were set up which checked the prices, and a shell for which the War Office, at the time the Ministry was formed, cost 22s. 6d. was reduced to 12s., and when you have 85,000,000 of shells that saved £35,000,000. There was a reduction in the price of all other shells, and there was a reduction in the Lewis guns. When we took them in hand they cost £165, and we reduced them to £35 each. There was a saving of £14,000,000, and through the costing system and the checking of the national factories we set up, before the end of the war there was a saving of £440,000,000."

When we remember the total production of the English armament industry during the war and the magnitude of the profits involved perhaps we ought not to be surprised that profiteering flourished in armament-making just as it flourished in many other industries in war time.

It is interesting also to note the share of the American armament firms in the profits of the European War. They are indicated in the approximate value of the contracts which were placed by Messrs. J. P. Morgan & Co. According to the history of the Ministry of Munitions they amounted to 2,063,350,000 dollars during the period 1914-1918.

In a world which prepares for war such a relationship as we have described between armament firms and Governments is of great value to both parties. The private firms sell to their own Government at good prices, they enjoy the benefit of having Government experts on their Boards who know exactly what the Government plans for war are and see that the firms provide for them ; the Government, on its side, knows that, by permitting the firms to sell abroad, they have within their boundaries an organisation far greater and more elastic than they could pay for out of taxation, and that its equipment includes just those types of weapons which its experts consider most necessary for the expected war. That this method also means that its enemies are similarly equipped seems only incidental.

Chapter V

WAR SCARES
AND
ARMAMENT CONTRACTS

COMPETITIVE arming is one of the acknowledged causes of war, and enough has been said in the preceding chapters to show that some of those who benefit financially from the sale of arms find various methods of stimulating such competition. The ramifications of armament firms into other businesses, the social influence of their titled directors, their connections with important personages, with Members of Parliament, and, most important of all, with the Press provide many opportunities for unostentatious persuasion and propaganda. The position of M. Wendel of the *Temps*, the *Journal des Débats*, and of the *Comité des Forges* on which is represented all the leading French steel and armament firms, has been already cited. In this country the connection of armament manufacturers with the Press is less obvious, though the attitude of several English newspapers during the Disarmament Conference has given rise to some speculation, and the fact that the Balkan representatives of one of the most famous English newspapers have been also the local agents of Vickers-Armstrongs is little known, but authentic. There are many other methods of propaganda. "Backward countries," for instance, have to be induced to buy arms and so prepare themselves for the "unavoidable" little frontier wars which occur on the edges of every Empire. When King Amanullah, the King of Afghanistan, visited this country, he was conducted round British armament factories and placed very considerable orders on his return to Afghanistan.[1] Since his dethronement, no doubt, the same arms have been serviceably used against British troops on the frontier. The cinema is one of the latest devices for increasing the traffic in arms. How would Balkan States know what arms to buy if they were not educated by the armament rings ? The *North Mail* (December 5, 1931) reports that :—

> "A special of British films was given to the King and Queen of Jugoslavia in their new palace at Dedinje. The films were productions made by a British firm of armament makers. There were tanks of all kinds, as well as field guns of all calibres and tractors.

---

[1] According to the *Daily Mail* of October 8, 1928, King Amanullah held a Durbar at Kabul after his return from this and other western countries :—

> "The King gave a short résumé of his travels abroad, emphasising the purchases made by him of factory equipment and armaments. Among the latter he enumerated 53,500 rifles, 106 guns, 6 machine guns as samples, 6 tanks and 5 armoured cars."

" A firm of shipbuilders also showed a film of the launching of a Jugoslav warship. These films were shown to the Jugoslav Minister and 200 of his senior officers.

" The *Evening Chronicle* learns that Messrs. Vickers-Armstrong, Ltd., are principally interested in Jugoslavia's pending naval contracts, and that the film referred to is probably one from Barrow-in-Furness. The Barrow works and shipyards of Vickers-Armstrong possess their own cinema theatre, where films are exhibited dealing with constructional works. A representative of the firm is in Jugoslavia at the present. The firm of Yarrow & Co., Ltd., on the River Clyde, were also interested in Jugoslavia, and are reported to have a warship under construction for the Government of that country at the present time."

Activities of this kind can be noticed by any observer. Occasionally accident brings to light other methods of salesmanship which are described as scandals and made the subject of public investigation. That activities of this kind may at any time be brought to light is suggested by the recent " Swedish Air Force Scandals," which *The Times* of November 11, 1931, describes as follows :—

" After eight months' inquiry the commissioners appointed by the Government to investigate alleged irregularities in the Swedish Air Force handed their report of 350 pages to the Minister of Defence yesterday. The findings have been given wide publicity to-day by the entire Press.

" The commissioners recommend that new officers should be appointed to succeed General Amundson, Chief of the Air Force ; Colonel Fogman, commanding the military section of the Corps ; Engineer Fjallback, technical officer ; and Commander Lubeck, Chief of Staff, whom they find unsuited for the posts. Proceedings will probably be taken against Commander Lubeck who will in that case be tried by court-martial. The commissioners found that bribes to the extent of 16,000 kronor had been accepted by Commander Lubeck in the form of ' long loans.' Some of the money, the report alleges, was received from the representative of an aircraft firm. The commissioners pass judgment on nothing for which there is no proof, and their report has revealed an almost incredible state of affairs within the Air Force higher command."

Big Navy Scare of 1909

1909 is the date of the best known of all armament scares. Trade was bad, unemployment rising and the dividends of armament firms beginning to fall.

At this point Mr. H. H. Mulliner must be introduced. Mr. Mulliner was then managing director of the Coventry Ordnance Co. In *The Times* of January 3, 1910, he published the " Diary of the Great Surrender " and these two entries provide an interesting insight into his work :—

" May 13, 1906.—Mr. Mulliner first informs the Admiralty of preparations for enormously increasing the German Navy. (This information was concealed from the nations until March, 1909.)

" May 8, 1909.—Mr. Mulliner, giving evidence before the Cabinet, proves that the acceleration in Germany for producing armaments, about which he had perpetually warned the Admiralty, was an accomplished fact, and that large quantities of naval guns and mountings were being made with great rapidity in that country."

In the autumn of 1908 Mr. Mulliner was able to reach the ear of one of the leading generals, who in the House of Lords subsequently prophesied " a terrible awakening in store for us at no distant date."

On March 3, 1908, Mr. Mulliner was solemnly received by the Cabinet in council assembled at Downing Street. Ten days later a statement concerning the Navy Estimates was published, showing a total of £35,142,700 for 1909-10, an increase of £2,823,200. These estimates and subsequent debates on them in the House of Commons give strong evidence of the success of Mr. Mulliner's secret campaign based on untrue information.

The calculations made on Germany's dreadnoughts and cruisers were so skilfully made and published in the newspapers, in Parliament and elsewhere that it produced the scare with its favourite slogan : " We want eight and we won't wait."

Events subsequently proved the falsehood of the charges against the German Government, and yet on July 26 four battleships (which, in March, the British Government had obtained contingent on its fears of German acceleration being justified) were announced, and one of the first contracts was given to Cammell Laird, which partly owned Coventry Ordnance Co. (managing director, Mr. H. H. Mulliner).

Mr. Mulliner subsequently admitted the authorship of the scare and his visit to Downing Street.

This indiscretion cost him his post and he was succeeded as managing director by Rear-Admiral R. H. S. Bacon, C.V.O., D.S.O., who had been Naval Assistant to the First Sea Lord and from 1907 to 1909 Director of Naval Ordnance and Torpedoes. This experience was no doubt useful to him: in any case he was subsequently able to obtain large Government orders for the Coventry Ordnance Co.

At the Annual Meeting of John Brown & Co. (which had large holdings in the Coventry Ordnance Co.) on July 1, 1913, Lord Aberconway said :—

"Coventry was improving, but it was a great drag on their finances, and would be for some time. The place was now fully recognised by the Government as an essential part of the national armament works. Last autumn he went over the Scotson works, where they made the heavy naval mountings, with Mr. Winston Churchill, who gave him an assurance—which he carried out—that Coventry would now be regarded as one of the most important supplying firms for the Government, instead of being cold-shouldered, as it was for many years past."[1]

The Mitsui-Vickers Case

The Mitsui-Vickers Case in 1914 is another illustration of the methods employed by armament firms to obtain orders. The *Japan Weekly Chronicle* during June and July, 1914, gave a detailed account of the case and showed to what extent bribery was used to get orders from Japan. This is the story.

---

[1] The whole story is told in *The War Traders* by G. H. Perris. But Mr. Perris somewhat overstates his case. Compare the account of the incident in the *Memoirs of Prince von Bülow*, Vol. II.

In March, 1910, the accused, Rear-Admiral Fujii, was appointed to visit England as officer for the Supervision of the Construction of Warships, with an order to report on the estimates and specifications sent by Armstrong and Vickers of a battleship-cruiser which the Japanese Navy Department proposed to build. He examined the estimates and specifications and reported to the Naval Stores Department on August 9, adding that the Vickers specification was the more precise and the price was lower. In October it was decided to order the ship from Vickers and the contract was signed between the Japanese Government and Vickers on November 17 at the cost of £2,367,100. Subsequently it turned out that the Director of Messrs. Vickers Works at Barrow, who was on intimate terms with Rear-Admiral Fujii, asked him to show his good will towards Vickers in obtaining the contract. After the accused's return to Japan, the Director of the Barrow Yard, with a view to reciprocating his good will, remitted over a period of years certain large sums of money to Admiral Fujii.

But although Vickers gave the biggest " remittances " for contracts gained, other firms used the same methods. For example, there is the following story concerning Messrs. Yarrow. At the beginning of 1911, when Naval Constructor Yanamoto Kaizo was visiting England, A. F. Yarrow, president of the Yarrow Shipbuilding Yard, saw him and explained the superiority of a destroyer fitted for the consumption of oil fuel which was the latest invention of the yard, and supplied a plan of it, expressing at the same time his desire to get an order from the Japanese Navy. The specification was sent to the Stores Department and following this further remittances were sent to Rear-Admiral Fujii. Subsequently the order was given to the Yarrow firm, and on December 27, 1912, a contract was signed between the Japanese Government and the Yarrow Yard for the construction of two destroyers.

But it was not alone from Vickers and from Yarrow that Rear-Admiral Fujii accepted bribes. Arrol & Co. paid him £1,750 on August 27, 1912, following an order for materials worth £33,621 16s. 9d. bought from them by the Japanese Government, whilst Weir & Co. sent a remittance of £1,000 in August, 1911, and this was followed by an order by the Japanese Government for six pumps and other machines used on a battleship which was in construction on their behalf.

These exposures were made in Court in 1914. Mr. Pooley, the correspondent of Reuter in Tokyo, bought from Richter, who was formerly an employee of Siemens-Schuckert, secret papers which showed the delivery, or promise of delivery, of bribes between Siemens Bros., London, and Rear-Admiral Fujii (Mitsugoro). During the case it was shown from the evidence of a Japanese named Kaga that there was an elaborate system of bribery in connection with armament firms and his evidence showed that the sums mentioned had been received by Rear-Admiral Fujii.

Corruption may not be the necessary consequence of private armament-makers, but it has unfortunately often been proved that armament firms have used corruption to secure Government contracts. In an article on the Japanese Naval Scandals entitled " Corruptive Competition," the *Japan Weekly Chronicle*, of July 23, 1914, observed :—

> " There is no nation which can afford to throw stones at Japan in connection with the existence of bribery and corruption in State services. Only recently a series of scandals in connection with the supply of stores to the British military canteens was brought into publicity in the courts, and the firm concerned . . . has been struck off the lists of Government contractors. In Germany and other

countries there have been cases equally unsavoury, until it has been made clear that the 'profession' of arms has become as sordidly money-grubbing as it possibly can. It would even seem that, in some countries, it is absolutely essential to resort to practices which, if not actually criminal, are grossly immoral, if any business is to be done by contractors anxious to get orders. Even when an order is obtained, it is sometimes necessary to resort to further corruption."

Armament Scandals in Germany

Several armament scandals were brought to light in the Reichstag by Karl Liebknecht in 1913. For instance, the work of a certain man named Brandt was exposed on April 18, 1913,[1] when Liebknecht explained :—

> " For several weeks now Krupp has employed an agent by the name of Brandt, a former artillery officer, whose business is to approach executive officials of the Government, of the Army and the Navy, and to bribe them for access to private papers in which the firm of Krupp happens to be interested, and able to discover the plans of the Government with regard to armaments, to obtain sketches of construction for internal defence, and to ascertain what rival firms were bidding or had bidden in the past. In order to carry out this purpose, Herr Brandt is, of course, granted a generous allowance."

The reports made by Brandt were signed by the name of Kornwalzer, hence the affair was called " The Krupp-Kornwalzer Affair." Liebknecht's exposure was verified and Brandt was sentenced to prison for four months on a charge of bribery. Eccius, a director of Krupp, was fined 1,200 marks for aiding and abetting.

The second scandal in Germany exposed by Karl Liebknecht and described in *War for Profits*, by Lehmann Russbüldt, concerned Herr von Gontard, one of the most powerful men in the German armament industry at that time. He was on the board of directors of the Berlin-Karlsruhe Industrial Works, Ludwig Loewe, Incorporated, &c., and was the chief secret witness in the Bullerjahn case. Bullerjahn was in charge of the warehouse of a magazine belonging to the Berlin-Karlsruhe Industrial Works and was accused of betraying secrets and, therefore, of being a traitor to his country.

In 1907, as it was shown in the Reichstag Debates (Vol. 147, page 5050) on April 23, 1913, a letter had been written from the German Arms and Munitions Factory in Karlsruhe, signed by the Director of Construction, asking that an article should be published in the French newspapers saying that the Chief of Staff of the French Army had decided to hasten re-equipment of the army with machine guns, and to order double the amount that had been previously contemplated. The intention was to stimulate the demand in Germany for machine guns.

The *Berliner Tageblatt* and the *Frankfurter Zeitung* openly referred to these commercial practices as " business unscrupulousness of an extreme sort, and a blind pursuit of pure egoistic and mercenary interests."

---

[1] *Reichstag Debates*, Vol. 143, page 4911. This is reported in full in *War for Profits*, by Lehmann Russbüldt.

The Putiloff Scandal

The Putiloff scandal concerns, mainly, France and Russia, although there is no doubt that English firms, particularly Vickers, through their agent, Sir Basil Zaharoff, were involved as well. In June, 1912, the Russian Duma had voted £130,000,000 for the building of a new fleet. Although the Duma demanded that orders for armaments should be given as far as possible to Russian firms, it was obviously impossible for them to carry out the whole scheme. Thereupon a race began on the part of international armament firms and Schneider-Creusot had a particularly good claim because the greater part of the money which was being spent on armaments had been raised in France. Further, in 1910, when the Putiloff Works in St. Petersburg were reorganised, Schneider-Creusot had taken over £1,000,000 of shares. But the biggest share of the order was obtained by Vickers through their agent, Zaharoff.

In January, 1914, the St. Petersburg correspondent of the *Echo de Paris* published a false report that Krupp was planning to acquire the Putiloff Works. The false report is said to have been provoked by Raffalovich in collusion with Suchomlinoff, the Russian Minister of War, after an understanding had been arrived at with Zaharoff. There was immediate panic among the armament firms in England, France and in Germany, and excitement in Paris was only allayed when subsequently the news was sent through from St. Petersburg that the Putiloff Works required another £2,000,000, and would be pleased if they could obtain it from Schneider-Creusot.

Schneider-Creusot accordingly put the required capital at the disposal of Putiloff and at the same time a new Russian loan of £25,000,000 was raised in France. Vickers, Ltd., were able to obtain their share, and *The Times* Paris correspondent of January 29, 1914, was able to announce that during the preceding months orders to the amount of about £6,500,000 had gone to Great Britain.[1]

The Shearer Case

Let us now consider the case of Mr. Shearer. This is the one great post-war scandal which has come to light. Its importance was not that it proved anything new about corruption in the United States, but that it showed that armament firms are willing to pay large sums of money to skilled propagandists to prevent the progress of disarmament at Geneva. Shearer is really the modern equivalent of Brandt, the agent of Krupps, whose exposure by Karl Liebknecht in the Reichstag before the war we have already mentioned.

Mr. Shearer was an American publicist who had had an eventful career as a lobbyist for a big navy and merchant marine, as a promoter of night clubs, theatres, and an ally of bootleggers. In 1929 Mr. Shearer sued the three largest shipbuilding corporations in America—the Bethlehem Shipbuilding Corporation, the Newport News Shipbuilding & Drydock Co., and the American Brown Boveri Corporation—for $255,655, the balance due to him for his services (which he held with reason to have been successfully rendered) in preventing any effective disarmament resulting from the Naval Conference in Geneva in 1927. He admitted that he had already received $51,230. He claimed the remainder as a reward for his skill in influencing orders for battleships that would never have seen the Atlantic if the Disarmament Conference had proved successful. Like the Mayor and

---

[1] The story is told in full in the *War Traders*, by G. P. Perris, and *Sir Basil Zaharoff*, by Richard Lewinsohn.

Corporation of Hamlin, the armament manufacturers were rid of the plague that threatened them and unwilling to pay their agent his full reward. Mr. Shearer had piped his tune and was not to be denied his guelders.

In September, 1929, President Hoover instructed the Attorney-General to make an inquiry, and shortly afterwards Eugene Grace, who was then president of the Bethlehem Shipbuilding Corporation, wrote to President Hoover explaining that he and Mr. C. M. Schwartz, chairman of the board of directors of the Bethlehem Steel Corporation (a subsidiary company), had employed Mr. Shearer as an " observer " at the fee of $25,000.

These duties have been conveniently summarised as follows[1] :—

(1) For the employment of an " observer " at the Geneva Arms Conference, who, whatever the terms of the " oral contract " under which he was hired, was notoriously engaged in violent anti-British propaganda, in doing his best to defeat arms limitation, in entertaining naval officers and American newspaper correspondents, in stimulating " the marine industry, both for navy and the merchant marine " (to use his own words, Sen. Doc. p. 450), in sending out literature designed to discredit American advocates of peace, and in inserting his " publicity " in reputable American newspapers, such as the *New York Times*, under the guise of news (*ibid.* p. 542).

(2) For the purpose of influencing federal legislation by maintaining a lobby in Washington in support of cruiser and merchant-marine bills pending in Congress.

(8) For the preparation of political articles to be published in newspapers and magazines.

(4) For lectures before patriotic societies and other civic organisations.

(5) For the employment of " experts " and other workers, whose exact activities are unknown.

(6) For addresses before the American Legion, Chambers of Commerce and similar organisations (*ibid.* p. 685).

But for the greed of Mr. Shearer, the fact that such methods were being used by armament firms to promote the sales of armaments would never have been known to the mass of persons likely to suffer violent deaths through the world's failure to disarm. It is interesting to note that Mr. Shearer has been seen in Geneva during the 1982 Disarmament Conference.

Without access to any private information we have been able to show that armament firms have been at one time or another open to each of the charges made against them by the League of Nations Commission. We have cited definite cases in which they have fomented war scares in order to increase the sale of arms, attempted to bribe Government officials, disseminated false reports concerning military and naval programmes in order to stimulate armament expenditure, sought to influence public opinion through the control of newspapers, played off one country against another in order to stimulate the traffic in arms, and induced Governments to pay more for their armaments than they would have done had the arms been under Government control. We have given specific instances of each of these activities. The scandals are instances which have happened to come to light.

---

[1] Vide *The Navy : Defence or Portent*, by Charles A. Beard. (Harper Bros. $2.) Mr. Beard analyses the whole Shearer inquiry.

Chapter VI

THE BLOODY INTERNATIONAL

WE have gained from this survey a rough idea of the interests at stake in this business of armaments; we have seen these firms with their international ramifications working with, above and against Governments, counteracting by means of propaganda and underground influence the feeble attempts so far made to promote disarmament. The science of warfare has become, as Mr. H. G. Wells has put it,[1] " a very active occupation. It is a sort of ugly and dwarfish twin sister of scientific research. The difference is that she tries to be secretive and her ends are murderous. She is perpetually seeking to seize and pervert scientific advances."

The Investment Class

Who reaps the harvest of this research and salesmanship ? Well, first, the Undershafts and Lazaruses, the Krupps and Zaharoffs, the international armament makers, multi-millionaires above patriotism or responsibility, men whose wealth and influence is incalculable and founded on the accomplished or prospective deaths of a large number of their neighbours. Secondly, the thousands of persons in all ranks of life who, as lesser shareholders, play no part in policy, but benefit by the sale of arms. In Vickers, Ltd., for instance, which is the holding Company for Vickers-Armstrongs, there are 80,000 shareholders. An examination of the lists of shareholders in Somerset House shows that there are persons in every class of society who stand to profit financially by an increase in the sale of arms. The list is an extraordinary one ; there are politicians and publicists, Cabinet Ministers, leading Members of Parliament, titled persons and humble people in every station of life. Oddly enough there is a noticeably high proportion of clergymen. It may be of interest to mention a few of the better-known shareholders, with the number of shares added after their names. These have been taken from the lists of shareholders in the Annual Return of Vickers, and were mentioned as holding shares on April 18, 1932 :—

Lord Hailsham, Secretary of State for War	210
[2] The Rt. Hon. Sir John Gilmour, M.P., Minister of Agriculture	8,066
Sir Robert Horne, M.P.	5,000
The Rt. Rev. C. L. Carr, Bishop of Hereford..	1,010
Earl Dysart	40,000
Lord Joicey, who is associated with the Lambton Collieries, Ltd., in Durham	20,000
Lord Plender, who has been engaged on many important committees dealing with military and civil matters, and was a Member of the May Economy Committee	7,050
Lord Dulverton	15,000
Mr. Wardlaw Milne, M.P.	3,000

---

[1] *The Work, Wealth and Happiness of Mankind*, by H. G. Wells. (Heinemann. 10s. 6d.)

[2] Now Secretary of State for the Home Department (October, 1932).

Other well-known names, selected at random, are The Rt. Hon. Mr. Justice Horridge, Mr. Stuart Bevan, K.C., M.P., and Sir John Lavery, R.A.

Naturally, the largest block of shares is held by the Vickers family. Mr. Douglas Vickers, who is one of the directors, himself holds 57,000 shares and shares with others over 90,000.

Now most of these persons must be quite innocent of any desire to slaughter their neighbours. Like the scientists who spend their lives in poison gas research without considering the purpose to which their skill is to be put, they draw their dividends without realising what kind of trade it is by which they profit. One may be sure that workers in the League of Nations Union who hold shares in armament firms are not conscious of any inconsistency ; they certainly do not want to increase the chances of war, but their interests and their financial influence are in fact directed to that end. Some who hold armament shares may believe that they are patriotic supporters of the Empire and might be surprised to learn that they are partners in an international business whose object is our mutual destruction.

There is a third economic interest concerned in the upkeep of arms, as Commander Kenworthy once remarked in the House of Commons[1] :—

> " It is not only a case of the capitalists who have money invested in armament-making firms being concerned, but there are also the employés and the satellites and all the people for whom they provide work and wages interested in this matter, and until the private manufacture of and traffic in arms can be controlled, or, better still, abolished, there will also be an agitation for more armaments, which in the long run means an agitation for war."

Any far-reaching proposals for disarmament will necessarily meet with opposition from those financially interested in the upkeep of arms. We have seen that there are three such classes of people. First, the employees of armament firms who have no interest in the matter provided other work is found for them. As to the argument that disarmament means unemployment, it has been calculated that if warships over 10,000 tons were abolished and if this meant paying 25,000 naval officers and men out of jobs and if these men were paid on pension (*all* of them regardless of employment) at an average rate of £1 *a day for life*, this would work out *much* cheaper than maintaining and replacing the ships. Secondly, the shareholders, most of whom are both innocent and ignorant of the nature of the armament business. Many of them would be horrified to be told that they formed an armament class. Neither of these would offer any opposition to disarmament if they understood the issue at stake.

Finally, we must consider the small body of big international capitalists who control the armament rings. Is the situation in this respect really very different from that described by Mr. Snowden in the speech we have already quoted ? He referred to a denunciation by Lord Welby of the people who were opposed to any better international co-operation. He said[2] :—

> " What . . . is the obstacle in the way of better understanding ? Lord Welby, who has held the highest and most responsible position as a permanent Civil Servant in this country . . . was speaking on this question a few weeks ago, and he said :—
>
>> ' We are in the hands of an organisation of crooks. They are politicians, generals, manufacturers of armaments and journalists.

---

[1] *Hansard.* July 14, 1924. Col. 149.

[2] *Hansard.* March 17, 1914.

All of them are anxious for unlimited expenditure, and go on inventing scares to terrify the public and to terrify Ministers of the Crown.' "

After referring to the M.P. for the Hallam Division of Sheffield who was then a debenture trustee for Vickers and also for Cammell Laird & Co., Mr. Snowden continued :—

"Now, who are the shareholders ? It would be too long for me to give more than a very short selection from the list, but I find that hon. Members in this House are very largely concerned. Indeed, it would be impossible to throw a stone on the benches opposite without hitting a Member who is a shareholder in one or other of these firms. . . . The hon. Member for the Osgoldcross Division of Yorkshire . . . I congratulate him on his election last week as hon. President of the Free Church Council . . . is the great imperialist. . . . I find that he is the holder of 3,200 shares in John Brown's and 2,100 shares in Cammell Laird's. Another of the Members for Sheffield figures in practically every list, as he figures in every debate of this House when there is a possibility of more money being spent on arms and ships. I refer to the Member for the Ecclesall Division (Mr. S. Roberts). He is a shareholder in John Brown's, a director of Cammell Laird, also debenture trustee of the Fairfield Co., and a shareholder in the Coventry Ordnance Works."

The Public Control of Armaments

We have said enough to explain why Lord Cecil said not long ago that " one of the most vital problems to be solved by the League is the suppression of the private manufacture of arms and the control of the traffic in arms." Thirteen years have passed since the people who drafted the Covenant of the League of Nations realised the importance of this question.[1] Ten years have gone by since the League Commission[2] summarised the evils that attend the private manufacture of arms. During the Disarmament Conference in Geneva proposals have been made from time to time that the question of private manufacture should be included in the agenda as a subject with some bearing on the general problem. Thus Spain suggested that in the Disarmament Convention there should be incorporated :—

    (i) The Convention of 1925 on the supervision of the trade in arms and ammunition ;

    (ii) A Convention providing for both international and national supervision of the private and state manufacture of arms and

---

[1] Article 8 of the Covenant reads :—

"The Members of the League agree that the manufacture by private enterprise of munitions and implements of war is open to grave objections. The Council shall advise how the evil effects attendant upon such manufacture can be prevented, due regard being had to the necessities of those Members of the League which are not able to manufacture the munitions and implements of war necessary for their safety.

"The Members of the League undertake to interchange full and frank information as to the scale of their armaments, their military, naval and air programmes and the condition of such of their industries as are adaptable to war-like purposes."

It was also agreed that regulations concerning the traffic in arms must be one of the objects of the League of Nations and Article 23, Clause D, reads :—

"The Members of the League will entrust the League with the general supervision of the trade in arms and ammunition with the countries in which control of this traffic is necessary in the common interest."

[2] See page 5.

ammunition, such manufacture to be subject to a system of licensing and publicity.

Germany proposed a strict prohibition of export and import of arms and ammunition and war material, except in countries which produced only small quantities, when special facilities would be given. A second proposal urged that manufacture should only be carried out in a limited number of recognised private or State factories.

Switzerland suggested that agreement should be concluded concerning manufacture, whether private or individual, and Norway suggested supervision of both private and governmental manufacture and trade. Czechoslovakia made a statement that she was prepared to adopt a stricter supervision than that allowed for in the Draft Convention. A reorganisation of armament factories with their wise distribution was advocated by Turkey, whilst Russia made important proposals, including detailed provisions for a Permanent International Commission of Control. There is as yet no sign that these proposals will be seriously considered.

And, with regard to the traffic in arms, seven years have passed since the Arms Traffic Conference in Geneva drew up the Arms Traffic Convention which only comes into force when fourteen Powers have ratified it. So far this has not happened, and " Great Britain, as has been frequently stated in the House of Commons, is not prepared to ratify unless the other leading arms-producing States agree to do so simultaneously."[1]

The advantages of making armaments production a State monopoly, which would necessarily follow any scheme to put arms under international control, but which could be carried out by individual States even without internationalisation, are sufficiently obvious. The sinister influence of armament firms would disappear ; the secret encouragement of fear and of militarism in each nation by armament firms ; the bribery of journalists and officials ; the opposition to disarmament by interested persons in every country—all this would disappear. The taxpayers' interest in economy would act as a more efficient check on militant patriotism. There would be no vested interest in war ; no class of persons waiting to reap financial advantages from slaughter.

So far the steps taken towards public control of armaments are only laughable.[2] Armament manufacturers have not been in any way inconvenienced as a result of the acceptance by the British and several other Governments of a rule that the manufacture and export of arms must be licensed by the State. So far this rule has been carried out to the complete satisfaction of manufacturers and Governments.

It is, in fact, nothing but a war provision. It provides the Government with useful information, and it would, if a war was imminent, enable a

---

[1] *Traffic in Arms*, 1928, No. 269. League of Nations Union.

[2] The First Sub-Committee of the Temporary Mixed Commission made several suggestions for the control of the private manufacture of arms which included the following :—

1. No manufacture without a licence.
2. No exports or imports of arms without a licence.
3. All licences to be registered at the League of Nations.
4. All company shares to be registered and no bearer shares to be issued.
5. All accounts to be publicly audited and published.
6. Those in control of private manufacture should be prevented from controlling or influencing newspapers, &c.

Government to stop the last-minute provision of arms to an enemy power. Similarly, it is childish to imagine that the compulsory publication of shareholders, also recommended by the League and already legally required in this country, can act as any safeguard. Few people know anything about the lists in Somerset House, and even those who consult them are not much wiser about the individualities concealed under the names of banks which hold large blocks of shares. Nor does the fact that the balance sheets of armament firms, most of which are public companies, have to be audited and published keep any armament manufacturers awake at night. Auditors combine discretion with accuracy and we have not needed a Hatry case to prove how easily even the most honest and efficient auditors can be prevented from discovering the less public or reputable activities of the firms whose accounts they audit. And if auditors themselves are ignorant, how much can the public know of the facts concealed by innocent words such as " depreciation," " reserve," " investments in subsidiary companies," and so on ?

The recommendation of the Commission that " those in control of private manufacture should be prevented from controlling or influencing newspapers " is a charming piece of *naïveté*. One does not need to hold shares in a newspaper in one's own name to influence its policy. It might be possible legally to prevent any one holding the position now occupied by M. de Wendel in the French Press, but even so you cannot prevent armament manufacturers being the friends and the financial backers of newspaper proprietors.

Nor have the subsequent efforts of the League proved more fruitful. The suggestion put forward by the Labour representative of the I.L.O. on the Temporary Commission that all private manufacture of arms should be prohibited was rejected by the Commission on the ground that it penalises those countries which could not manufacture all the arms they required for themselves. In other words, the sale of arms would be directly subject to public policy and small countries would be unable to arm except with the good will of the big Powers. Would that be a bad thing ? It would at least make the arming of a small Power a deliberate act of will on the part of the great Power ; it would no longer be possible for a Government to ride off on the excuse that it could not interfere with private enterprise.

Subsequent discussions at Geneva have shown a tendency to move backwards rather than forwards as far as private manufacture of arms is concerned. In December, 1930, when the subject was included in the Draft Convention on the Limitation and Reduction of Armaments, the recommendations were actually less drastic than in 1925. They proposed that publicity for war material was to be allied to *value* only, whereas it had been suggested in 1925 that Governments should give figures of number and weight as well as of value.

Conclusion

It is indisputable that private armament firms, no matter how reputable and incorrupt, depend for their prosperity on the perpetual exasperation of international fears and suspicions : they live upon that armament competition which saps the world's economy, they thrive upon war scares, and they must have occasional wars. It is indisputable, too, that the private armament firms, with their potent financial and political backing, can and do maintain such fears and suspicions between the nations, and do thus continually endanger the world's peace. It is indisputable that they afford to the War Departments in the countries where they operate the means for the rapid expansion of armament production in time of crisis : and Governments which can rely upon thus augmenting their war supplies are the more likely and the more ready to strike a sudden blow against their neighbours.

If Governments wish us to believe in their sincerity when they preach peace and discuss disarmament, they must begin by abandoning their unholy alliance with the vested interest in arms. As rulers who have renounced war, they must also renounce the supposed advantage of having a private organisation capable of immediate expansion and use in the event of war. They must cease to pretend that a Disarmament Conference is a meeting of statesmen to adjust minor differences and openly proclaim themselves the enemies of the vested interests in armaments. These vested interests are powerful enemies, not stage dummies and their defeat and subjugation is an essential part of any genuine scheme of disarmament.

If Governments fail to abolish the private manufacture of arms, what is the alternative ? Another war for " King and Country," for " Fatherland," for " Liberty " and all the other time-dishonoured battle cries ? Perhaps. But there is another possibility—the possibility of which M. Vandervelde spoke at the Disarmament Conference when he declared that the workers would not again take up arms—at least not against each other. He appealed significantly to the " prudence " of statesmen. If that " prudence " is lacking, if armament firms are allowed to continue to foment national fears and hatreds, to create scares of war between populations which have no quarrel with each other, may not the next appeal to the warlike passions of the nations prove and justifiably prove to be the signal not for war, but for revolution ?

Published by the Union of Democratic Control, 34 Victoria Street, London, S.W.1, and Printed by the London Caledonian Press Ltd., 74 Swinton Street, Gray's Inn Road, London, W.C.1, England,
w34854